MEN AND THINGS

BY

HIRAM P. BELL

Hiram P. Bell

MEN AND THINGS

BY HIRAM P. BELL

BEING REMINISCENT, BIOGRAPHICAL
AND HISTORICAL

PRESS OF THE
Foote & Davies Company
ATLANTA: 1907

Originally published by Foote and Davies Company,
Atlanta, Georgia, 1907, © H.P. Bell.
Reprinted with an index by
Col. Hiram Parks Bell Camp 1642,
Sons of Confederate Veterans, Cumming, Ga., 2004,
from an original volume in their collection.

Library of Congress Control Number: 2004102840
ISBN # 0-9717466-2-1

With sincere gratitude to the
City of Cumming
for their appreciation of our heritage

Additional copies of this book may be ordered from:
SCV Camp 1642,
2055 Foster Drive, Cumming, Ga. 30040

Made in the Good Old United States of America

Preface to the Second Edition

by

Ted O. Brooke

I am humbly honored at this accomplishment, yet knowing there is nothing I can add to or take away from the finished work of a man the stature of Hiram Parks Bell. He was a self made man, a patriot when it was not popular, a soldier who bled for his Country, a statesman among statesmen and a Christian who lived his faith; a model man for all times and ages.

This new edition of *Men and Things* contains a new name and location index, epilogue, an additional photograph of Hiram P. Bell and a revised and expanded Table of Contents, all of which are designed to improve the usefulness of the book. The original content of pages 1 to 449 as penned by Colonel Bell has not been changed.

I sincerely hope that the modest efforts I have made will help *Men and Things*, in his words, "be interesting to the present generation, and useful to future ones."

Ted O. Brooke,
March 2004

PREFACE.

The author has lived in eventful times. He presents to the public in this unpretentious volume, sketches—biographic, historic, reminiscent and analec tic of some of the men and things that have made them eventful. He does so in the ardent hope that they may be interesting to the present generation, and useful to future ones.

Cumming, Ga., HIRAM P. BELL.

March 7, 1907.

TABLE OF CONTENTS

MEN AND THINGS

CHAPTER I.

Parentage and Birth of the Author.

I was born in Jackson County, Ga., January 19th, 1827.

My father was of English extraction. He was a native of Guilford County, North Carolina. He was born July 22, 1794. His name was Joseph Scott Bell. His father, Francis Bell, removed from North Carolina, and settled in Jackson County, Ga., about the year 1800. He died in 1837, at the age of ninety-one years. He was a non-commissioned officer in the Continental army, and failed to be in the battle of Guilford Court House, by reason of being in command of a squad on detached service. My father was a man of iron constitution, physically, of high temper, strong impulse, resolute will and fearless courage. His education was limited, being such only as could be obtained by a short, irregular attendance upon inferior schools in the back-woods. He was by occupation, a farmer; never held a civil office, and was never a candidate for one. In politics he was a "State's Rights Whig." He was no trader. His communications were " yea, yea," and "nay, nay." He was the genius of manual labor. I do not remember to have known him to spend an hour in idleness.

My mother was Rachel Phinazee, a native Georgian, and of Irish descent. Like my father, she was brought up in a newly settled country, from which the Indians had but recently disappeared, and therefore, her education was meagre. With poor people, in a newly settled country, bread-winning was the watchword. She was born on the second day of November, 1794. Her mother, whose maiden name was Sarah Harris, died at the advanced age of ninety-one years, which age, my mother also attained. She was distinguished for plain, practical common sense, unremitting industry, devotion to duty and faith in God. Her spirit was quiet and gentle as a May zephyr, and even her reproof was in tones sweet as the "Spicy breezes of Araby the blest." Success did not elate, nor defeat depress her, but always and everywhere she maintained that self-poise which is the offspring of philosophy and Christianity.

My father and mother married young, probably in 1813 or 1814; and located in a cabin in the woods, on a small tract of land given to my father by his father. This was in the northeast portion of Jackson County, Ga., fifteen miles from any town. Here they lived and toiled in agricultural avocation, until 1838, when, immediately after the removal of the Cherokees to the West, my father bought a few hundred acres of land in the woods, unmarked by human invasion, except an Indian trail, leading from the Chattahoochee to the Etowah River, in the county of Forsyth, to which a part of his family removed in the early part of the year

1838. The remainder of the family joined this colony in the spring of 1840. Here he repeated the experience of his early life,—the building of a home, and clearing a plantation in the woods, unscarred by the civilizing touch of the axe and ploughshare. Here he wrought, until he "crossed over the river, to rest under the shade of the trees."

The family of my father and mother consisted of six sons and six daughters, all of whom lived to attain majority, and a majority of whom passed the allotted threescore and ten years. The senior son, Joseph T., died at the age of twenty-two years. His death left a scar in my mother's heart that never healed.

My parents were both deeply religious. They united with the Methodist Church shortly after their marriage. My earliest remembrance is associated with the visits of ministers of the Gospel at our home, which was always open to them; and with the regular and systematic family worship. Such was their admiration for them, that they gave to each of their six sons, the name of a favorite preacher.

My father was an official of the church—either steward, class-leader, or trustee—practically all his church life. He was a man of extraordinary power in prayer. I have heard him often, at the family altar, pray with an earnestness and power and pathos, that seemed to me to make the foundation of the house tremble. Faithful, earnest, consistent, devoted Christians, they lived together in harmony, peace and love, for more than sixty years, until all of their children became grown, and married; and passed away without a cloud upon their spiritual horizon.

On a calm, moonlight night in May, 1876, I witnessed my father's translation; with a face all radiant with the light of high communion, his last utterance was: "I leave the world in triumph," and gently exchanged the cross for the crown. My mother survived him nine years. In September, 1885, at the home of her daughter, in Cumming, Ga., she closed a long life, with the stainless record of duty faithfully done, sufferings patiently borne, wrongs freely forgiven, and faith unfalteringly kept; and passed sweetly into the joys of the true life. I honor my parents for their character and their virtues; I bless their memory for their love and benefactions to me, in a thousand different forms.

CHAPTER II.

BOYHOOD ON THE FARM.

Those familiar with the history of Georgia during the first half of the nineteenth century, will remember that, at the close of the Revolutionary War, but a small part of the State, extending from the coast up the Savannah River, was occupied by white inhabitants; the bulk of the territory, of what now constitutes the "Empire State of the South," was wild woods, occupied by hostile Indians and wild beasts. The absence of money and commerce, the continental war-debt, apprehension of failure in organizing successfully the new system of civil government, and the general demoralization resulting from the war, and the disorganized state of society generally, created the conditions to be met. These conditions developed the cardinal factors in achieving our present advanced type of civilization —enterprise and industry. Men and women went bravely to work to win bread and better their condition. Controversies were adjusted, and treaties negotiated with the Indians, population poured in, new counties were formed, forests subdued, the wilderness reclaimed, churches and school-houses built—cheap and humble at first, it is true, but they were the seed of a harvest to be gathered later.

That portion of Georgia lying west of the Chattahoochee River, known as Cherokee, Georgia, was the last portion of the State opened for settlement by the white people. It was occupied by an industrious, hardy class of people, with small means, very speedily. There were few slave-holders among them. The settlement of this section of the State took place at the time when President Jackson's removal of the deposits from the national bank, and specie circular burst the bubble of "flush times" sent the wild-cat banks, which had sprung up like Jonah's gourd, to grief; and left the people in debt without a circulating medium. Under these conditions—from 1840 to 1847—and between thirteen and twenty years of age, from sunrise until sunset, in winter and summer, I was engaged, without intermission, in work on the farm, which consisted in the winter season, in clearing and fencing the land, cutting, hauling logs, and erecting buildings. The county was heavily timbered, which was wasted with reckless prodigality. Each neighborhood had its circle of fifteen or twenty neighbors; and every spring, as regular as the Ides of March, each neighbor had his regulation log-rolling; and in the fall, each within the circle had his corn-shucking. The house-raising was another institution of these primitive times. This was carried on either in the winter or in the summer, between the crop-finishing and fodder-gathering season.

These good people wrought hard and constantly, without money; and strikingly illustrated the truth that: "Man wants but little here below." They were plain and simple in their dress; the cotton patch, flocks, cards, spinning-wheel, loom-room, and deft hands of good, virtuous house-wives, supplied the wardrobe. It was not long, however, until the farm, herd, orchard, garden and dairy, poured their treasures into the refectory in a variety and profusion that would satiate the appetite of Milo, or eclipse the board of Lucullus. They lived like princes on the proceeds of honest labor.

In those days many communities had its little log church, built after a vigorous controversy over the place of its location, at which they held their Sunday-school and attended preaching, which was often on a week day, and to which the men would go from the field and the women from the loom—all in fatigue dress. They went to hear the Word of Life, and were generally thrilled by its power, and comforted by its solace. They lived in peace, all, or most of them, unconscious of what was transpiring in the great big world around them. If they were denied the blessing of different environments and a more advanced state of civilization, the law of compensation exempted them from the annoyance of an army of cooking-stove, sewing-machine, and insurance agents, and peddlers of rat poison and Chinese grips. It was not long, however, until the thin-nosed, irrepressible wooden-nutmeg Yankee clock-peddler put in his appearance.

It is written: "In the sweat of thy face shall thou eat bread." My boyhood life on the farm is a striking illustration of the truth of this divine statement. An accident to an elder brother in the spring of 1834, sent me to the plow at the age of seven years. Other hands put on the gear and tied the hamestring, and a friendly stump or fence corner, after climbing, enabled me to reach the back of the horse. In 1843, in the absence of my father, I bossed the farm. The weather was phenomenally cold in the winter and spring, forage was scarce, live-stock died—a magnificent comet stretched across the southwestern heavens. Miller's prediction of the approaching end of the world alarmed the superstitious. It snowed in March, and the ground was deeply frozen as late as the 5th of April; and vegetation indicated no sign of appearance at that date. A little later, an indiscreet neighbor put out fire on an adjoining farm in dry, windy weather, which caught the dead timber on my father's farm, set the fence on fire, and necessitated the tearing down and rebuilding of between two and three hundred panels, to save the rails. I felt something of the consternation of Napoleon, when he discovered the blaze of Moscow. I did not retreat, but saved the fence. How much trouble, labor, expense and solicitude we could save others by a little caution at the proper time! In the winter of 1842-43 my elder brother and myself made the rails and enclosed a forty-acre lot of land, thirty acres of which was mainly a chinquapin thicket. When the crop of 1843 was finished, my father returned home from a mining enterprise in which he and my elder brother had been engaged, and constructed a threshing-machine, the band of which my two brothers and myself turned, in the month of August, until we threshed out the wheat crop of one hundred bushels, at the rate of five or six bushels per day. In the winter of 1843-44, my elder brother having attained his majority, left home and entered school. My two younger brothers and I devoted our time to the clearing of the thirty acres of chinquapin thicket, which consisted in cutting off the bushes near the ground with club or pole-axes.

Early in the month of May, 1844, the brush was burned, the ground was laid off, without breaking, and planted in corn. After wheat harvest, on the twentieth of June, my brother Matthew and I commenced to plow it for the first time. Father and a negro woman followed with the hoes. The rows were nearly a quarter of a mile in length. The water-sprouts were as thick, and very nearly as tall, as ordinary wheat at maturity—so thick and tall that we frequently lost the row in running the furrow next to the corn. The corn having grown in the shade, was about eighteen inches high, and the stalk but little larger than a well-developed sedge-broom straw; so slender indeed, that when the sprouts were taken from around it much of it fell down. We had been plowing, or trying to plow, for about three hours in this wilderness on an immensely hot day, when I discovered an immensely large rattlesnake making an effort to disengage itself from entanglement with the foot of my plow. I shall not attempt to describe my horror, for the reason that there are some things beyond the attainment of human power. I killed the snake, reported at once the adventure to my father, and begged him to abandon the field, urging that it was tempting providence to take the risk of the snakes. But my father had more faith than I, and scarcely gave my importunate plea a respectful hearing. We ploughed on for nearly a week; and passing each other near the centre of the field, we stopped and engaged in conversation. I noticed in a moment my brother's face turned white as cotton. He had discovered a large rattlesnake lying under a bush in the row between us. We loosed our horses, despatched the rattler, and turned to hitch them, when I discovered, under another bush nearby, a companion snake of equal size, which was also promptly despatched. After ten days of ploughing in new ground covered with a wilderness of bushes, permeated with roots and stumps, and inhabited by rattlesnakes—suffering all the agonies of mental crucifixion—we finished the job, with *Nil* as the result, so far as the crop yield was concerned. A few years ago, as I closed my brother's eyes in death—within an hour after I reached his bedside in Milledgeville—these struggles, toils and associations of our boyhood came trooping down the dusty aisles of memory, with a power and pathos for which language has no expression.

The year 1845 was eventful in most of the Gulf States, on account of the absence of rain, and the failure of crops. Hundreds of families, especially from South Carolina and Georgia, sought homes in the West. Four weeks of the summer of this year is epochal in my history. I had, for that period, the benefit of my brother's instruction. The preceding year, he had the instruction of a first-class teacher, and was himself an accomplished grammarian. This month's instruction from a competent teacher laid the foundation for what little I may have attained in the way of education.

In 1846 my father took a new departure in his farming enterprise. He had tried cotton, which his boys had shivered with cold in picking during Christmas week and in January and which he had hauled with an ox-team to Madison, Ga., then the head of the Ga. R. R., and sold at two and one-half cents per pound. This departure consisted in substituting a tobacco for a cotton crop. He planted ten acres in tobacco plants. The land happened to be in the most favorable condition to produce its largest yield of crab-grass. The season was unusually wet, the growth of the tobacco was retarded, that of the grass, not. After much toil, the crab-grass, late in the summer, was subdued. If there is any one thing for which a farmer-boy ardently pants, it is a few weeks of rest, after the crop is "laid-by," and the peach and watermelon season puts in an appearance. But just as this halycon heaven of boyish delight was reached, the tobacco plants must be topped, and the worms and suckers removed. This process consists in pinching off the top bud, and suckers with the fingers; and knocking off the great, green, loathsome worms with a stick, and mashing them with the foot. The operator is bent forward in the broiling sunshine, besmeared with the gum and stench of this plant, and disgusted with the sight of the worms. This is anything but a delightful exercise. It was completed, in this case, some days after the drying fodder had suffered for gathering. Then the tobacco-house was to be built and daubed, the plant to be cut, placed on sticks and cured, stripped from the stalk and bound into hands. What the crop yielded in money I do not now remember. I am sure it was the only experiment my father ever made with tobacco. He went back to cotton.

Having attended school—all told, only six or eight months in snatches of two or three weeks at a time—in the old field school, most of that time to very inferior teachers, even for this grade of school; and having attained the age of twenty years, without education, I proposed to my father to serve him another year if he would send me to school for one year; or, that if he would release me from the service, I would discharge him from the obligation to give me a year's schooling, as he had done for my older brother, and take the chances of educating myself. He generously accepted the latter proposition. It is due to the memory of my dear father to say that he had a high appreciation of his obligation to educate his children, and ardently desired to discharge that obligation. But having a large family to support, always necessarily in debt, settling in the woods remote from schools fitted to be entrusted with one's education, it was utterly impracticable for him, with these environments, to carry out his wishes in this respect. It is a matter of solace to me, that most of his children, somehow, secured a good English education.

Before I close this chapter, allow me to say that there is one phase of the life of the average country-brought-up boy, that it would do him great injustice to omit. It is about the time, in his history, when the first application of a dull razor is made to his upper lip, designed to elicit the appearance of an infantile mustache, and he is, or thinks he is, desperately in love with a neighbor's pretty daughter. My observation convinces me that this event in a boy's life constitutes a rule of general, if not universal application. I was not an exception to the rule. On a bright Sunday morning, having blacked my shoes—that is, the top of the front portion of them—with a mixture of cold water and chimney soot—as much as I could induce them to mix—donned my best suit, saddled and mounted a small mule, something—but little larger, than a full grown Texas jack-rabbit—(it was a very small mule), and set out on the Don Quixotic adventure of calling to see the object of my supposed idolatry. Within a quarter of a mile from the house the road crossed a creek with rather precipitous banks. The mule, as it soon afterwards became apparent, was thirsty. As soon as it came within reach of the water, it very naturally but very suddenly and decidedly unceremoniously, put its mouth to the water, which left its body in an angle of something over forty-five degrees. The result was, the rider was tumbled over the mule's head into the creek, followed by the saddle, which fell on him. This mishap was then esteemed a calamity. It is now regarded as the poetry of the ludicrous. It would present a picture that would shame the genius of Nast, whose artistic skill as a cartoonist broke the heart and caused the death of Horace Greely.

CHAPTER III.

The Old Field School.

The old field school, like some other institutions of this country, has, in its peculiar way, served its day and generation, and by common consent has been relegated to memory and history. In these days of public school fads, higher educational pretentions, college and university base and foot-ball games, and punch-bowl banquets, reference is seldom made to an institution which, though lowly in origin and humble in claim, has made possible all these institutions as well as our advanced state of civilization. When it is referred to it is usually with the sneer of derision or the smile of amusement. It seems that such a spirit of ingratitude is capable of repudiating the love of a mother, or reproaching the misfortune of poverty. It met a condition of society at a time and under circumstances which could not have been met without it. It kindled a light that makes the opening years of the twentieth century all radiant with the glow of intelligence. The "old field school" possessed three distinctive sides—the ludicrous, the sentimental and the useful. Its houses, furniture and comforts, as well as the extent of its curriculum and the qualifications of its teachers, compared with those of the present time, appear ludicrous in the extreme.

The school-house was usually located in the corner of an old field cleared by the Indians, or in the woods, constructed of small round oak or large, split pine logs, notched down at the corners and covered with clapboards. The orthodox dimensions were 24x16 feet. The larger part of one end was devoted to what is known as a "stick and dirt chimney." Economy in labor and money was promoted by dispensing with sleepers and floor, and substituting the ground therefor. The furniture consisted of a small, rough pine table and a superannuated chair in the rear of it. This was the throne of the intellectual sovereign. The seats for the pupils were made of oak or chestnut logs about six inches in diameter, split open in the center and pegs driven into auger holes from the round side of the half-log. These pegs were of a length that would prevent the feet of the urchins occupying the benches from reaching the dirt floor by a distance of from six to eight inches. To occupy such a seat for a long, hot summer day was a penance that ought to atone for a multitude of sins. The remaining article of furniture was the writing bench. This consisted of a rough plank nailed to the top of a frame, as nearly on a level as practicable, twelve inches wide and ten feet long, and a plank of similar dimensions joined to each of its edges, slightly inclining downwards.

The aesthetic will perceive that this equipment, in the line of convenience and comfort, was neither expensive nor elaborate. The curriculum was not extensive but it had the merit of being in harmony with its surroundings, and confined, within the constitutional limitation, to "the elements of an English education only." It embraced spelling, reading, writing and arithmetic The standard text-books were: The *American Spelling-book,* the *American Preceptor* and *Dilworth's* or *Fowler's Arithmetic.* A little later, as this class of educational institution advanced, the *Columbian Orator* and *Weems' Life of Washington* were added.

The teachers, in the main, were men of advanced age, too lazy to work and too poor to live without it. Having appeared after the age of Raphael, Titian, Angelo and Reynolds, and passed away before the discovery of Daguerre, the world has lost the pleasure of looking upon their pictures and must rely only upon such faint and imperfect pen-pictures as memory alone can supply.

I have in mind with some degree of distinctness, the image of four of them who are strikingly typical of the class. For fear of marring the pleasure of some filial descendants in tracing his heraldry, for the discovery of his ancestral escutcheon, I refrain from stating names. Indeed, the given or Christian name of the first one to whom I refer is forgotten. I only remember that his students, by common consent, substituted for it, whatever it was, the name "Nipper," so that he was known only as Nipper A——s. I do know, however, that he was a tall, ungainly, bald-headed, sour-tempered old man, with no magnetism and but little intelligence. He was not deficient in physical force, as two certain boys who engaged in an innocent game of "hard-knuckles" during study hours when he was supposed to be asleep, after having visited, at the noon recess, a neighboring still-house, discovered to their mortification and discomfort.

The next one, W——, whose only possession was a homely wife and a bad "small boy," was an Irishman of exuberant cheerfulness. No conditions seemed to discourage or dishearten him. He secured his support, principally, from his neighbors by borrowing such articles of food as were necessary to prevent actual starvation, under the pretext that "to his surprise, he had ascertained that the articles desired had just been exhausted at home," and with the munificence of a prince bestowing an "order" or conferring a proconsulship upon a grateful subject, he promised to return it with manner that simply defies description, except to say that it was done in a way of Irish shrewdness that made the lender feel that he was the beneficiary. This feeling was the only benefit he ever received for the loan. His theory of teaching seemed to consist, judging from his practice, in the belief that light could be communicated to the mind by the application of force to the body.

H——, unlike W——, was a man of some means. He had a wife, a very large family of children, five or six dogs and two rifleguns, the stocks of which were well worn by long use. Mr. K—— was a man of large frame, dark complexion, of slow motion and deliberate speech; though of robust health he seemed to be averse to motion, and the act of breathing appeared to be irksome to him. If the "law of the Lord" was not his delight the law of inertia was. His uncharitable neighbors entertained the suspicion that he was afflicted with an attack of remediless laziness. Of the truth of this imputation, posterity must judge. I only state the facts in the case.

F——, the remaining member of this quartet of famous pedagogues, was a man of decidedly marked, if not unique, personality. His stature was low, his head large and of peculiar form, his lower limbs short and bent with a regularity that fitly represented the segment of a circle, the convex side being outward; his feet inclined to the club variety; his walk was sort of hobbling and shuffling movement. The conception of a cross between a chimpanzee and a dwarf would present the nearest an ideal picture, of which his figure was susceptible. In bestowing her gifts, Nature had been parsimonious with him; some—and among them, beauty—had been entirely withheld. An officiating clergyman said at a vagrant's funeral, that "Whatever else might be said of the deceased, all would admit that he was a good whistler." So I can say of this dead pedagogue (and it is about all that could be said), he wrote a beautiful hand.

These great men of the olden time were differentiated, mainly, if not solely, in their personality. They were all old men. They were about on an equality in scholarly attainments, perhaps I should say, in the absence of scholastic attainments. They all taught at the same place, used the same books, practiced like methods and quenched their thirst at the common "still-house."

As the branches taught were few, the methods employed were simple. The lessons were studied vocally, not silently, and by far the largest portion of the study consisted in the hubbub of mingled voices in every variety of key. The full measure of vocal power was developed in preparing the "heart lesson" preceding the evening adjournment. With favorable atmospheric conditions the hum of this noise could be distinctly heard at the distance of a mile, and the peculiar shrieks of one boy's voice (Duncan Campbell's) could be easily distinguished at that distance. The useful art of writing was taught by commencing with a so-called "line of straight marks" across the top of a leaf of coarse, unruled paper. This, of course, was made by the teacher and called the "copy." The beginner, equipped with a goose-quill pen and the juices pressed from oak-balls (well known among the scholars as ink-balls) for ink, commenced the process of copying the marks. The second lesson was the mark, as in the first, curved at the bottom and traced upward. This mark, in the figurative language of the teacher, was called "pot hooks." The third copy was a line of "pot hooks" with the second line curved at the top and brought down to evenness with the lower curve; then followed copies of capital letters of the alphabet, etc. It was a singular fact that the students almost invariably in making these curves, slightly twisted and protruded the tongue, and kept the tongue and eyes in a movement precisely corresponding to the motion of the pen. I never did understand, and do not now know, which was the dominant motor in this operation—these members or the pen. I had the privilege of securing early instruction from each of the worthies here mentioned, in an institution which I have endeavored to describe. Whatever mistakes in instructions or discipline they made I forget and forgive. For whatever of good they did me, I give them the thanks of a heart, which I trust is incapable of ingratitude.

THE SENTIMENTAL SIDE OF THE OLD FIELD SCHOOL.

"A land without sentiment is a land without liberty." The short resolution adopted by the Pilgrim fathers in the cabin of the "Mayflower" was the prophecy of our magnificent structure of democratic constitutional government. They symbolized the religious faith of the United States as they stood on "Plymouth Rock."

> "And shook the depths of the forest gloom with
> hymns of lofty cheer."

The old field school was our present civilization in embryo. It was the beginning of what now is. Pioneer settlers were always distinguished for their energy, industry, fearlessness and faith. This school was theirs. Indeed, it was the pioneer educational institution of the North American wilderness.

On a Monday morning, late in July or early in August, coming from all directions, in a circle within three miles around the school-house, from forty to fifty children of both sexes, ranging in age from five to twenty years, might be seen to meet at the school-house. They were simply and cheaply clad in such apparel as their good mothers could manufacture. They were all barefoot, except the few grown girls. They were all bronzed by the mingled force of hard labor and hot sunshine. The commissariat consisted of bacon, or steak, sandwiched between slices of corn-bread, or biscuit, neatly wrapped in a clean napkin and placed in a small tin bucket, or basket, and a black quart bottle—which had seen other service—filled with butter-milk and closed with a corn-cob stopper. The dessert—peaches and apples—were carried in the boys pockets. There was no difficulty in arranging classes. All that was necessary was to point out and assign as lessons, the alphabet, the lesson in spelling and the multiplication table. A few lessons being recited, the noon recess reached and lunch over, they assembled on the play-ground, and speedily renewed old and formed new acquaintances. They cared little for the ceremonious etiquette of courts, or the military discipline of camps. These children on the play-ground presented a scene on which idle angels would delight to look for.

"They also serve, who only stand and wait."

The games they played, if lowly and rustic, were healthful and harmless. Their section of the country, at least, had not been favored with the entertainment of the cock-pit, the bull-fight, nor foot-ball. Nor had a powerful daily press then delighted the public with columns of detailed description of the bloody "rounds" of Jeffries and Fitzsimmons. To preserve the facts of history, a list of them is given; they were: Base, tag, cat, marbles, bull-pen, town-ball, shinny, roly-hole and mumble-peg. Both sexes joined in the first two named, therefore base and tag had precedence in popularity. I always thought, for the reason, that the execution involved the thrill of touch. These children had a common experience in labor and poverty; had learned self-denial and self-sacrifice; had waded in the branch and been charmed by the ripple of its tiny waterfalls; had gathered autumnal fruitage in the tangled wildwood; had breathed alike the fragrance of the rose and honeysuckle; had listened in ecstacy to the chorus of the birds and gazed in wonder upon the stars that deck the diadem of night. They had communed with Nature and reveled in its charms until their life had become an unwritten idyl. They had likewise realized in their short, young lives all the emotions of hope and fear, of success and defeat, trial and triumph, and gratification and disappointment.

As they stood on the play-ground about to advance a step in the social and intellectual world, each felt the consciousness of a force within that was not understood, and that could neither be defined nor described, still it throbbed in the brain, pulsated in heart-beats and gurgled through the veins. It was present in their ambitions, aspirations, admirations, envyings, rivalries, likes and dislikes. What was this force? Was it the struggling of the mind for higher attainments in knowledge, the panting of the restless spirit for the solace of peace, or the thirst of the soul, clamoring for one full draught of immortality? No body can tell. No one knows. Whatever it was, it was the power, dying

"Ion caught from Clemanthe's eye"

that assured him of a reunion of love,

"Beyond the sunset's radiant glow."

If they never heard the name of the poet, nor read the couplet, they all felt the sentiment that

"Kind words were more than coronets,
And simple faith, than Norman blood."

It was very soon discovered that in playing the game of base some boys were very easily caught by certain, particular girls. It was further observed that the same boys and girls, in going home in the evening, would linger at the parting of their ways and play, or pretend to play, "tag." They parted with the compact, that whichever one reached the place first on the succeeding morning, in returning to school, would make a cross-mark or drop the twig of a green bush in a particular place in the road. This sign always accelerated the movements of the party of the second part. I never heard of any complaint of violating the stipulations of this treaty. It may be, after all, that these trivial, simple little things shed light on the solution of this great problem that has baffled the learning and exploded the theories of psychologists. It was a little thing to dip seven times in "Jordan" but it healed a leper.

In long after-years and from far-away places, many a heart has sent memory back to the old play-ground, and silently sighed for

"The touch of a vanished hand,"

and the sparkle of an eye forever closed.

The Useful Side of the Old Field School.

It must be remembered that the school under consideration, was the educational initiative, the first grade or primary species of the genus old field school. This grade did not, and necessarily, could not exist long. It was subject to the great law of gradation, progress and development, which seems to have dominated the process of creation, as well as the disclosures of revelation. As the good people improved their conditions, increased their means and enlarged their views, they built better houses, used superior books and employed more capable teachers. Occasionally, in a more wealthy neighborhood, an academy would spring up, and as new counties were formed the law provided for the establishment of an academy at the county-seat. In the meantime the University was struggling up to the guerdon of triumph; later the great churches built colleges for both sexes; finally public sentiment crystalized into constitutional provision for the public school system.

The first grade of the old field school, as described in these pages, is the granite bed-rock upon which this superb superstructure rests. It was the small seed from which this luxuriant harvest within the period of a century was gathered. The children of this school, belonging to the same grade of society, identified in common environments, and the sympathies which result from early association (at least many of them), married and organized homes in the quiet country, in which peace, gentleness, affection and contentment exemplified the only remnant of Eden, unblasted by the fall. They became the parents, and grandparents, of a race of men and women that subdued the wilderness, beautified it with gardens, orchards, farms, towns and cities, and crowned it with temples of worship and learning, and hospitals and asylums. A race of chivalrous patriots, who in 1812, dispersed the boasted navy of England, sent back to her, from New Orleans, the pickled corpse of Packenham; scaled the rocky heights of Cherubusco, Chepultepec, Milino del Rey; floated the American flag from the dome of the capitol of the Aztecs, and spangled the "milky way" of national glory with a gorgeous jewelry of stars.

The people provided the old field school for themselves. It was the best they could do, and they deserve the grateful thanks of all the coming ages for what they did.

There were two other potent factors co-operating with the old field school in laying the foundation for these achievements. They were the Decalogue and the Sermon on the Mount. Side by side with the school appeared the irrepressible Methodist circuit rider, with his much-used and well-worn Bible, hymn-book and "Discipline," preaching every day in the week, at the little log church or school-house, and at night frequently at some house of a brother in the neighborhood. At the same time the Baptists appeared, preaching on Saturday and Sunday. The preaching of that day dealt with the doctrines of depravity, repentance, faith, regeneration and obedience, as taught in the Bible, with occasional reference, by the Baptist brethren, to some of the dogmas of the ironclad theology of Geneva, such as election and reprobation, final perseverance, mode of baptism, etc. These combined forces formed the character of a good people and directed the course and shaped the destiny of a great nation. The power of many of these men finds fit expression in Wirt's description of the blind preacher: "They spoke as if their lips had been touched with a live coal from off the Altar." They accepted the Mosaic cosmogony. They taught that "the Son of Man came to seek and to save that which was lost," and that He brought "life and immortality to light." They indulged in no speculations on the "glacial" and tertiary periods, nor did they waste any time in searching for "protoplasm," nor tracing their paternity, through the processes of "evolution," to a monkey progenitor.

Schools, academies, colleges and universities can not educate. They can only supply the means to aid and enable people to educate themselves. Education, in its last analysis, is a personal work, facilitated by the aid of helpful agencies, or retarded, of course, by their absence. To become thoroughly educated, comparatively, requires a life-long, unremitting, systematic process of observation, reading and thinking; and this can only be done by the student himself. The great and learned Newton said that he "had only picked up a few shells on the shore, while the great ocean of knowledge lay, unsailed, beyond him." The old field school did its work, and did it well. Like the "Mother of the Gracchi," she can present George Washington, Benjamin Franklin, Andrew Jackson, Henry Clay and Abraham Lincoln, as her jewels, and proudly challenge Harvard or Yale, Oxford or Cambridge, Leipsic or Heidleberg, or all of them combined, to duplicate this quintet of American immortals.

CHAPTER IV.

EDUCATION, ADMISSION TO THE BAR, AND MARRIAGE.

At the age of twenty years, with an attendance, altogether, at school, of six months—four at the old field of the first grade, and two of the second grade. I left home with the blessing of my parents, and entered on the battle of life. My wardrobe was such as my dear, good mother could provide. I had a purpose (this was all), owned no property, did not have one cent of money; bought books and secured board and tuition on credit; and entered the academy at Cumming, in February, 1847. It should be stated that my school instruction had been supplemented by studying during the long winter nights, with my brothers and sisters. We had many and most interesting "spelling-bees," and recitals, in English grammar and geography. I made it a point to read every book upon which I could put my hands; and in 1845, I had the advantage of very superior instruction from my brother, for five weeks, who taught near Sheltonville, Ga., the odor of whose lessons has lingered for threescore years, in the community, "like the fragrance of roses that have once been distilled." The principal of the Academy, Joseph K. Valentine, was a professional teacher, in middle life; a fine scholar and a gentleman. He was so thorough in the Greek and Latin languages, that he read the text-books in the course as promptly and with as much facility, as he read English. The students, in constant attendance, numbered about one hundred, half of whom, approximately, were grown. It was a mixed school. In arranging the classes, it was my good fortune to be assigned to a class of five grown girls, in three or four studies. In preparing the lessons in these studies, we occupied seats together. Being further advanced, especially in English grammar, than any of them, I was helpful to them in that study. I had parsed most of Milton's "Paradise Lost," and when surrounded by this coterie of beautiful girls, I felt as if I was in "paradise found." One of the most interesting and valuable lessons, was the "Heart" spelling lesson. The class was a large one, more than twenty, of the grown students. The book used was "Town's Speller and definer," a book of something over 300 pages, containing the words in most common use, with accurate definitions. The first thing after the noon recess was this lesson, which had been carefully studied during the recess. The class stood in a line; the teacher called the word, and the class spelled and defined it. At the formation of the class, each student took his place at the nearest point at which he reached it; before the end of the second lesson the five girls and myself were the first six in the class, counting from the head—four of them above and one below me. We stayed there for one year—not one of the six missed the spelling or defining of a word in the book for that period. These girls were: Virginia M. Lester, Martha Erwin, Josephine Strickland, Virginia Sims, and Mary Sims. They all had been trained by practical, sensible, good parents; were all of nearly the same age and size, were social chums, ardent personal friends, free from malignity and envy, bright as stars, and animated with ambition and rivalry to excel each other. A year's class and social association with them failed to discover the slightest defect or weakness in the character of any one of them. The respect, confidence and friendship of all of them, and the priceless love of one of them, have been the blessing and solace of my life. And now, the precious memory of them comes to my spirit, sweet and sad, as the tremulous echoes of a nightingale's dying song.

Within three months from the day I entered that class, Virginia M. Lester and myself were engaged to be married so soon as I finished my education, and was admitted to the bar. As unwise and reckless as this engagement may have then seemed, time and trial vindicated its wisdom. Her bright smile, like light on "Memnon's lyre," set my heart to throbbing with the music of love, that was as resistless as a decree of destiny. She was in the bloom of young womanhood. The ease and grace of her pose, the simple elegance of her manner and the beauty of her face and figure, would have delighted an artist, as a model for his masterpiece. Added to these charms was a spirit radiant with the light of hope and joy; and a heart, pure as love, and faithful as truth. For thirty-seven years she made more than one heart contented and happy, and one home a paradise of peace and love. She merited the highest eulogium ever pronounced on woman—that which came from the lips of the Nazarene, when he said of Mary of Bethany: "She hath done what she could." I loved her, living, with an ardor for which language has no expression; I mourned her, dead, with an anguish for which earth has no consolation.

Josephine Strickland married John B. Peck, of Atlanta, Ga., and was the first of the class to pass away. Mary Sims married Lewis D. Palmer, now of Nashville, Tenn. She and Virginia M. Lester died on the same day, April 30, 1888. Virginia Sims married Mr. Backman—both are dead. Martha Erwin, who married Mr. W. H. Camp, now of Floyd County, Ga., is the only survivor of this class of splendid girls and noble women. She is now in "the sere and yellow leaf," but possesses all the sweetness, gentleness, modesty and sly humor of the long ago.

My studies were grammar, geography, philosophy, chemistry, logic, rhetoric, composition, history and the Latin language. In spare hours I read "Plutarch's Lives," Irving's "Life of Columbus," Prescott's Conquest of Mexico," Seneca's "Philosophy," and Locke on "The Understanding." I pursued these studies in this school during the year 1847 and the greater portion of 1848. In 1849 I taught in the Academy at Ellijay, Ga.; and read law. I was admitted to the bar, at Spring Place, Ga., on November 28, 1849, by Judge Augustus R. Wright, after an examination in open court of four hours, by a committee consisting of Judge W. H. Underwood, Judge Turner H. Trippe, Warren Akin, J. W. Johnson, William Martin, and R. W. Jones. I entered upon the ordeal of that examination with a trepidation that makes me shiver to think of now, but my good angel was not nodding at his post; and it so happened that I did not fail to answer every question correctly. In pursuance of our engagement, Virginia M. Lester and myself were united in marriage in Cumming, Ga., on January 22, 1850. I taught that year, in Ellijay; and continued my study of law. In the latter part of that year, we settled in Cumming. I possessed only two things—the best of wives, and the noblest of professions.

On June 11, 1890, I was united in marriage to Miss Annie Adelaide Jordan, in Eatonton, Ga., at the home of her aunt, Mrs. M. L. Reid. She was the daughter of Warren H. Jordan, of Noxubee County, Miss.—a native Georgian—and her mother was Miss Julia L. Hudson, of Eatonton, Ga.—both of whom died before she was grown. She is an accurate scholar, and an accomplished pianist. Her sweet and gentle ministries of love and devotion to me, in joy and sorrow, in health and in sickness, have imposed upon me an obligation of gratitude I can never recompense.

CHAPTER V.

The Bar of Georgia in 1850.

At the time I was admitted, the bar of Georgia, compared most favorably with that of any State in the Union—indeed, with that of any age or country. At its head were John M. Berrien, Robert M. Charlton, William Law, Francis S. Bartow, John E. Ward, Charles J. Jenkins, George W. Crawford, Andrew J. Miller, Robert Toombs, Alexander H. Stephens, William C. Dawson, Francis H. Cone, Joshua Hill, Augustus Reese, Linton Stephens, Augustus H. Kennan, William McKinley, Eugenia A. Nisbet, Barnard Hill, Washington Poe, Samuel P. Hall, Absalom H. Chappell, Henry G. Lamar, Seaborn Jones, Walter T. Colquitt, Martin J. Crawford, Hines Holt, Henry L. Benning, William Dougherty, Hiram Warner, Robert P. Trippe, Herschel V. Johnson, Edward Z. Hill, Benjamin H. Hill, Charles Dougherty, Junius Hillyer, Howell Cobb, Hope Hull, Thos. R. R. Cobb, James Jackson, Cincinattus Peeples, Thos. W. Thomas, B. H. Overby, Nathan L. Hutchins, Charles J. McDonald, David Irwin, Andrew J. Hansell, George D. Rice, William H. Underwood, Turner H. Trippe, Warren Akin, Augustus R. Wright, George N. Lester, John W. H. Underwood, Edward D. Chisolm, Joseph E. Brown, Logan E. Bleckley, Dawson A. Walker, William H. Dabney, John B. Floyd, O. A. Lochrane, James L. Calhoun, James Starke, William Martin, and the first Chief Justice of the State, Joseph Henry Lumpkin. This list of illustrious lawyers furnished cabinet ministers, senators and representatives in the United States Congress, equal to the best in the Union; governors, judges of the supreme and superior courts of the State; and ministers to foreign countries. It contained many of the ablest statesmen and most eloquent orators of the age. In their day, they led the public sentiment, and moulded and shaped the public policy of the State, and largely, of the nation. They were the leaders of the bar. Yet there were hundreds of lawyers, very nearly, if not quite, their equal in legal learning and professional skill, in the management of causes in the courthouse.

The country will never know its wealth of talent and capacity for public service, for two reasons—the modesty of meritorious men, and the lack of opportunity. Public position, like the clown's measles that "struck too large a family to go round," can not furnish the opportunity to all the capable and meritorious.

As a class, lawyers are the closest thinkers, and best logicians in the world. The reasons are obvious. The science of law trains its votaries in the best methods of securing its object, which is the ascertainment of truth and the enforcement of right.

The definitions of the law are clear. Its distinctions being fine, must be accurately observed and drawn, conflicts (or seeming conflicts) reconciled, language construed, doubts resolved, and its application to facts—infinitely varied—made; all to be done with reference to the rights of an anxious client; and involving the reputation of the lawyer, and frequently the bread of his family. His profession is a direct intellectual combat with an antagonist that may be relied upon to do his best to defeat him. The struggle is in the open—before the public—with a judge present to decide who is victor or vanquished. The practice of the law is the best possible training in the art of successful disputation. It has the incentives to thorough research and thought, to the examination and study of both sides of a case or question. He studies the strength and the weakness of his adversary. He learns much of human nature and human infirmity by contact with parties, witnesses and jurors. It has been urged that the study and practice of law contracts and narrows the mind. Precisely the contrary is true. It expands the horizon of mental vision, enlarges the field of investigation, of inquiry, and liberalizes the process of thought. Law, in its different departments, of international, national, civil, criminal, military and maritime, comprehends every right and interest of man absolute and relative, in all his relations. Familiarity with it and the knowledge of it, therefore, extend the range of thought, and increase the domain of knowledge. Jefferson and Hamilton, Pickney and Wirt, Webster and Choate, Clay and Crittenden, Prentiss and Douglass, and Stephens and Toombs, illustrate and demonstrate this truth.

Able and upright lawyers are no unimportant factors in conserving the moral interests of society and elevating the tone of public sentiment to proper standards. The vindication of rights, the denunciation of wrongs, the maintenance of truth, and the exposure of falsehood, in the discussions of the courthouse, involving, as they do, the interest and rights of every spectator, is an education by no means lost on the public mind. Discussions of moral questions in the pulpit and on the platform deal with them in the abstract, in the courthouse, in the concrete.

It has been urged that lawyers were ambitious and inclined to seek office and honors. This is not true of them as a class, any more than it is of any class or profession. It is perhaps true that more offices in the government are filled by them, than any other class. Civil government is an institution of law; and a knowledge of the law is an important, if not a necessary, qualification for the duties of the office. In all judicial offices it is absolutely indispensable, and legal training and knowledge is a qualification for wise and intelligent legislation, as experience has abundantly shown.

Lawyers have always led the van in the assertion, maintenance and defense of liberty. They have always stood for human rights and against the tyranny of despotism. It was a lawyer who sounded the first note of hostility to British oppression in the Virginia House of Burgesses, in a resolution written on the flyleaf of a law book. That sound had its last echo in the surrender of the British at Yorktown. A lawyer wrote the Declaration of Independence. The Constitution of the United States is mainly the product of two lawyers—James Madison and Alexander Hamilton. These two great and patriotic lawyers were the representatives and exponents of two opposite schools of political thought and theories. They were equally able, honest and patriotic. They each urged their views with the emphasis of conviction. The Constitution of the United States embodies the compromise of these opposing theories of civil government.

John Somers, in a five minutes speech, procured the acquittal of the Bishops, in a trial, that drove the last of the Stuarts from his crown and kingdom. The learning and eloquence of Halifax and Somers obtained in the Convention Parliament, the limitations upon power and prerogative, secured in the Act of Settlement, and the Bill of Rights. The powerful denunciations of oppression by Webster and Clay, in the American Congress, thrilled and incited the Greeks to the resistance of Turkish despotism in Europe, and the Latins in opposing Spanish tyranny in South America.

In the late war between the States, Bartow fell in the first fray and Cobb soon thereafter; and hundreds of lawyers of perhaps less learning and eloquence, but with equal valor and patriotism, "poured out their generous blood like water" in defense of the right of self-government, on more than five hundred fiercely fought fields.

History amply vindicates the claim of the profession, to the highest niche in the temple of fame, for devotion to learning, liberty and patriotism.

CHAPTER VI.

Changes in the Law and Its Procedure Since 1850.

At the time of which I write, Joseph Henry Lumpkin, Eugenius A. Nisbet and Hiram Warner occupied the Supreme bench. Such men as Edward Y. Hill, David Irwin, Junius Hillyer, John J. Floyd, Garnett Andrews, Herschel V. Johnson, Francis H. Cone, Augustus R. Wright, and many others of equal ability, presided on the circuit bench.

The Supreme Court was established in 1845, after a protracted struggle. The earlier volumes of its reports contain monumental evidence of the independence and learning of the first three judges. Lumpkin was learned, eloquent, impressive and humorous. Nisbet was equally learned, dignified and elegant; Warner was cold as a Siberian icicle, and clear as a tropical sunbeam. I confess that he was my ideal of a judge. I never think of him, as he sat upon the bench, struggling, sometimes alone, to uphold the constitution and the law against the debauchery and dishonesty of so-called relief legislation, without applying to him, the magnificent eulogium pronounced by the Attorney-General, on the dead vice-president, when Cushing said of King: "He stands to the memory, in sharp outline, as it were, against the sky, like some chiseled column of antique art, or consular statue, of the Imperial republic, wrapped in his marble robes and grandly beautiful in the simple dignity and unity of a faultless proportion."

The last fifty years have wrought marvelous changes, in Georgia, in the law, its forms of procedure, and the questions with which it deals. The War and the altered conditions resulting from it have contributed greatly, if not mainly, in producing these changes.

Before, the principles, practice and forms of equity and the common law were separate and distinct; now, they are merged. Then, the English common law forms in all their "vain" repetitions, and technical refinements and distinctions in pleadings, were followed; now, the pleader states his client's case—in law or equity, whatever it may be—in short, pithy paragraphs. Then, all persons interested in the event of the suit were incompetent witnesses; now, all parties living and sane (with a few exceptions) are competent. Then, only the parties to the record could be heard in the case; now, anyone, in any way interested, may intervene and be heard.

There has been as decided change in the subject-matter of litigation as in the forms of proceeding. The institution of slavery was the fountain of a stream that carried fortunes to the profession. The farmers became rich, breeding negroes, buying land and making cotton. The validity and construction of wills, breaches of warranty of the soundness of slaves, action of trover for their recovery and debt for large amounts of indebtedness upon their sale—these and the trial of disputed land titles, as population increased and settlements were extended raised the questions upon which the legal giants fought their battles and won their fame and fortunes.

This was the agricultural age of Georgia. The abolition of slavery eliminated from the courts this source of litigation, and substituted a totally different kind of questions and controversies. The ordinance of the convention of 1865, providing for the adjustment, by the courts of Confederate contracts, upon the principles of equity and justice, the depredations and trespasses of home guards and robbers during the last years of the War, and the relief legislation of the reconstruction period, filled the courts for a few years with a flood of litigation. But this was necessarily temporary, and soon passed away. Now (1904), commercial and corporation law and practice are regnant, and confined, principally, to the cities and larger railroad towns. In the rural counties the practice arises from the levy of distress warrants and executions upon the foreclosure of liens, and the defense of negroes for larceny, robbery and burglary usually by assignment of the court. How the hundreds of young men, annually brought to the bar by colleges, universities and otherwise, are to win bread, by the practice, in the light of the present outlook, is their problem; not mine. It is alleged that *some* of the more enterprising members of the profession—especially in cities—have henchmen employed to hunt up business, and that they follow a train wreck, like vultures, the scent of a carcass. I hope, for the honor of the profession, that this allegation is a slander.

This progress, reform, or certainly change in our law,

commenced in 1847 upon the passage of the act which substituted, for the common forms of pleading, the short forms, popularly known as the "Jack Jones forms." The law allowing appeals in the superior court was repealed. The marital rights of the husband as to property owned by the wife at the time of marriage or acquired by her after marriage were wholly changed. The homestead laws enlarged from their pony proportion up to sixteen hundred dollars worth of property—real and personal—which, however, is practically nullified by the creditor invariably taking a waiver note and mortgage on everything that the debtor owns or ever expects to own. The school law which humanity provided for the education of the poor has given place to a system that imposes annually, upon the people of the State, a tax of nearly two millions—a large portion of which is devoted to training negro children in idleness and crime, under the pretext of qualifying them for useful citizenship. These and numerous other radical changes have been made in our law to such an extent that if a Georgia lawyer had fallen asleep in 1850 and waked up in 1904 Rip VanWinkle would have been no more remembered! Whether these changes were all wise and promotive of the public interest raises a question upon which opinions will differ.

The British government sent an agent to this country to investigate the question of law reform, who carried back copies of the "Jack Jones" forms of pleading, which were enacted into law by Parliament. The youngest of her American colonies, in less than one hundred years from the establishment of its independence, furnished to the Mother of the common law her form of pleading.

CHAPTER VII.

Secession and Reconstruction.

On the sixteenth day of January, 1861, the people of Georgia, by their chosen delegates, assembled in convention at the capitol in Milledgeville.

This was perhaps a body of the ablest men ever assembled in the State. The magnitude of the issue to be considered and determined induced the people to select the men supposed to be best qualified to determine wisely.

The people were prosperous; many of them rich; all of them peaceful and happy. They owned African slaves, numbering hundreds of thousands. Their barns were crowded with fullness and plenty. They exhibited the finest type of society civilization ever presented. This prosperity had been achieved in the Union, under the protection of the Constitution of the United States. The practical nullification of the fugitive slave provision of the Constitution, by the hostile legislation of fourteen States, and the election of a President by them from one section of the Union, upon the issue of hostility to the institution of African slavery as it existed in the Southern States, convinced a majority of the convention that their safety and preservation of their rights could only be secured by dissolving their relation with States thus faithless to constitutional obligations. Three days after the convention met—on the nineteenth of January, 1861—it adopted, by a vote of 166 yeas to 130 nays, the Ordinance of Secession, and thus withdrew from the Union, in the exercise of the right of self-government asserted in the Declaration of Independence. This opened "Pandora's box," and a tragedy was enacted that General W. T. Sherman rightly named "hell."

On the twenty-fifth of October, 1865, another convention of the people assembled at the same place. The environments were different. The slaves had been freed by force; the barns were empty; the fields, gardens and orchards had been trampled down; dwellings robbed; cities sacked and burned; live stock slaughtered or stolen; mills and factories demolished; churches profaned and cemeteries desecrated; the flower of Southern chivalry dead; the land groaning in poverty, widowhood and orphanage; and crushed by the iron heel of a relentless military despotism; the people put under the government of military satraps. This convention, like the former, was composed of able and patriotic men. Herschel V. Johnson presided over its deliberations and Charles J. Jenkins led them upon the floor.

President Johnson had adopted his plan of readjusting the seceded States in their relations to the Union. James Johnson, an able and conservative citizen of the county of Muscogee, had been appointed Provisional Governor, and the convention assembled for this purpose. The Ordinance of Secession was promptly repealed by a unanimous vote, the payment of the War debt prohibited and the emancipation of the slaves expressly recognized. The presidential program of reconstruction was literally carried out. A State constitution was adopted in conformity to the Constitution of the United States. A general election for Governor, members of Congress and members of the General Assembly was held. Charles J. Jenkins was elected Governor.

"The pure of the purest,
The hand that upheld our bright banner, the surest."

The legislature assembled on the fourth of December and unanimously ratified the thirteenth amendment to the Federal Constitution, prohibiting the existence of slavery. Charles J. Jenkins was inaugurated Governor on December 19, 1865, and Provisional Governor James Johnson relinquished the conduct of the State affairs to the authorities thus constituted. The legislature elected Alexander H. Stephens and Herschel V. Johnson United States Senators. The people supposed that constitutional civil government was restored, that military domination would cease, and that they could persue their avocations in peace and hope, if in toil and poverty, but this was a mistake. The legislature met on November 1, 1866. The fourteenth amendment to the Constitution had been submitted to the State for ratification. Governor Jenkins, in his message to the legislature, made a masterly argument against ratification. The legislature declined to ratify by a unanimous vote in the senate, and by a vote of 132 to 2 in the house. Major-General John Pope assumed command in the third military district, containing Georgia, Florida and Alabama, on April 1, 1866. Civil government having been restored and in successful operation in the State, Governor Jenkins made an effort to bring the question of the constitutionality of the reconstruction act before the Supreme Court for adjudication. This effort failed. The State of Georgia presented the anomalous spectacle of being under two governments—a civil government under constitutional law administered by Governor Jenkins, and a military despotism, in violation of law, enforced by Major-General John Pope.

On the sixth of January, 1868, Major-General George G. Meade assumed command in the third military district. Congress had repudiated the Presidential scheme of reconstruction and adopted that provided in the several reconstruction acts; and impeached the President.

On January 11 the State officers were admonished under color of authority, not to interfere with the exercise of military authority in the States composing the third district. Governor Jenkins and State Treasurer Jones were ordered to pay out of the public treasury the public money, under military order, which they declined to do for the reason that they had taken an oath to support the Constitution, which provided that "No money shall be drawn from the treasury of this State, except by appropriations made by law. Whereupon General Meade issued the following order: "Charles J. Jenkins, Provisional Governor, and John Jones, Provisional Treasurer, of the State of Georgia, having declined to respect the instructions and failed to co-operate with the Major-General commanding the third military district, are hereby removed from office.

Brevet Brigadier-General Thomas H. Ruger appointed Governor and Brevet Captain Charles F. Rockwell to be Treasurer of Georgia."

A constitutional civil government in a time of peace was thus summarily abolished by an order, on the ground that its officers refused to violate their official oaths and allow the treasury robbed, and a military despotism substituted in its place and the treasury opened to the robbers.

Under the congressional plans of reconstruction, a registration of voters, under the first civil act, was ordered, and an election for delegates to a constitutional convention. One hundred and eighty-eight thousand six hundred and forty-seven voters, white and black, were registered. The white majority was about 2,000. The election of delegates was held from October 29th to November 3d. Of the delegates chosen, 133 were white and 33 black. John E. Bryant, of Skowhegan, Maine, was one of the whites, and Aaron Alpeoria Bradley and Tunis G. Campbell, from the southern coast of Georgia, were two of the blacks. This white and black spotted convention assembled in Atlanta, under the supervision of General Meade, made for Georgia the organic law, known as the Constitution of 1868. On March 14, 1868, a military order was issued for an election commencing April 20th, to continue four days, on the ratification of the Constitution, and for State officers, representatives in Congress, and members of the General Assembly, of which three Senators and twenty-five representatives elected were negroes. On July 4, 1868, "pursuant to General Order No. 98, issued from Headquarters, Third Military District, Department of Georgia, Alabama and Florida, dated Atlanta, Georgia, July 3, 1868," the Legislature met in Atlanta, and was organized by R. B. Bullock, under military order of Gen. Meade.

On July 29th, Joshua Hill and H. V. M. Miller were elected United States Senators. The fourteenth amendment to the Constitution was ratified, and all the conditions of Congressional reconstruction complied with. On July 28, 1868, the State was declared to be restored to the Union.

Upon examination of the Constitution of the State, no provision thereof expressly gave to the negroes the right to hold office; the negroes were therefore expelled from the Legislature. On December 22, 1869, Congress passed "An Act to promote the Reconstruction of the State of Georgia." Whereupon Rufus B. Bullock issued the following order: "Atlanta, January 8, 1870. In pursuance of the Act of Congress (to promote the reconstruction of the State of Georgia), approved December 22, 1869, it is ordered that J. W. G. Mills, Esqr., as Clerk pro tem. will proceed to organize the Senate. He will call the body to order at 12 o'clock M., on Monday, the tenth instant, in the Senate chamber. The names of the persons proclaimed as elected members of the Senate, in the order of General Meade, dated "Headquarters, Third Military District, Department of Georgia, Florida and Alabama, Atlanta, Ga., January 25, 1868, General Order 90. As each name is called, the person so summoned will, if not disqualified, proceed to the clerk's desk, and take oath or make affirmation (as the case may be) prescribed in the said act, before Judge Smith, United States Commissioner, who will be present and administer the oath. When the oaths are so executed, they will be filed with the Honorable, the Secretary of State, or his deputy, who will be present; when all the names mentioned in said order of General Meade, have been called as before provided, such of the persons as shall be qualified will thereupon proceed to organize by the election and qualification of the proper officers."

RUFUS B. BULLOCK,
Provisional Governor.

On February 15, 1870, the General Assembly proceeded to elect three United States Senators, after having already elected two—Messrs. Hill and Miller, who were in life, had not resigned, were at Washington applying for their seats, and whose term of service had not expired. But, of course, official oaths and constitutional obligations were cobwebs, with the majority of the Legislature. Foster Blodgett was declared elected for the term of six years, to commence on March 4, 1871. Henry P. Farrow was declared elected for the term expiring on March 4, 1873, and Richard H. Whitely was declared elected for the term expiring March 4, 1871. Georgia had seven Senators in life, elected—not one of whom had been permitted to qualify, and take his seat. The patriotic members of the Senate entered upon the journals their indignant protest. But Provisional Governor Rufus B. Bullock had the protection of Brevet Major-General Alfred H.

Terry, commanding the military district of the State of Georgia.

On July 18, 1870, the Provisional Governor informed the General Assembly that he had secured unofficial information of the passage of an act to admit the State to representation in Congress, and adding that he was informed that "the General commanding will make no objection to the General Assembly proceeding with legislation." The Governor and Treasurer, presented against each other, respectively, charges of high crimes and misdemeanors, which were investigated by a joint committee of the two houses of the General Assembly during the months of May and June, 1870. The evidence, and the report of the committee, which appears on the journal of the General Assembly, establish the guilt of both. Reconstruction in the seceded States, was a reign of falsehood, lawlessness, robbery and despotism. It is due to a few able and patriotic members of that historic Legislature, to say that they made a manly and gallant stand for constitutional liberty and common honesty, for which the country owed them a debt of gratitude it will be difficult to discharge. Finally the State was allowed representation in Congress. Gov. Bullock found it necessary to his safety to retire from the State before the expiration of his term of service. A new election installed an honest democratic administration.

In 1877, the people of Georgia held a constitutional convention, over which that incorruptible statesman and patriot, Charles J. Jenkins, presided; and established a Constitution that secured white over black domination, and restored the supremacy of the civil over the military authority.

The men who invoked, imposed and enforced Congressional Reconstruction upon a brave and patriotic people—defeated in war—in the anguish of grief, and thralldom of poverty, sacrificed honor, race and liberty for power and plunder, and have gone to history, embalmed in infamy.

CHAPTER VIII.

Conditions after the War—Lawyers.

The reconstruction regime packed the judiciary, as far as possible, with judges in sympathy with their policy. That policy had greatly demoralized the public sentiment. This was especially true in certain sections of the State. The people of the mountain region of the State were opposed to secession. They lived remote from cities and railroads, owned few slaves, made an honest living by hard labor, and distilled their corn and fruit without revenue. They did not care whether slavery was established or prohibited in the territories; the government was beneficent to them. They honored its founders, loved its traditions, and were proud of its flag. Their delegates in the convention were nearly unanimous in opposing secession. Several of their delegates declined to sign the ordinance after it was adopted. These people had bright intellects, strong convictions and high prejudices. They were true and faithful in their friendships, bitter and relentless in their enmities, generous in hospitality, and full of resources in the execution of their purposes. When the war came they were divided. Most of them joined the Confederate, but some the Union army; and many sought to avoid service in either. During the war, Home Guards, representing both sides—under the pretext of protecting—plundered the people. When the war ended, and the men returned home with four years' training in the nursing and indulgence of passion, it will be readily perceived that collisions and conflicts were inevitable. The influence of reconstruction principles, practices and ethics, superadded to the partisan prejudices and passions engendered by the war, left the people in a state of demoralization that found expression in disorganization and crime. Men appeared at public gatherings and superior courts with uniforms and army, or navy pistols buckled around them, looking daggers at those supposed to be or to have been enemies, and anxious for an excuse or an opportunity for revenge. The Union element felt that they had triumphed in war, and seemed to exult in the oppressions of reconstruction, relying upon those in power to protect them in whatever line of conduct they saw proper to adopt or pursue. Inoffensive men were shot down unceremoniously in open daylight, at the supper table, at night, or from ambush while at work in the field. A conviction for murder could not be secured. Judges, solicitors and jurymen were of the party temporarily in power. William P. Milton, at Ellijay, while sitting at supper at his home, was shot through a window, and killed. Worly sneaked up behind William Ellington, and shot him in the back. Hately rode into town in open daylight and shot James G. Inlow through the head as he sat on the sidewalk, killing him instantly. Near "White path," Bartley Pinson, while ploughing in his field, was shot from ambush and fell dead in his tracks; and not one of the criminals was convicted. At Morgantown, James Morris, a kind-hearted old gentleman over seventy years of age, was aroused about midnight by the screams of a woman in distress, and walked across the public square to the house of Spencer Pruitt, ordinary of the county, whence the cry of distress proceeded. He stepped into the house, and asked: "In the name of God, what does this mean?" Whereupon Pruitt, a very large, strong man,—who was shamefully abusing his wife, seized Morris and held him until he made his two boys stab him to death. The next day Pruitt pointed to the boys, and said: "There are the brave chaps who stabbed the d— old rascal to death." Pruitt and his boys were indicted. He escaped, and was never tried. The boys were tried, of course, before a Republican judge, prosecuted by a Republican solicitor-general, and a Republican jury. James R. Brown and I were employed to aid the prosecution, which we did, to the utmost of our ability. Unknown to us and the court, Pruitt's friends had armed themselves, and formed a conspiracy to kill Brown and myself in the courthouse as soon as a verdict of guilty was returned. Samuel Ralston was informed of it, armed a number of his friends, and notified the leader of the conspiracy that he and his crowd were under observation, and the first motion towards violence they made would cost them their lives. The defense was that they were under fourteen years of age, and acted in obedience to the order of their father. They were acquitted. Later, Duke Palmer, a lawyer living in Cleveland, was returning home from Towns superior court, and was shot in the back by an assassin concealed in the bushes on the roadside. It so happened that he and I occupied the same room at the hotel, in Hiawassee. He was a brave man, and of superior intellect. The night before he was killed, he gave me an account of his life, and especially his adventures in Mexico, which were both thrilling and romantic. We sat up until midnight, in conversation. The next morning he bade me: "good-bye," seeming cheerful and happy—little dreaming of the tragic fate awaiting him. That afternoon at 2 o'clock I organized an inquest over his dead body, as it lay in the road, covered with dust and blood. The assassin was concealed behind a stump about ten paces from the road. A party was indicted and tried in Towns superior court, but acquitted. These cases are mentioned as a sample of many others—as illustrating the disorganized state of society, growing out of the secession and reconstruction of the State.

The courts in the counties of Gilmer, Fannin, Union and Towns were held in May and October. The soft, balmy zephyrs, the murmur of sparkling waterfalls and the fragrance of roses, azalias and laurel blooms in May; and the variegated hues of extensive and magnificent forests, and the brisk, healthful breezes of October, were delightful beyond the power of expression. Environment, with these charms and beauties of nature, ought to mollify the malignity of hate; and purify and etherealize the spi rit of love; and doubtless it did. The spirit and discussions of the bar had a most favorable influence in allaying party animosities. The lawyers were a jolly, noble set of fellows, full of good humor, and from envy, perfectly free. The lawyers who practiced in the mountain counties of the Blue Ridge Circuit, were: Geo. D. Rice, James R. Brown, William P. Price, C. D. Phillips, C. J. Wellborn, Wier Boyd, Marshall L. Smith, E. W. Chastain, J. E. Alsabrook, W. H. Simmons, J. A. Jervis, and James Butt, Democrats; and John S. Fain, John A. Wimpy, W. T. Crane, W. T. Day, Samuel C. Johnson, James M. Bishop, Republicans. These men fought like tigers over their cases in the courthouse, but when the intellectual combat was ended—being personal friends—their social intercourse with each other and with the people was of the kindliest and most pleasant character. Their conduct, prompted by a high sense of obligation to the public, did much to restore a better state of feeling among the people. They were greatly aided by a class of substantial citizens of each of the parties, who stood for the right and against the wrong; who had wisdom enough to see the folly of the strife, and patriotism sufficient to endeavor to stop it. When the war cases were disposed of in the courts, an honest Democratic administration of the State government inaugurated, and capable Democratic judges placed on the bench, peace was restored and the wrongs and passions of these stormy and turbulent times relegated to the historian. Most of these men—either before or after the time of which I write—held high office. Chastain and Price were representatives in Congress; Rice, Brown and Wellborn, judges of the Superior Court; and Smith, judge of the City Court of Gainesville. Phillips, Johnson, Bishop, Wellborn and

Greer, solicitors-general. Eight of them were State Senators. Three, Rice, Chastain and Day, were members of the Secession Convention. Seven of these men, Rice, Chastain, Alsabrook, Fain, Johnson, Boyd and Bishop, have crossed the silent river. They lived in a time of peace, and through the storms of war. They each did their duty as they understood it. Honor to their memory and peace to their ashes!

Rice was a very able lawyer, deeply read in the law, devoting his entire attention to its study and practice. He prepared his cases thoroughly, briefed the questions of law and fact—both leading and collateral—elaborately, and therefore entered upon the trial well equipped. When he went upon the bench of the Western Circuit, he turned over to me five cases in Lumpkin Superior Court. They were so well prepared that I found it easy to win all of them.

Brown was a superb lawyer and practitioner. It was delightful to be associated with him in a case. He studied and practiced law as a scientific system, devised for the enforcement of human rights, in conformity to certain established rules. He seized with promptness, the controlling questions in the case, fortified his position with authority and logic, and usually carried the strong points of his adversary by assault.

Chastain was admitted to the bar without reading law, in middle life. He possessed a fine intellect, handsome person, and was brave as Roland. He was a born politician, and the leader of his section. He was Representative and Senator in the State Legislature, and twice a Representative in Congress. He was intensely

Southern. His friends were devoted to him, and his enemies respected and feared him. He was a fluent speaker, knew men, and was formidable before juries.

Price was a good lawyer, but it seemed to me that he never enjoyed the disputes and contentions of the courthouse. As a lawyer, he was open, manly and fair. In his practice, he sought the triumph of the truth and the right. He rendered invaluable service to the State as a member of the Legislature, in reconstruction time. As a member of Congress, he secured the Mint at Dahlonega, from the Government, and the establishment of the North Georgia Agricultural College, a service that merits the gratitude of the people, and enshrines him in their affection. He is a cultured, courtly, Christian gentleman.

Boyd was unique, admitted to the bar past middle life, while Clerk of the Superior Court of Lumpkin County, he was more familiar with the forms of practice than the principles of jurisprudence. He never had the slightest conception that his client could possibly be in the wrong or his adversary in the right. He was intensely ardent in his convictions, absolutely honest; saw a case or legal principle only from his standpoint, and never dreamed that any other view was admissible, or any modification possible. His view of the settlement or compromise of a case was to demand a bonus for taking all he claimed. His antagonist might therefore rely upon a fight to the bitter end. His character, earnestness and honesty made him a power before a jury that knew him.

Smith was a jurist, not an advocate. He was a close

student, with a clear, incisive intellect; and reveled in the complex and abstruse subleties of metaphysics. If he had lived in the time of Aristotle, the Greeks would have voted him an Apotheosis, as the divinity of technicalities. He saw—clear as a sunbeam—defects and objections to pleadings, proof and everything the other side did, alleged or said. His style was cold, clear and conversational. He was perfectly conscientious. While he enjoyed winning a case on its merits, he was charmed and delighted to triumph on a technicality. As associate counsel, in consultation, as you would state the strong points of your case, he would suggest a thousand questions that might arise in your case, and was equally fruitful in suggesting difficulties in the adversary's way. Occasionally he made points of inestimable value. It was always much more safe to have him with you than against you.

Phillips, unlike Smith, cared nothing for technicalities. He was rather a loose pleader. His mind quick in action, his person imposing, his humor exuberant, his invective withering—all taken together, made him an advocate of decided power. His speech in the prosecution of Rogers for murder, in Fannin Superior Court, the presiding judge (Lester) thought was the finest he ever heard.

Wellborn was a good lawyer, of finely balanced mind and character. His pleading neat, he presented his proofs clearly, and sought the triumph of right and justice in the administration of the law.

CHAPTER IX.

Amusing Incidents in Court.

It often happens that in the contention of strife and anxieties of court proceedings, something will occur to excite mirth, and relieve the tension of counsel and litigants. The spectators are always on the "qui vive," for something of this sort. It is astonishing how quickly they catch a sally of wit, a felicitous retort, or an exhibition of the ludicrous. They listen to the judge and lawyers, and scan the witnesses, in the expectation of hearing something either interesting or amusing. A witness was on the stand in Cherokee Superior Court. He was a minister of the Gospel. I have observed that a certain class of that sacred profession (I hope a small one), on the witness stand, always seek to impress themselves upon the court and country—they generally succeed. I never understood the reason for it. But it has been true since the time of the Rev. Burwell Shines. The witness in question was a master in the figurative style of speech, as the sequel will show. He had made his statement in answer to questions, on the direct examination. The late Judge George N. Lester, conducting the cross examination, said: "Do I understand you to state so and so," repeating the statement made by the witness to which he replied with an air of offended sacradotal dignity: "Mistur Lustur, I have chawed my terbacker."

On a certain Tuesday morning, in Ellijay, just as I entered the courtroom, the judge called the case of George Ellis vs. William Cole, trover, and announced Greer for the plaintiff. The parties announced "ready." Counsel read the declaration to the jury, and swore the plaintiff as a witness, who went upon the stand. He had an expression of peculiar sadness that engaged my attention, excited my curiosity, and presented an imploring appeal for sympathy. He was tall, angular and bony in physique, with very black hair and bear. His head had the appearance of having been just taken from a charcoal heap; his arms were long, and hands and feet large. His trousers lacked about four inches of reaching to his shoes, which were homemade and of primitive style. He was in his shirt-sleeves—that is, he was without coat or vest—the collar unbuttoned. The buttons on his bosom were manufactured of coarse, cotton thread. His shoulders were so round, or rather bent, that when they touched the wall his head projected about one foot from it, as he stood upon the stand. As he stood thus he was the living personification of sorrow. From his testimony, which was delivered in monosyllables mainly, it appeared that he did a certain amount of ditching, for which Cole was to pay him a cow and calf and a rifle-gun. The gun was delivered; Cole refused to deliver the cattle. The calf had died, but another calf had succeeded it. The action was brought to recover the cow and her increase. Greer (feeling that he had proven a strong case), turned the witness to the other side for examination. "Ah, stop a moment, Mr. Ellis. What became of that cow and calf?" With an expression of anguish, that he would be supposed to show in looking for the last time upon his wife's coffin, he answered in these words: "They tell me that the cow are dead, and that the calf what she had superior to that time were in the same fix."

Unity in variety seems to be a universal law of nature. Of all the multitudinous leaves of the forest, no two of them are precisely alike. The same is true of the forms, features and intellectual attributes of the human race. Men appearing very much alike in many respects, yet differ widely in an infinite variety of characteristics. We meet, occasionally, a man of no merit, but great ignorance and self-assertion, who moves among his fellows with a sort of "hail, the conquering hero comes" air that advertises him as a candidate for the popularity and fame among men, for which he has already given himself credit. His manners and movements are as pompous and bombastic as a Pronunciamento, of Santa Anna, in revolutionary times in Mexico. Whether this characteristic results from a high soul, with lofty aspirations, that has been starved and dwarfed by the want of opportunities for expansion and development, or whether it is the offspring of narrow, contracted ignorance, stimulated by an unworthy and unattainable ambition, presents a problem that is referred to the psychological, for solution. These reflections have been suggested by the character of a witness for the State in the case of the State vs. Richard Ratliff, charged with the offense of assault and battery, in Gilmer Superior Court. This witness was a man of striking appearance and manner. He was slightly above medium height, a little rotund but of shapely figure, with rather a springy, yet dignified movement. His complexion was florid and nose decidedly red. He wore a black Prince Albert coat, a beaver hat, standing collar, supported by a rather wide black stock. Taken altogether, he was by no means a man of repulsive appearance—rather the contrary. His great pretention was his facility in the use of words; his strength lay in his capacity to coin them, and his weakness in his total ignorance of their meaning. The trouble out of which the indictment grew, occurred at a "road working." Of course a "road working" without at least one fight would be justly esteemed a failure. There was but one on this occasion, but this one had in it (according to the statement of the witness) the element of what the lawyers call a "continuendo," when the witness related the first part (for it took place in installments), and stopped. "Go on," said the solicitor-general, "and state what next occurred." Straightening up himself, and adjusting his stock and standing collar, with an expression on his face which gave the public notice, that something important was about to happen, he said: "Previous aufter that, I was follering along before, and seen the priminary gwines on."

In Union Superior Court the case of John Doe ex dem. Brown, et al. vs. Richard Roe, cas. ejr., and Smith, tenant, etc., was on trial. The defense was the statute of limitations. The late witty, humorous, eloquent John W. H. Underwood, was counsel for defendant. A witness on the stand had stated clearly and intelligently about the possession of the lot sued for, how much was cleared, etc., when the following occurred. Counsel: "Mr. Witness, you say Smith is in possession of this lot of land, claiming it as his?" Witness: "Yes, sir." Counsel: "You say Smith cleared twenty acres of the lot?" Witness: "Yes, sir." Counsel: "When did Smith first enter into the possession of it?" Witness: "I don't remember the time." Counsel: "See if you can not refresh your recollection?" Witness: "Well, Squire, really (scratching his head just behind the right ear), I can't remember. Counsel: "Was it in the spring, summer, fall or winter?" Witness: (In a deep study for a moment), then, brightening up, answered: "Ah! I remember now, Squire, it was the time that March Addington wintered John Butt's bull."

In the rural districts of the country, before the advent of railroads, telegraphs, telephones, daily mails, common schools, and cheap watches, even the most intelligent paid but little attention to dates. There was nothing in their surroundings that made it especially necessary to store away in the garret of memory the rubbish of dry and useless dates. It was convenient for them to regulate their calendar by important events, occurring under their own observation. Very few knew or cared anything about the day on which Columbus sailed from Palos on his great voyage of discovery, or when he discovered San Salvador, or the date of the inauguration of the Reformation, or when the last of the "Stuarts" was driven from the throne, the British dynasty changed and the "Bill of Rights" adopted by the Convention Parliament. But, "Big Court," the "Camp-meeting" and the "Fourth of July Barbecue," they attended and remembered. These events became epochal in their history, as the bases from which they reckoned time. The fact that March Addington "wintered John Butt's bull," was perhaps of less importance than these historic events; yet it was by no means of insignificance in vindicating the truth of a question involving time. There is a deep philosophy underlying these facts. It is found in the statement that if you wish to interest a person in any matter, you must identify him with its activities. It is upon this principle that a wife never forgets the date of her marriage, or a mother the birth of her child. The question of time arises in some form, in the trial of every case. The case of the State vs. Hugh Porter, for malicious mischief was no exception to the rule. The fact alleged as constituting the offense was the killing of Shade Green's cow by Porter, in his corn-field. Mr. Green was a man of some humor which, though in the rough, would sometimes sparkle. He was an honest man and a truthful witness; which, unfortunately, can not be said of all witnesses. The cow was found dead in Porter's cornfield; the damage to the corn, the habit of the animal and the height of the fence, were under investigation. John Echols, a witness, had described the height of the fence by stating that "he could stand astride of it." Mr. Green, the prosecutor, was on the stand. I asked him, as follows: "How high was Porter's fence?" to which he replied: "It was about up to

John Echols' fork." To the question: "When was the cow found dead?" he answered: "It was summers along in tatur diggin time." I asked: "When do we dig potatoes?" He replied: "Ah! Well now, that depends entirely on when the bread gives out."

Augustus M. Russell was a man of strongly marked characteristics in many respects. In person, he was tall—six feet and two inches—his hair straight and black, with brown eyes and symmetrical form. His intellect was of a very high order, bright, active and vigorous. By affinity, his relations and connections were, socially and intellectually, high; by the law of moral gravitation, his associations were otherwise. With his mental superiority, steady habits, close application and extensive research would have easily placed him among those at the head of his profession anywhere. As it was, his professional reading did not extend far beyond Hotchkiss' Codification and Cobb's Analysis and Forms. His clients and cases were of a class that did not yield a revenue equal to the "steel trust" and "Standard Oil Company." To contemplate him as a whole was suggestive of royalty in ruins. The Hon. Alexander H. Stephens told me of an adventure he had with him at Calhoun, Ga. Mr. Stephens made a speech during a political campaign at which Russell happened to be present. When he concluded, Russell's friends and chums called on him to reply, which he did, and in which he most recklessly assailed Stephens with all sorts of charges without the slightest regard to truth—to one of which, that greatly nettled Mr. Stephens, he sharply said: "I deny the fact." Russell paused a moment, and then said, "Yes, fellow citizens, that is the gentleman's trouble, he always denies the facts." Mr. Stephens added that that lesson taught him the importance of caution in the use of words.

In Lumpkin Superior Court, Russell was defending a client, charged with an offense by special presentment of the grand jury. The presentment had not been entered on the minutes of court, as the law required. He moved to quash the presentment on that ground. The solicitor-general moved an order to enter it on the minutes of court "Nunc pro tunc," to which he responded: "May it please your honor, I have examined all the authorities, searched Hotchkiss and Cobb (and your honor knows Mr. Cobb was a very sharp man), and I can not find in the books any authority for the making of a nunc pro tunc business out of a special presentment." The judge ruled that there was such authority.

Emancipation changed many things. Among them, the definition of the crime of disturbing religious worship. The change was from a "Congregation of white persons, assembled for public worship" to "A congregation of persons assembled for Divine service." Before this change, J. P. C. was indicted and tried in Lumpkin Superior Court for the offense of interrupting and disturbing "a congregation of white persons, lawfully assembled for public worship." He was defended by Mr. Russell. There were two witnesses in the case, the Rev. Mr. Roberts, and the Hon. Eli Wehunt. The former was a primitive, or "Hardshell" Baptist clergyman. The crime was alleged to have been committed while he was preaching on a certain Sunday, at his own house. It appeared from the evidence that Mr. Roberts' home was a combination of dwelling and still-house, and that the products of the still-house were stored in the smoke-house, located at some distance from where it was made. The preaching was in that part of the combination used as the dwelling. It did not appear what the theme of the discourse was. Whether it was a learned digging in search of the Greek roots of immersion, or of the decree before the foundation of the world, that foreordained whatsoever comes to pass, was left, by the testimony in the case, to conjecture. It was probably both. It did appear that Mr. Roberts and his neighbors had fine orchards and that the apple crop was abundant, and that it was a "pity" to allow the fruit to rot and waste. It further appeared that the neighbors frequently met at Mr. Roberts', especially on Sunday (as it was a leisure day), though the visits were by no means confined to that day. It did not appear that any females attended that service. Nor did it appear whether the crowd of men met for the service, or whether the service was improvised because the crowd had assembled. Mr. Roberts, in his testimony, stated clearly and distinctly that neither he nor his congregation were disturbed in the slightest degree. The Hon. Eli Wehunt, who, after the time of the trial, obtained the high honor of representing Lumpkin County in the General Assembly of the State—a county that had been represented by such men as the Honorable W. P. Price and Honorable Weir Boyd—had been denied the advantage of an early education. Indeed, I am informed that he did not know a letter of the alphabet. He was of Dutch descent, and of marked personality. He was of medium height and size; his eyes grey, and set far back; his cheek-bones high, and his forehead low; his beard long and red, carefully divided in the middle, each half neatly platted and skillfully tied into a knot under his chin. The color of his hair was immune from the power of description; the nearest approach to description is to say that it seemed to be a combination of pale claybank and Albino pink. There was nothing peculiar in his dress except that at the time of the trial, he wore a vest, made of spotted, tanned fawn-skin; and it was a picturesque garment. He testified that while Mr. Roberts was preaching, on the Sunday in question, in his dwelling, he and defendant met behind the smoke-house, in which the brandy was stored—some distance from the dwelling—with no one but himself and the defendant present. The defendant abused him, and they had a private quarrel. With this evidence the State closed; the defendant introduced none, and the court took a recess for dinner. Upon resuming the bench after dinner, the judge said: "Gentlemen, proceed with the argument of this case. Mr. Russell, state your points to the solicitor-general." Russell rose from his seat with some difficulty, and balancing and steadying himself as well as he could, responded to the judge's order as follows: "M-M-may it please your h-honor, my point in the defense is that Eli Wehunt is not a congregation of white persons assembled for public worship." The verdict of the jury sustained the point.

Almost every superior court has pending, a case that

attracts more than ordinary public interest. This was true of a case in Gilmer County, popularly known as: "The Granny King case." Mrs. King was a kind-hearted old lady, who practiced a profession that made her especially popular with the married ladies, in a thickly settled community, with a rapidly increasing birth-rate. Mr. and Mrs. King owned a plantation containing some very fine bottom land, on "Owltown Creek." They had no children. Mr. King died. Most people have observed that it is not difficult to find those who desire the possession of what the late Judge Dawson A. Walker was accustomed to call "rich flat-land." It turned out to be true in this case. The Ahab who sought this vineyard was a collateral relative who resided in Dawson County, whose name was "Montgomery." He applied for letters of administration. Mrs. King resisted the application on the ground that she, as the widow, was entitled to it. Rice, Boyd and Smith represented Montgomery; James R. Brown and H. P. Bell represented the widow. Pending the controversy over the administration, Montgomery filed a bill in equity to recover the property. It turned out on the trial of the right to the administration, that Mrs. King had been previously married. She claimed to have been divorced, but could only show one verdict granting it. Montgomery won the administration. Mrs. King set up in her answer and cross bill, that her money, earned by her profession, paid for the land, that the deed was taken in his name, and that he held it as an implied, or resulting trust for her. On the trial, Boyd moved to dismiss his bill, to which counsel for

Mrs. King objected, on the ground that she had set up cross equities. In support of his motion, Boyd, among other things, said: "May it please your honor, we have met the gentlemen on the other side of this fight, and vanquished them on every field; and now, may it please your honor, when we want to retire across the "Amicalola mountain," and enjoy in peace our victory, the gentlemen won't let us." The motion was refused, the case tried, and Mrs. King won. Fannin, Union and Towns followed the circuit, closing with Towns. Boyd and Smith, returned home in the same buggy. After a long silence, Boyd suddenly said: "Bro. Smith, we have no cause to complain of our luck during this riding; we have lost but one case." "That is true, Bro. Boyd, but we have tried but one," replied Smith—the "Granny King case."

It is as refreshing to a lawyer, as a fountain in a desert, to a caravan, to meet with a party in a case, who will "swear the truth to his own hurt." In an age distinguished for its avarice, it is seldom a party in interest can be found who will not discolor the truth in favor of his interest. Occasionally, however, a rare exception to this general rule will occur. Such an instance took place in Fannin Superior Court. John A. Jervis, Esqr., sued John Brown, in ejectment, for the recovery of a lot of land. The defendant was an octogenarian—his hair white as snow, his rather small person slightly bent with age. The expression of his face placid and benevolent; he looked the very embodiment of peace and innocence. Jervis presented his evidence, showing his absolute right to recover. No counsel was marked or appeared for the defendant. Col. Wier Boyd, sitting by, seeing the situation, and humanely desiring to do a kindness to an aged, worthy, poor old man, or share with him in a division of the land in the event he recovered, or both, held a brief consultation with the defendant, said: "Your honor will please mark my name for the defendant;" administered the witness's oath to defendant and said to him: "Uncle Johnny, go on the stand," and proceeded to examine him as follows: Counsel: "Uncle Johnny, do you know the land sued for in this case?" Witness: "I do." Counsel: "Who is in possession of this land?" Witness: "I am." Counsel: "How long have you been in possession?" Witness: "Nine or ten years." Counsel: "What improvements have you put on this lot?" Witness: "I built a cabin and cleared twelve or fifteen acres." Counsel: "Did anybody ever disturb your possession?" Witness: "No, sir." Counsel: "You state, Uncle Johnny, that you have occupied this land without disturbance, continuously, for nine or ten years, built a house on it, and cleared twelve or fifteen acres of it,—all the time claiming it as your own?" Witness: "I just went on the land and cleared, and built the house, and lived on it. I never claimed it. It is not my land." Counsel: "What! Do you say that this is not your land?" Witness: "Yes, sir; I say that this land is not mine, I never claimed it. It belongs to the plaintiff." Counsel: "Come down, Uncle Johnny."

Charles Alston, of Towns County, was insulted, or supposed himself insulted, to an extent that, in his opinion, demanded blood in atonement. He therefore challenged the offender. Whether the challenge resulted from the gravity of the offense, the homicidal impulse, supposed to be irresistible, in the constitutional organism of a certain class of the genus homo, or from hereditary chivalry (for he was a native South Carolinian), was never satisfactorily ascertained. The grand jury of the county, less in sympathy with the punctillios of personal honor than the enforcement of criminal law, indicted him for an alleged violation thereof. This rude action of the grand jury amused the people of the community, but disgusted the defendant. He employed Col. Weir Boyd to defend him. The case, from its novelty in this section of the State, created great interest in the public mind; and from its importance, weighed heavily upon the thought of his faithful counsel. After its continuance for several terms of the court, it was finally tried, resulting in the triumphant acquittal of the defendant, to the disparagement of the code penal, and to the honor of the code duello. After the adjournment of the court, at which the trial took place, Boyd and Marshall S. Smith were returning home in a buggy, together as usual, Boyd driving the regulation mule, and Smith intensely absorbed in an effort to untangle the knotty kinks in a skein of metaphysical abstrusities, and "Distinguish and divide a hair, 'twixt north and north-west side." Boyd said to him: "Brother Smith, what do you think of my speech in the Alston case? Smith replied: "Brother Boyd, it was a failure." Boyd said (with solemn emphasis): "Brother Smith, I carried that speech too long, it soured."

Men do not always show wisdom in choosing an avocation. They sometimes disregard the advice of the Roman philosopher "to consult capacity and follow inclination," and follow inclination without consulting capacity. This truth finds a signal illustration in two applications for admission to the bar. They were made at different times, but to the superior court of the same county. One of the applicants was an ignorant, pretentious, pedantic pedagogue. He was tall, of very dark complexion, and elaborately and gaudily dressed. When the court met in the morning for the examination, he arose, with a pompous, magisterial sort of movement. Having very much the appearance of a combined advertisement of an animal and circus show, he addressed the court as follows: "May it please your honor, as I have recently been engaged in the very interesting study of philology, I ask the privilege of answering the questions, in this examination, in a paraphrastic manner." The privilege was accorded. He answered the questions so very paraphrastically that the judge advised him to withdraw his application. C. W., the other applicant, had passed middle life by at least a decade. He had failed to realize his ambitious hopes for distinction in defeat, for numerous small offices which he sought. He had taught singing-school without discovering a bonanza in melody, but was not without power in politics, in his militia district, which was remote from the county courthouse. In stature, he was a little below medium size, in intellect, below mediocrity; and in culture, still lower. His two upper front teeth were missing, and the color of his hair was of the claybank variety. His application was duly filed, and the order of court, appointing the committee of examination, regularly passed, and entered on the minutes of court. The committee met the applicant, G. L. conducting the examination on Common Law. After asking, "What was law in general? What was civil law; what natural, and what revealed law was?" And various questions about rights—alienable and inalienable, absolute and relative—all of which was Egyptian hieroglyphics to W., G. L. turned to the "economic or domestic relation, when the following occurred: G. L.: "Mr. W., how many kinds of persons are there in law?" No answer. G. L., explaining, stated, "there are two, natural and artificial." G. L.: "What are natural persons?" No answer. G. L., explaining again: "Natural persons are such as the God of nature formed; you and I are natural persons." G. L.: "What is an artificial person?" "A woman," promptly answered W. G. L.: "Mr. W., how many kinds of children are there in law?" "Two," answered W. G. L.: "That is correct. Now, Mr. W., what are they?" W.: "Boys and gals." He was admitted, and a license certifying "that after examination he was found to be learned and well skilled in the knowledge of the law; and authorized to practice in all the courts of law and equity in this State, except the Supreme Court." Somehow litigants managed their business without his assistance. I never knew nor heard of his receiving a retainer, or appearing in a case.

Young men may avoid breakers ahead by choosing a life-work with deliberation and decision and pursuing it with integrity and industry.

CHAPTER X.

Secession.

The Secession Convention at Milledgeville, adjourned January 29th, to meet in Savannah upon the call of the president. On February 9th I reached Nashville, as Commissioner of Georgia to the State of Tennessee. That State, at an election, though recently held, had refused to call a convention to consider the grievances of which the Southern States complained, by a popular majority of ten thousand votes.

The Legislature was not in session. The only means I, therefore had of official communication with the authorities was with the Governor of the State. That chivalric, patriotic, sterling statesman, Isham G. Harris, was governor. The Ordinance of Secession, together with the reasons for its adoption, were officially and formally presented to him in the executive office, and the co-operation of Tennessee, with the seceded States, in the formation of the Southern Confederacy, invited. Gov. Harris was in thorough and hearty sympathy with the movement, but surrounded with great obstacles. The people had refused to call a convention to consider the matter; the legislature was not in session; the border States peace conference was in session in Washington, and a condition of apprehensive uncertainty and alarm reigned supreme. The Governor could only await the logic of events and conform his action to their results.

While I was in Nashville, Gen. Leslie Combs, of Kentucky, addressed an immense concourse of people at night, in the public square. His speech was an eloquent and impassioned appeal for the Union. Pending its delivery, the mayor of the city read a fake telegram from Washington, stating that Lewis T. Wigfall, of Texas, had killed Andrew Johnson in a duel. The excitement of the multitude defies description. My report of this mission appears in the journal of the Convention.

On my return from Nashville, I met at Chattanooga, Jefferson Davis, with his party, on his way to Montgomery to assume the presidency of the Confederacy. The crowds at the different railway stations to Atlanta were numerous and enthusiastic. Though the night was far advanced, at Dalton, upon the vociferous and continued demand of the crowd, he came out of the car, and made a short and thrilling speech.

By proclamation of President G. W. Crawford, the Convention reassembled, on March 7th, at Savannah; and after ratifying the permanent constitution of the Confederate States, revising the constitution of the State, and the passage of such ordinances as were necessary to adjust the State to its new relations and provide for such exigencies as the changed order of things might create, adjourned sine die, on March 23, 1861.

There followed a restless, feverish state of the public mind. Secession orators and leaders assured the people "That we were in the midst of the most remarkable revolution of history—remarkable because peaceful." The intuition of the common people taught them better. The coming event had "cast its shadow before." They had no doubt but that war would result, and were far from being a unit in favor of the policy of secession, until the fire upon Sumter, and the proclamation of President Lincoln calling for 75,000 men to suppress the insurrection, dispelled the peace delusion, and united the Southern people from "many as the billows, to one as the sea," in the defense of their firesides, their altars and their homes.

Lincoln's proclamation determined the course of Virginia and Tennessee; and they joined the Southern sisterhood. Robert E. Lee and Albert Sydney Johnston resigned their commissions in the United States Army, and tendered their stainless blades to the land of their nativity and allegiance. The latter was at San Francisco, Cal., at the time, and made his way in midsummer, across the desert to Texas, the State of his adoption and his love. His escort was thirty brave young men (some of them army officers), who had formed the resolution to cast their fortunes with the South, without any knowledge of his purpose to do so. They were only too glad to be joined by such a comrade. They ran the gauntlet of a cordon of Federal garrisons from Los Angeles to Fort Fillmore, infested with hostile Indians, robbers and marauders, under a temperature that was burning, and a thirst consuming, for a distance of fifteen hundred miles, moving mostly during the night, requiring six weeks time, and accomplished the march without a serious mishap or adventure.

The brave people of Kentucky, Missouri and Maryland, writhing in the crucifixion of a conflict between the sentiments of love for the Union and hatred of oppression, stood for the neutrality of their respective States until the policy and power of the Federal Government bound them in the chains of slavery and trampled them in the dust and blood of despotism, and secured from the border States two hundred and fifty thousand of the best troops in the Union Army. It was then too late to correct the mistake. The States of Kentucky and Missouri then had democratic administrations, and if these great States had united with the Confederacy at the beginning, the final result might, and probably would, have been different.

The promptness with which Maj. Anderson surrendered Fort Sumter, intensified the enthusiasm of the excitable and impulsive, and increased the delusion that the conflict would be short and successful. Among the young men, especially, there was a restless rush to enter the military service. The unreflecting esteemed it a sort of holiday recreation, and hungered and thirsted for the excitement of the fray. People of thoughtfulness, familiar with history, and who understood the character of the American people, knew better. It is due to this class of young men who entered the service early, unburdened with families and business obligations and relations, to say that they developed into the finest soldiers the world ever saw. Trained by discipline to subordination, thrilled by the impulse of an ardent patriotism, led by soldiers like Robert E. Lee, Albert Sydney Johnston, Stonewall Jackson and

Bedford N. Forrest, they were invincible to any antagonist but death. The author joined the first company of volunteers raised in the county of Forsyth, but a large mass-meeting of the people requested him, by resolution—unanimously adopted—to withdraw from the company and remain at home for the present, to aid in raising troops and in making provision for the families of such as might need assistance, with which resolution he complied.

The battle of Manassas, July 21, 1861, was a brilliant triumph of the Confederates and gratifying to Southern pride and complimentary to valor; but it increased the delusion under which the Southern people labored as to the continuance and result of the war. The masses of them knew nothing of Gen. Scott's plan to overwhelm the Confederacy with three grand armies, one to move against Richmond, another down the Mississippi River, and the third to bisect the Confederacy diagonally from Louisville via the L. & N. railway to the sea. Nor did they know of the vast efforts and resources employed for the organization and equipment of these immense armies; nor were they fully aroused to a sense of their danger until the disaster of Forts Henry and Donelson; and the retreat of Albert Sydney Johnston from Bowling Green, to the south bank of the Tennessee River, brought them to a realization of their peril.

The year 1861 was fruitful in local strife in the border States, and elaborate preparation for the fearful struggle to follow. In October I was elected to the Senate. This was the first general election under the revised constitution, by which the Senators were reduced to forty-four in number. The counties of Cherokee, Forsyth and Milton formed the thirty-ninth district. The Legislature met in November. It was the first General Assembly after the secession of the States, and the formation of the Confederacy. All classes, professions and avocations in the State were represented by typical men—men of high personal character, eminent ability and unselfish patriotism. Warren Akin was elected speaker of the House of Representatives. On its roll of members appears the names Elbridge G. Cabaniss, Thos. M. Norwood, George N. Lester, Thomas G. Lawson, George T. Barnes, Osborne L. Smith, Milton A. Candler and many others of merit and ability. The Senate was organized by the election of that accomplished and scholarly gentleman, John Billups, president, and James M. Mobley, secretary. The agriculturalists had superb representatives in the Senate in Wm. M. Brown, Wm. M. Hill, Timothy Furlow, Richard Lane and Samuel Y. Jamison; the bar in James L. Seward, Miles W. Lewis, William Gibson, George Gordon, A. J. Hansell, James P. Simmons, Samuel D. Killen and Weir Boyd; medicine in Drs. Winn and Beasley; and scholarship in Joseph H. Echols. The Senate was a body of very able and patriotic men, animated with the single purpose of faithfully discharging their duty to the State, in the hour of existing and impending national calamity. They were distinguished for their ability and moderation, their wisdom and patriotism, their courtesy in official and social relations, their vigor and fairness in debate, and unselfish devotion to the public interest. This Legislature sought, as far as possible, to husband the resources of the State, mitigate the burdens of her people, and strengthen the arm of the Confederate government.

So far as he is informed, the writer is the only survivor of that body of patriotic public servants. The personal friendship and delightful association with these Senators has always been and continues to be, a most pleasant memory to him.

CHAPTER XI.

In The War.

The picnic phase of the war passed with the year 1861.

The following year opened, with the conviction universally prevailing, that it would be protracted, stubborn and bloody. The call of the government for more troops was urgent; and in response thereto, the Governor of Georgia issued his order for twelve regiments of volunteers, to serve for three years, or during the war. Henry C. Kellogg raised one company of 100 men and the writer another of an equal number in Forsyth County. These companies repaired to Camp McDonald early in March, 1862, for organization into regiments. These two—"E" and "I"—Captains, Kellogg and Bell; two from Cherokee—"A" and "B"—Captains, Mullin and Grantham; two from Jackson—"G" and "H"—Captains, Story and Howard; two from Hall—"F" and "H"—Captains, Law and Reeves; one from Pickens—"C"—Captain, Harris, and one from Banks—"D"—Captain, Ragsdale, were formed into the Forty-third Regiment of Georgia Volunteers. The field officers elected to command it were: Skidmore Harris, Colonel; H. P. Bell, Lieutenant-Colonel, and Henry C. Kellogg, Major. Early in April the regiment was ordered to Chattanooga, where it soon entered upon the usual experience of raw recruits—in sickness, superinduced by the change of the habits and comforts of home-life, to the exposure, privation and duties of life in the camp. Measles, flux, dysentery and brain fever attacked the troops; some died and nearly all, were more or less, sick. In this condition of affairs, Brigadier-General Ledbetter, who was commanding at Chattanooga, was ordered to Bridgeport to defend the railroad bridge against General Mitchell, who, with a column, six thousand strong, from Buell's army, was advancing to seize it. General Ledbetter gathered all of his soldiers that were able to move, not exceeding 500 in number, crossed the river and formed his line of battle on the west bank, sending out scouts under Lieutenant Rheinheart to ascertain and report the movements of the enemy. Starnes' cavalry reported that the enemy was rapidly approaching in forces. Convinced of his inability to resist it, General Ledbetter ordered his troops to fall back across the river, which they did in order. Their camp equipage, knapsacks, etc., were placed on a hand-car to run over the bridge. After all had crossed except those in charge of the hand-car, and General Ledbetter, Lieutenant-Colonel Jackson and the writer, who were awaiting the return of the scouts, the enemy's battery opened fire on us from the top of the hill, with a storm of grape and canister. Rheinheart had been wounded and he and his scouts captured. We walked across the bridge in a tempest of balls and splinters from the battery, not 400 yards distant, without being struck. It was not a comfortable experience. The hand-car was behind us, near the middle of the river. It struck me and knocked me from the plank, upon which I was walking, and but for the accident of falling diagonally across the bridge-timbers I would have gone to the bottom of the river. This episode added nothing to the comfort of the occasion. Just as the hand-car reached the end of the bridge it ran over a soldier and cut off, entirely, both of his lower limbs at the trunk, and the poor fellow was wallowing in his blood and gasping in the agonies of a horrible death.

The bridge was blown up and the advance of the enemy, by that means, arrested. This was my introduction "to the pomp and glorious circumstance of war."

When I entered the army, with the opinion entertained of the magnitude and duration of the war, I did not cherish the slightest hope of escaping death. In middle life, without military training or predilection, and honored with command, my only resource was to obey orders, do my duty and perish rather than soil the escutcheon of my wife and children with the stain of cowardice. This I resolved to do, and never faltered in keeping this resolution. The first test came at Bridgeport. I was in command of the regiment, but so sick that I could scarcely stand on my feet, but I did stand all day, though in agony, and without complaint. When a field officer pleads sick, in the hour of danger, the burden of proof is upon him. The result of this affair was an attack of fever that kept me in bed for three months, with the balance quivering in uncertainty most of the time. I rejoined the regiment the last of July, still feeble, in East Tennessee, near Morristown.

The regiment, then in Reynolds' brigade, was ordered to Cumberland Gap, then strongly fortified, and occupied by the Federals under Gen. Morgan. There was a fight with the Federals, under DeCoursey, at Tazewell, resulting in DeCoursey's defeat, and his withdrawal and return to the gap. Nothing of interest occurred except occasional firing between the pickets and foraging parties of the hostile forces, until the last of August, when, in conjunction with Bragg's invasion of Kentucky, Kirby Smith's column crossed the Cumberland Mountains at Rogers' Gap and the Federals evacuated their stronghold and fell back toward the Ohio. Smith had a sharp engagement early in September with Nelson at Richmond, in which he won a brilliant triumph over superior numbers, capturing many prisoners and a large amount of arms, etc., and completely routed the Federal forces. Bragg captured Mumsfordsville, moving in the direction of Louisville; Smith moved to Lexington. We were then in the far-famed "Blue grass region of Kentucky." The counties of Fayette, Bourbon, Madison, Scott, Jessamine and Harrison form the most beautiful country I ever beheld. Its broad, macadamized pikes, its palatial homes, its baronial farms, its expansive fields of blue grass, with their fat, slick, grazing herds; its beautiful forests of walnut, beach, maple and elms, touched with the first tints of autumn —all conspired to heighten its charms. But I confess to being absorbed in other thoughts. We were in the birthland of Lincoln and Davis, among a people, the valor of whose forefathers, at Broadaxe, Wisconsin Heights, Tippecanoe, Thames, New Orleans, Buena

Vista, Cerro Gordo, Cherubusco, Chapultepec and Molino del Rey, had shed the light of imperishable glory upon the chivalry of Kentuckians and the history of Kentucky—a State whose glorious history is illustrated with a long list of illustrious jurists, orators, statesmen, heroes and poets—with her Clays and Crittendens, her Marshalls and Breckenridges, her Prestons and Johnsons, her Prentices, Warfields and Welbys—a glorious list of names that eclipse the proudest that emblazon the escutcheon of Norman heraldry. A land whose men are brave as Cæsar, and whose women, more beautiful than "the star-eyed Sorceress of the Nile," was now hopelessly divided, and trampling the flowers of this Eden in the blood of civil strife and fratricidal slaughter.

Smith advanced to Covington, causing consternation in Cincinnati. I established and commanded the Confederate picket line in front of Covington.

The result of this campaign was the evacuation of Nashville and Cumberland Gap by the Federals, the inauguration of Hawes, Governor at Frankfort, the capture of Mumsfordsville by Bragg, the victory of Smith over Nelson, at Richmond, and the bloody battle of Perryville. This battle was fought by Bragg after the Confederate retreat and Federal pursuit began. The Confederates captured a large number of prisoners and arms, besides securing and sending out a vast amount of commissary stores. Bragg returned to Murfreesboro; Smith, to Knoxville, and the Federal army to Nashville. I resigned my seat in the Senate, at Georgetown, Ky., in September, 1862, in time to elect a successor before the meeting of the General Assembly. Hon. James R. Brown was elected to fill the vacancy. I shall never cease to cherish kind and tender memories of the hospitality of Kentucky Confederates. Riding along a street in Lexington, literally covered with dust, a beautiful woman came out of a handsome cottage, to the gate, and asked me to alight, "Come in and have breakfast." The want of harmony between her appearance and mine induced me to make an effort to excuse myself, which proved unavailing. I went in, and met the hospitality of a sparkling julep and a delightful breakfast, dispensed with the charming grace, dignity and elegance for which the sex is distinguished. I felt something of the sentiment which, I suppose thrilled the heart of the Indian when he discovered the Alabama, and christened it into the name of "Here we rest." Near Paris, I was attacked violently with bilious fever. I was taken to the elegant home of Frank Ford, who, with his good wife, gave me special attention and tender nursing for eight or ten days; at the same time keeping up with the movements of the opposing forces, with the view of preventing my capture. Finally he informed me that the movements of Woolford's cavalry made it vital to me to leave. He put me into his buggy and drove me, in the night, a distance of twenty miles, to Lexington, with a negro boy to ride a horse which he had given to me. I found at the hotel a member of Bragg's staff, sick, and much exercised for his safety. The next afternoon I left Lexington in the direction of Nicholasville, on horseback. After proceeding five or six miles I broke down and could proceed no further. I stopped at the home of Elijah Bryan and remained here more than a week. Mr. Bryan had another guest, in the person of a pale, sick, slender youth, who belonged to Churchill's Brigade. He had been in the battle at Richmond. His age, size and condition, with his intelligence, coolness and courage, impressed me greatly.

The retreat of the Confederates was a severe blow to Southern sympathizers. As the Federals fell back and the Confederates advanced, they hoped the war would be transferred across the Ohio. They were jubilant at the coming, and in tears at the departure of the Confederate army. It was to them unexpected and disappointing. Everybody was on the qui vive for news. All sorts of rumors were flying in every direction as to the movements of the troops of the respective armies. Under the observation and information of Mr. Bryan, I finally ascertained the location and movement of my command, and convinced that if I escaped capture, no time must be lost, I determined to make the effort to rejoin it. Mr. Bryan repeated precisely the kindness of Mr. Ford, by putting a negro boy on my horse, and taking me in his buggy, delivered both at the bridge across the Kentucky River just as it was being set on fire by order of the Confederates. With a grateful heart I bade my friend "good-bye," mounted my horse and was the last to cross the bridge. I held up better than I expected that day, and stopped at a comfortable Kentucky home, where I had some rest. I awoke in the morning to find that someone, during the night, had swapped horses with me. My horse (the present from

Mr. Ford), was large, fat and able. In his place I found a very thin colt, utterly broken down, with a horribly sore back, and so weak that it staggered in walking. The only thing to be done was to take the chances with the colt. So, shortening my saddle-girth a few feet and putting on the saddle, I mounted the crippled colt, to escape the Federal army. When I reached the command and removed the saddle, the colt tumbled down, where it was left when the camp moved. The comforts of that day's travel were not promoted by the kind (?) assurance of everyone I passed, or met, that "I was gone up," that the "Yankees will get you." With my facilities for movement, it was a little tantalizing to be constantly advised as I was, to "hurry up." After resting a few days at Lenoir's Station, we were ordered to Readysville, and thence, on December 19th, took the train at Tullahoma for Vicksburg, where we arrived on the evening of December 27th, and marched from the train, into line of battle, at Chickasaw Bayou, where the fight was in progress. I was in command of the regiment. The troops on that part of the line all next day (Sunday), were under constant fire of shells and sharpshooters.—About sun-up, I was ordered to change the position of the regiment, and while moving to the new position, was shot by a sharpshooter. I was carried to the rear, and at night removed to the hospital in Vicksburg.

Singular coincidences often occur. Maj. Humble, of Louisiana, was shot in the knee; Lt.-Col. Timmons, of Texas, in the ankle, and I in the leg, equidistant from the knee and ankle, on the same day, and met at the hospital at night. Maj. Humble died that night. Lt.-Col. Timmons and I were removed to a private house in the suburbs of the city, and placed in the same room. His foot was amputated and he died. The ball that hit me, ranged between the two bones of the limb, lodging in the knee-joint, destroying the periosteum, caries of the bone succeeded, and gangrene in its most malignant type, supervened, defying arrest by the surgeons. The sloughing progressed with a rapidity and to an extent that was startling. Half a dozen army surgeons, upon consultation, adjudged the case hopeless, and so informed my wife by telegram. My hostess, Mrs. Eberline, told the doctors that pulverized loaf-sugar would arrest the sloughing, which of course, they ridiculed. But when they surrendered the case as hopeless, they told her she could try her sugar. She pulverized a plateful, sifted it through a muslin cloth, and applied it to the wound. I never had any idea of the intensity of agony until then; the only way to conceive of it was to feel it. The third application entirely arrested the sloughing, and within two or three days the wound, which was a large and ghastly one, began a healthy granulation. It turned out that Mrs. Eberline was one of those inspired geniuses in the discovery of simple remedies for emergent ailments with which we sometimes, though rarely, meet. That she was the human agent that saved my life, I have never entertained the slightest doubt. I have been thus particular in recording in detail, what may seem to others a very small matter, in the hope that sometime, somewhere, the facts may be of value to somebody. On

March 8, 1863, occupying a litter, I was placed on the train, under the care of that true soldier and faithful friend, M. H. Eakes, now a useful member of the North Georgia Conference of the M. E. Church, South, and reached home a week later. During the year, with two exceptions, capture and death, I had passed through all the vicissitudes and experience of soldier-life, of hunger and thirst, heat and cold, dust and mud, weary marches and sleepless bivouacs, sickness and wounds; and perhaps had suffered more, and done less, than any soldier in the Confederate service. Col. Harris was killed at Bakers' Creek. I was promoted to the Colonelcy and resigned. Kellogg was promoted, and was wounded at New Hope; but, with Joseph E. Johnson, surrendered the shattered remnant of the Forty-third Georgia Volunteers at Greensboro, N. C., in 1865. Frank Simmons concealed the regimental flag, and brought it home. He concealed it by wrapping it around his person, under his shirt. Its tattered fragments are now with the Archives of the Regimental Association.

CHAPTER XII.

SECOND CONFEDERATE CONGRESS.

In October, 1863, I was elected representative from the ninth district, to the second Congress of the Confederate States. The Congress met in Richmond in December. The House of Representatives was composed of the following gentlemen, from:

ALABAMA—Thomas J. Foster, William R. Smith, M. H. Cruickshank, David Clopton, F. S. Lyon, W. P. Chilton, James L. Pugh, James S. Dickinson.

ARKANSAS—Felix I. Batson, Rufus K. Garland, T. B. Handley, Augustus H. Garland.

FLORIDA—S. St.George Rogers, R. B. Hilton.

GEORGIA—Julian Hartridge, W. E. Smith, M. H. Blandford, Clifford Anderson, John T. Shewmake, Jos. H. Echols, James M. Smith, George N. Lester, Hiram P. Bell, Warren Akin.

KENTUCKY—W. B. Machen, George W. Triplett, Henry E. Read, George W. Ewing, James S. Chrisman, H. W. Bruce, Humphry Marshall, E. M. Bruce, James W. Moore, B. F. Bradley, John M. Elliott.

LOUISIANA—Charles J. Viller, Charles M. Conrad, Duncan F. Kenner, L. J. Dupree, John Perkins, Jr.

MISSISSIPPI—J. A. Orr, W. D. Holder, Israel Welch, H. C. Chambers, O. R. Singleton, E. Barksdale, John T. Lampkin.

Missouri—Thomas L. Sneed, N. T. Norton, John B. Clark, A. H. Conrow, G. G. Vest, P. S. Wilks, R. A. Hatcher.

North Carolina—W. N. H. Smith, R. R. Bridges, James T. Leach, Thomas C. Fuller, Josiah Turner, John A. Gilmer, James M. Leach, James G. Ramsay, B. S. Gaither, George W. Logan.

South Carolina—James H. Witherspoon, Wm. Porcher Miles, L. M. Ayer, W. D. Simpson, James Farrow, W. W. Boyce.

Tennessee—J. B. Heiskell, W. G. Swan, A. S. Colyar, J. P. Murray, H. S. Foote, E. A. Keeble, Jas. McCallam, Thomas Menees, J. D. C. Atkins, John V. Wright, M. W. Clusky.

Texas—S. M. Darden, C. C. Herbert, A. M. Branch, F. B. Sexton, John R. Baylor, S. H. Morgan.

Virginia—R. L. Montague, R. H. Whitfield, W. C. Wickham, Thomas Gholson, Thomas S. Bocock, John T. Goode, Jr., W. C. Rives, D. C. DeJannette, D. Funsten, T. W. M. Holliday, John B. Baldwin, W. R. Staples, S. A. Miller, Robt. Johnston, C. W. Russell.

DELEGATES FROM THE TERRITORIES.

Arizona Territory—M. H. McWillie, Cherokee Nation; E. C. Bowdinot, Choctaw Nation; R. M. Jones, Creek and Seminole Nations; S. B. Callahan.

Thomas S. Bocock, of Virginia, was elected speaker, and A. R. Lamar, of Georgia, clerk.

The First Congress under the permanent Confederate Government had been in session often during its term, and had made provision by law for the use of all our men and means in supporting the prosecution of the war. That body had enacted the Conscript law, which placed every able-bodied man and boy between the ages of eighteen and forty-five, in the Confederacy (except in the border States), and established the Constript Bureau, charged with the duty of their enrollment in the military service of the Government. It had imposed enormous taxes upon the people, including a heavy tax in kind; in a word—it had reaped the field of resources and but little to glean, by the Second Congress, had been left. Up to July, 1863—in the language of the French Minister, M. Douyrs de l'Hays, the "struggle seemed to be balanced" with the scales inclining in favor of the Confederacy. But upon the result of the battle of Gettysburg and the siege of Vicksburg, "gravitation, shifting, turned the other way" and with separation from the trans-Mississippi portion of the Confederacy, by the Federal control of the river, and the loss of supplies drawn therefrom; for that reason, the fortunes of the Confederacy had something of the appearance of desperation. The proposition of France to the English and Russian Governments, to unite with her in an effort to secure an armistice, with the view of myolitions for peace, had been declined. Foreign governments recognized under their interpretation of International Law, the sufficiency of the blockade of Confederate ports. The neutrality of these governments prevented our privateers from entering their ports with their captures for adjudication as prizes; and therefore, they had to be burned or sunk, at sea

The railroads were worn out and transportation crippled. The constant withdrawal of labor from the farms was diminishing the production of supplies; great numbers of so-called "homeguards," and "details" were scouring the country in search of conscripts and deserters. Trusted leaders like Johnson, Jackson, Polk and a host of others of inferior rank, but equal courage, like Ashby, Morgan, Barksdale, Cleburne and hundreds of others, had fallen. The women and such children as were large enough to aid them, were making a most heroic struggle to keep the wolf away. The State governments, as fast and as much as they could, were doling out pittances of corn, flour and cotton-cards to aid them in the fearful effort for food and clothing. The men who had passed middle life and raised families, who were accustomed to peaceful pursuits of agriculture, and the enjoyment of domestic life, without military aptitude or ambition, were unfit for soldiers. Soldiers are made as well as born, and more made than born soldiers. The city of Richmond was practically beleagurered by an army of overwhelming numbers amply equipped, bountifully supplied, and ably commanded. It was defended by a force wholly inadequate in numbers, badly clothed and poorly fed. Judge Geo. N. Lester and myself called on a certain Sunday, to see our friends in the trenches, around the city. The late Judge N. L. Hutchins, Jr., the Colonel commanding a battalion of sharpshooters, invited us to dinner. The spread consisted of thin, green, sour sorghum syrup and coarse corn bread. This was no fault of the Government, nor its officials. It was the misfortune of our situation. The government exhausted all of its powers and resources, in the effort to provide for the necessities and comforts of its heroic defenders, yet these brave men stood by their flag and defended their convictions with a valor never surpassed, under the leadership of a General without an equal. It was under these conditions and surroundings that the Second Confederate Congress met, transacted the public business, and witnessed the dying agonies of a Government, instituted to preserve and perpetuate the inalienable right of civil self-government.

It is interesting to consider the military operations around the city of Richmond, while Congress was in session. In the latter part of the winter, and early portion of the spring, Grant and Lee were confronting each other, north of Richmond. The former, with an army of 141,160 troops and an available reserve of 137,602. The force of the latter numbered 50,000, with no reserves. The campaign was opened by a movement of Kilpatrick, Custer and Dalgreen to cut Lee's communication with Richmond, and by a sudden dash, release the Federal prisoners, assassinate President Davis, and his Cabinet, and sack and burn the city. Dalgreen was met by the War and Treasury Department Clerks and volunteer citizens, not liable to military duty, at the outer defenses of the city, and repulsed with considerable loss—he being among the killed. Custer retreated, burning the bridges behind him; Sheridan, with 8,000 tropps, was approaching when Stewart gathered up a force of 7,100 men, harassed his rear, and by a detour, and forced marches, flanked him and appeared in his front at "Yellow Tavern," six miles from Richmond, where, being reinforced by the department clerks, he was engaged and repulsed. The brave Stewart, at the head of his column, with every chamber of his pistol empty, fell, mortally wounded. On May 1st, Gen. Butler arrived at Bermuda Hundred.

On May 3rd, Grant and Lee fought the great battle of the "Wilderness," which continued for three days. The United States forces being driven back, Grant withdrew and swung around to Spottsylvania Courthouse, where Lee promptly met him, and the fight was renewed and the field made historic by a baptism of blood. The armies confronting and fighting almost daily, moved in the direction of Richmond until they met in the terrible death grapple of slaughter and blood at Cold Harbor. I shall never forget the feelings I experienced while standing on Capitol Hill, in Richmond, listening at the guns sounding the death knell of the Confederacy.

While these environments were not favorable to calm and deliberate legislation, the Congress was undismayed end entered in a business-like way, upon the discharge of its duties. In fact, its duties were few and simple—only to provide for the increase of the army and its support, and for these purposes there were no means or resources of men, money or supplies to be obtained. The only thing that could be done, therefore, was to go through the form of legislation. This, Congress proceeded to do. The questions of leading interest, discussed and considered, were the increase of taxation, the extension of conscription, the suspension of the writ of Habeas Corpus, the employment of negroes in the ranks, and the appointment of a Peace Commission.

It must be remembered that the men in the trenches had families at home, struggling against starvation. When the tax bill was under consideration, I submitted an amendment exempting the products of the garden, orchard and dairy, when used for the support of the family, and not for sale. Hon. Charles M. Conrad—not distinguished for comeliness of person, who wore a wig of rather long, faded hair, of nondescript color—by way of ridicule, proposed to amend my amendment by adding "butter and eggs." Another statesman, who had been imbibing freely (it was in night session), moved to add "bees-wax and tallow." Quite a ripple of amusement passed through the House, at my expense. When it subsided, I arose and spoke as follows:

Mr. Speaker: "I accept both amendments, for the reason that they extend the aid which my amendment is designed to give to the toiling women and children of the country, to prevent their starvation. I apprehend that their gallant husbands and fathers in the trenches around this beleaguered capitol, upon whom we depend for our personal safety, will not appreciate the statesmanship that would deride by ridicule, an effort to help those dearer to their hearts than the blood they so freely give for our protection. Nor will their respect be increased for the wisdom and gravity of legislators who can derive amusement from such derision. I confess my surprise at this feeble effort at wit, coming from the gentleman from Louisiana. He is a sort of favorite with me. I was charmed by his appearance the first time I saw him. Indeed, I had come to the conclusion to beg of him the favor of a lock of his beautiful hair, to keep as a souvenir of both his exalted statesmanship and his personal pulchritude."

After thoroughly discussing the bills to increase taxation and extend conscription, with the certainty that neither could be done, Congress passed them both. The first law provided for the enrollment of those between the ages of eighteen and forty-five years. The new law included those between seventeen and fifty years of age. While the chairman of the committee on military affairs, Hon. W. P. Miles, was discussing the conscript bill with regard to including ministers of the Gospel, a member asked him the question "did not St. Paul labor? Was he not a tent maker?" to which, in much confusion, he replied, "I will say to the gentleman, that I can not answer his questions at present, as I am not fresh from the authorities upon the subject." Perhaps the ablest discussion of the Congress was that upon the suspension of the writ of Habeas Corpus. It was not suspended. The question of enlisting the negroes into the ranks as soldiers was long disputed, and the bill for that purpose finally passed. Grant had said that the Confederacy had "robbed the cradle and the grave" to recruit its armies, and had calculated on success with mathematical certainty on the basis that when the last Confederate soldier was dead, the United States would still have an army left. The argument was that they could not conquer the Confederates, but that by holding on long enough, they could destroy them. And it was for this reason that the United States Government, under Grant's advice, refused to exchange prisoners. Every Confederate held in prison was equivalent to a dead soldier. The Confederacy had put its last man into the field. The Union had an army that quadrupled its numbers, already in the field, with large resources of men at home; and the world from which to recruit its depleted ranks, with agents abroad actively engaged in enlisting mercenaries. The United States Government, therefore, cruelly allowed thousands of brave men on both sides to suffer, languish, and die in prison, rather than exchange them, in conformity to the usage of civilized warfare. To put the negroes into the ranks in sufficient numbers to do any good would have soon diminished the production of supplies to the starvation point. If they had the capability of becoming soldiers, the time required for their organization and training, made their employment too late. The Confederacy was rapidly tottering to its fall.

The members of the House of Representatives were, in the main, able men. There was among them a small class of impulsive, enthusiastic optimists, inclined to radicalism. There was another class of wise, practical, conservative men, who knew that it required men and money to prosecute successful war; and that the Confederacy had neither. This class clearly saw that the end was near. Anxious to save whatever could be secured, from the final wreck, and make a last desperate effort to accomplish that object, they favored an effort at negotiation, the appointment of a commission to the Government of the United States, to ascertain upon what terms peace could be made and the war ended. Four men, Adkins, of Tenn., Echols, Lester and Bell, of Ga., were quietly active and prominent in originating this movement. It was soon discovered that many members favored it.

In the meantime, Francis P. Blair appeared in Richmond from Washington, upon what was understood or conjectured to be, a sort of unofficial peace mission. The sentiment in favor of an effort at negotiation grew rapidly. A meeting was held at the "Ballard House," over which Hon. W. A. Graham, Senator from North Carolina, presided. At this meeting, after full consideration, it was resolved to introduce and press the passage in the House of Representatives a resolution authorizing and requesting the President to appoint a commission for that purpose. The morning after the meeting the *Richmond Sentinel* came out in an article with the sensational head-lines: "Treason! Treason!" bitterly denouncing the meeting as a traitorous conspiracy against the Confederacy.

When President Davis was informed of this movement, he stated promptly and frankly that if it was thought best, he would appoint the commission at once, without awaiting the action of Congress. He had an interview with the vice-president upon the subject, in which it was determined to appoint the commission. The President asked Mr. Stephens to suggest a commissioner; he named Judge Campbell. The President then named Senator Hunter and asked Mr. Stephens to be a member of it, to which he agreed. And the Hampton Roads Commission was raised.

It was a bright Sunday morning when the commissioners left Richmond to meet the United States Commission, upon this high embassy. The result of the meeting is history. When the Confederacy embarked on her career, one of her first acts was the dispatch of commissioners to the United States Government at Washington, to settle all matters of controversy peaceably by negotiation. They were rejected. In the final catastrophe she went down with the olive branch held out to her foes. Surely she is exempt from responsibility for the bloodshed and slaughter which negotiation might have avoided.

The friends of this movement, to secure peace, had but little hope of success, but they felt better after exhausting their last effort in that direction. The failure seemed to intensify the determination to die in the last ditch. Mr. Davis made a stirring speech to a large crowd in the African Church. Dr. James A. Duncan, the eloquent pastor of the Broad Street Methodist Church, preached a masterful sermon, from the text: "The Sword of the Lord and Gideon" intended to strengthen the spirit of resistance, and rekindle the light of dying hope. But great speeches and eloquent sermons can not beat great armies, led by able generals. Soldiers, supplies, arms, equipments and money, are the instruments that win battles. President Jefferson Davis and his Cabinet and Congress, General Lee and his officers and men, did all possible to be done, to insure success. And what they did with the means at command will forever stand the wonder of history.

An agricultural people, without a government, an

army, a navy, a treasury or factory, and their ports closed by blockade, improvised all these in an incredibly short time, and prosecuted a war of defense, against an enemy numbering three to their one, for four years. They fought six hundred battles, winning a greater number of them than they lost—a record without a parallel. And at last, when their beloved Confederacy went down, it fell like Sparta at "Thermopylæ," when its defenders had poured out liberty's "last libation."

It appears to a layman incapable of military criticism, who necessarily forms his judgment upon facts and results, that some Confederate commanders exhibited a skill and genius, that if equalled, was certainly never surpassed. Such is shown by Jackson, in his celebrated valley campaign, in which, by divining the intention of the enemy, information of his strength and location, accurate calculation of time, and the celerity of his own movements, with vastly inferior numbers, he defeated a large Federal Army, by attacking in detail, under Banks, Milroy, Freemont and Shields. And then he threw his troops, at the critical moment, into the Confederate lines at Frazier's Farm, Gaines' Mill, and Malvern Hill, and aided in the defeat of McClellan.

By the same high quality of military leadership, Lee, with three troops to his one against him, repulsed Grant at the Wilderness; met him at Spottsylvania; slaughtered him at Cold Harbor, and kept him out of the Confederate Capitol. Lieutenant R. W. Dowling, commanding the garrison (forty-four Irishmen), at Fort Grigsby, a weak earthwork, armed with fifteen guns, located at Sabine Pass, was attacked by a Federal fleet of twenty-three vessels, and a force estimated at from ten to fifteen thousand men. In an engagement lasting an hour and thirty minutes, the garrison sank two gunboats, crippled a third one, killed fifty, captured eighteen heavy guns, besides small arms, supplies, etc., and one hundred and fifty prisoners, including the commander of the fleet. The fleet was driven away and not a man hurt. This simple story reads like the wildest romance.

About the last of February or first of March, 1865, Congress having done all it could do—suffering from my wound, and seeing that the impending doom must soon come—I left Richmond, with the Hon. Warren Akin, and two Alabamians, for my home. When we reached Greensboro, N. C., we learned that all the railroad bridges had been burned by the military, or washed away by the floods. We went to Newton, to the end of the Western N. C. Railway, and thence took the chances. After much effort and difficulty, we succeeded in hiring a four-horse wagon and team, which the rain and mud made necessary, to carry four men, with light baggage, to Spartanburg. From this place, we proceeded by rail to Abbeville. Akin's family had refugeed to Elberton, and mine to Jefferson. From Abbeville to Elberton we were taken by another wagon "and four."

Strange and unaccountable things sometimes occur in human history. Riding along in the wagon from Newton to Spartanburg, Col. Akin told me a dream he had the night before he left Richmond. He dreamed that he was at home, and picked up his son Elbert, a boy of fifteen years, lying on the ground, the blood flowing from his mouth, and found him dead. Sitting on the hotel veranda at Abbeville, he arose, stating that he would go to the postoffice across the public square, and see if he could get any news from home. I noticed him as he left the office, open a letter, which he read, walking slowly. I discovered, in a moment, from his movements (though fifty yards distant), that it contained sad news. Mrs. Akin had sent him a letter to Richmond, which he failed to receive, giving particulars. In the letter just received from Mrs. Akin, among other things, she incidentally said: "Since our beloved Elbert's death," without any other or further allusion to the subject. This was the first news of his eldest son's death. Although he maintained his calmness, I could see that his feelings were intensely wrought up with the mingled emotions of grief, anxiety and uncertainty.

When we reached the Savannah River, it was so swollen by recent rains that the ferryman preemptorily refused to put us across. After earnest importunities of argument, and extravagant offers of pay, at last Col. Akin said to him, with an emphasis that touched his heart and overpowered his will: "I live in Elberton; my son is dead, and I am going to reach Elberton this night." "What is your name?" asked the ferryman. "Akin," replied the Colonel. "Are you any kin to the man who was killed in a horse-race the other day in Elberton?" asked the ferryman. The ferryman, against his judgment, finally consented, with our aid, to put us across. By running the boat near the bank, whose friction neutralized the force of the current, to a proper distance, he shot it like an arrow diagonally across the raging flood, and struck the opposite landing. I spent that night in the hospitable, but bereaved home of my friend. No allusion was made to the sorrow during the night. Next morning, as I bade him good-bye at the gate, he pointed to a large locust tree near, and said it was against that tree that Elbert was thrown and killed. The dream precisely revealed the facts. Elbert and another boy had ridden the horses to water. Returning, for amusement, they undertook to see which was the faster horse, with the result here recorded. To me, sometimes it seems a wonder that a boy was ever raised to manhood.

I had the adventure of a train wreck near Athens, but escaped injury, and after a journey of ten or twelve days—which can now be made in a shorter time—I reached home. A few days thereafter, at Appomattox, the curtain fell upon the bloody tragedy. It was soon followed by two crimes of monstrous enormity—the assassination of President Lincoln in Ford's Theatre, at Washington, and the shackling in irons, of President Davis, in Fortress Monroe, upon the basely false charge of complicity therein.

CHAPTER XIII.

Personnel of the Members of the Second Congress.

The study of a people, their opinions, principles, passions and prejudices, as reflected through their representation, as well as the character, capacity, and personal peculiarities of the Representatives themselves, was to me always interesting and instructive.

The seething, boiling passions of revolutions, like volcanic eruptions, often cast to the surface unknown men, endowed with high capacity for command and leadership. However this truth may have been illustrated in the military history of the Confederacy, it finds no confirmation in the civil service department of the government. The President and his Cabinet were distinguished statesmen, well known for their ability and long and faithful public service. This is also true of a number of the members of both houses of Congress.

The House of Representatives was a body of able, brave, earnest men, ardently devoted to the success of the Confederate cause and unusually free from selfish ambition. Of course there were divergent views and opinions upon the wisdom of particular measures, but the members were a unit in the desire and purpose to promote the public interest. In ability, the members approximated as nearly equality as could be found in any body of the same number. The Georgia members were: Julian Hartridge, a graduate of Brown University, a fine lawyer and polished orator. He had served his State as legislator and prosecuting attorney with decided ability. He was a strong debater and a courtly gentleman. William E. Smith was a practicing lawyer, with a strong will, clear discriminating judgment; rarely spoke, but always voted. He had lost a leg in battle. Mark Blanford, rugged, rough, blunt and bright, was a lawyer, striking square from the shoulder, and never surrendering. He lost an arm in the war. After the war, he was associate justice of the Supreme Court of Georgia, and was distinguished for his brevity, clearness and correctness of his decisions. Clifford Anderson was a lawyer. He took his stand, while yet a young man, at the head of the profession. He was a pleasing speaker, had represented his county in the Legislature, before the war, and ably served the State as attorney-general, after the war was ended. John T. Shewmake was a quiet, cultured gentleman, who thought much, and spoke little. He was always present and gave close attention to the business before the House. Indeed, he kept a book in which he made a careful memorandum of everything that was done. Joseph H. Echols, an educated gentleman, was an extensive planter. He had presided over a female college at Madison, Ga. He was a State Senator in 1861-2. He was an accomplished gentleman, a genial companion, a faithful friend and an ardent patriot. James M. Smith, vigorous and robust in mind and body, was an able lawyer. Though not inclined to speech-making he thought closely and logically and had strong and decided convictions, which he did not hesitate to avow and defend, and, as occasion was supposed to require, with the emphasis of certain expletives that do not appear in Sunday literature. He was the first Democratic governor, after the Hegira of Rufus B. Bullock and his carpet-bag menagerie. George N. Lester was admitted to the bar at the age of nineteen, by special act of the Legislature. He had been Supreme Court reporter. He served two terms as chairman of the Judiciary Committee of the House of Representatives in the State Legislature; lost his right arm in the battle of Perryville, Ky. After the war, he was judge of the Superior Court in the Blue Ridge Circuit, and Attorney-General of the State. Hiram P. Bell received an Academic education, secured by his own efforts; was a member of the convention that seceded from the Union. He opposed secession; was elected to the Convention, Commissioner to the State of Tennessee; was elected State Senator in 1861, served one session, and resigned to remain in the army; was Lt.-Col. of the Forty-third Regt., Georgia Volunteers; was desperately wounded and permanently disabled for further service at Vicksburg. After the war, he served in the Forty-third and Forty-fifth Congress of the United States, and one term each in the House and Senate of the Legislature of Georgia. Warren Akin was probably the ablest lawyer in the Cherokee Circuit. He was a strong debater. He opposed Governor Brown for the Governorship, and, though defeated, he made a brilliant campaign.

He was speaker of the House of Representatives of 1861-2, and won reputation as a presiding officer. It will be seen, that of the members of this delegation one, James M. Smith, became Governor; two, Lester and Blandford, Judges; two, Anderson and Lester, Attys.-General; three, Hartridge, Bell, and William E. Smith, members of the United States Congress.

Governor Brown's controversy with President Davis on the constitutionality of the conscript law and the right to appoint military officers in certain cases, had brought the Governor and the State, into disfavor at Richmond. The members from Georgia, being new men, were supposed to have been chosen because of the Governor's views and their sympathy therewith, or because they had been mangled in battle, and that, in either case, the delegation could not be relied upon. This suspicion or speculation was successfully dissipated when Akin, Lester, Hartridge and Anderson tackled them in debate. This fact, I accidentally ascertained by overhearing a conversation that I could not avoid hearing, between Judge Gholston, a member of the House, and another gentleman. Gholston, after stating the distrust of the Georgia members, as above-stated, added that after hearing these gentlemen from Georgia and becoming personally acquainted with them, he was never more astonished in his life; that he found the delegation as able, faithful and true as any one in the House.

What is called oratory, or eloquence, has never been, and can never be, accurately defined nor described. There is no common authoritative standard of perfection established for the adjudication of its merits. Styles of speaking, and the impressions produced, are as different as those of a flower garden and a thunder storm; a battle and a landscape. Patrick Henry's "Give me liberty, or give me death," and William Wirt's answer to "Who is Blannerhassett?" are the illustration. The pictures of attitudes in books, that profess to teach the art of public speaking, are only ludicrous cartoons. Each auditor is a judge, and every auditor has an equal right to judge what constitutes it. Three professors will disagree in awarding the medal in a contest between a half-dozen college boys. Some speakers, by mellifluous voice and chaste, smooth flowing diction, will charm the weak esthetic; others, by clear, cold logic, will convince the judgment and control the reluctant will of the stubborn; still others, by the sympathetic earnestness of pathos, will excite and control the passions of the emotional. The possession, by a speaker, of all these powers, in harmonious combination, in my opinion, makes him an orator. Few men possess them. Bishop George F. Pierce possessed them all in a larger degree than any speaker it was ever my privilege to hear. And Sargent S. P. Prentiss, in a more eminent degree than any orator of whom history or tradition, gives any information. The nearest approach to a true definition of oratory, eloquence included, that can be attained, is that it is that form of speech, from living men to living men and women, that convinces the judgment, controls the will, masters the emotions and incites to action.

Most legislation is considered and formulated in the

committee-room, and reported by the chairman to the House. The chairman, usually, engineers the report through the House, and is therefore, often on his feet engaged in discussion, and for this reason, the uninitiated think he is a great man. This may or may not be true. Sometimes chairmen are appointed because of their ability; often because of favoritism. Valuable men in legislation are those who think wisely and work constantly. Francis S. Lyon, whose character is so finely drawn, under the name of "The Hon. Francis Strother," by the master limner, Joseph Baldwin, in his "Flush Times of Alabama and Mississippi," was chairman of the committee on Ways and Means; W. P. Miles, on Military Affairs; John A. Gilmer, on Privileges and Elections; Charles W. Russell, on the Judiciary; and Frank B. Sexton, on Postoffices and Post-Roads. As accomplished speakers, I think Hartridge and Vest excelled. Marshall, Lester, Akin and Baldwin were the strongest parliamentary debaters. W. N. H. Smith, Machen, Gilmer, Chilton and Colyar, were the wisest practical legislators. Barksdale, Dupree and Perkins were able, optimistic extremists. Charles W. Russell was a man of coldness, courage, and ability. It was understood that the administration relied on him for leadership. Two men greatly impressed me for the possession of what I regarded as high qualities and capacity for legislation. They were W. N. H. Smith, of N. C., and W. B. Machen, of Ky. They were watchful, wise, cautious and practical. They were both modest, unobtrusive and able. They understood the use of language, and in a few plain words, successfully exposed the wrong, sustained the right, or explained the doubtful. William C. Rives was the Nestor of the House in age only. He had been United States Senator, and Minister to France, and at that time, stood with the first statesmen of Virginia; but age had palsied the sceptre of his power. There was one member of the House who, for uniqueness and picturesqueness, stood, like Adam's recollection of his fall, alone. This was Henry S. Foote. His intellect was bright, his information large, his experience varied, and his courage invincible. He had been shot in a duel with Prentiss, had the memorable scene with Benton in the United States Senate, and had defeated Jefferson Davis for Governor of Mississippi. He represented the Nashville District, Tenn. He had lost all hope (if he had any), in the success of the Confederate cause. He was a Don Quixote, a sort of free lance, that would fight a windmill or a mogul engine with equal alacrity. For some cause which I never understood, or it may be without any cause, he was exceedingly bitter in his feelings toward Mr. Davis and Mr. Benjamin. He allowed no occasion to pass; and with or without excuse, he never spoke without indulging in denunciatory invective against them, pronouncing their names with a vicious malignity of tone, and a contemptuous sneer of derision and distortion of expression of face, that baffled description. A resolution to expel him was introduced and referred to the committee on privileges and elections. All the members of the committee—the chairman and myself excepted—promptly adopted a report in favor of the resolution. We submitted a minority report against the resolution. He was not expelled. A short time after this he left Richmond. It will be understood that the mention of certain members of Congress by name, is not to the disparagement of those not referred to by name. I wish I had the data, time and space to give to those who come after us, the history, of every member of this body of true men, who participated in the last scene of the play, and witnessed the fall of the curtain upon the bloody tragedy of Civil War.

I am unwilling to close this chapter without referring to one member of the cabinet; the last one appointed by Mr. Davis. I refer to John C. Breckenridge, Secretary of War. I had a matter of business for a constituent before the department and happened to be present when he was sworn in. Being immediately introduced to him, I congratulated him, and the Confederacy, upon his appointment, to which he replied that he could not say as to the Confederacy, but that certainly, in view of the momentous responsibilities of the office, he was not to be congratulated personally. He invited me to a seat, took one himself in my front, and at once began, in an easy way, a most charming conversation. He inquired what district I represented, and in what section of the State it was located. He asked particularly about the state of affairs in Georgia, the condition and sentiments of the people in my district. Knowing the pressure of business, and the weight of responsibility upon him, as well as the value of time, as soon as a pause occurred in the flow of his delightful conversation, and I could do so without rudeness, I stated what I wanted. He said: "Really, I do not know whether this matter is under the jurisdiction of the Secretary, or the Chief of the Conscript Bureau. You see this business is all new to me; I will see." Calling his chief clerk by the tap of his bell, who at once responded, he asked him "which had jurisdiction, the Secretary or the Chief?" "Both," replied the clerk; whereupon, in a moment and without a word, he took up his pen and granted my request. This is the man who contests, with Henry Clay, the premiership of affection in the heart of Kentuckians; that presided over the highest legislative body in the world, and of which Clay had been the most illustrious member. He was scholar, soldier, orator, statesman and patriot. The memory of this brief interview has lingered with me for almost half a century, fresh as the dew of the morning, and sweet as the fragrance of roses. His superb physique, his versatile accomplishments and excellencies, his intellectual, moral and social qualities—all in symmetrical and faultless combination—made him, in my conception, the most magnificent specimen of manhood I ever beheld. When the Confederacy fell, the United States requited his long and brilliant public service with malignant hate and relentless persecution, and thus compelled him to seek refuge among strangers. On entering the boat on the coast of Florida, which was to bear him away, he thanked a Confederate private who had served him; adding that he wished it was in his power to requite his kindness. "It is," replied the private. "Corporal A. has abused and lorded it over me because he is an officer and I a private, I want to outrank him;" whereupon he was brevetted Captain on the spot, and made happy. This was the last official act of the Confederate Secretary of War.

CHAPTER XIV.

Lincoln and Davis.

No two men in the last half of the Nineteenth Century engaged a larger share of public attention than Abraham Lincoln and Jefferson Davis. Future generations will be anxious to know their history, actions and achievements, without the time and labor required to gain the knowledge, by searching the numerous volumes in which it is to be found. They were both born in Kentucky, not far apart in distance, and near in time, Davis in 1808 and Lincoln in 1809. They were born under the same moral, social and civil institutions, but under diverse conditions; Lincoln, in abject poverty, Davis in comparative affluence. Lincoln, without education in his boyhood, went to the wilderness of Illinois to earn his bread by the toil of his hands and the sweat of his brow. Davis went from Transylvania University to West Point for military training. After a few years they met in the Blackhawk War, Lincoln the awkward, untrained captain of a company of three-months raw militia; Davis, the scholarly, polished lieutenant of the regular army. Lincoln next appears, successfully practicing the profession of law in the county of Sangammon, Ill.; Davis, at the head of the "Mississippi Rifles," winning victory for his country at

Buena Vista, in Mexico. Lincoln, a free-soil Whig, became a leading lawyer in the Northwest; Davis, a pro-slavery States Rights Democrat, became a planter, in the Southwest. They were both intensely patriotic and ambitious. They had experienced alike the triumph of success and the chagrin of defeat. Trumbull and Douglass each had defeated Lincoln for the United States Senate; a Warren County Whig had defeated Davis for the Legislature, and Henry S. Foote had defeated him for Governor of Mississippi. Both had been Representatives in Congress. Lincoln was an ardent supporter of the father-in-law of Davis, Gen. Taylor, for the Presidency. Davis supported Gen. Cass for that high office.

The compromise measures of 1850 and the Kansas-Nebraska Legislation of 1854, formed the volcano, whose eruption deluged the land in the burning lava of human passion which was soon to be crimsoned into seas of human blood.

While Davis was quietly and ably administering the affairs of the War Department in Pierce's Cabinet, Lincoln was busily and earnestly engaged in organizing the anti-slavery elements of all parties into the Republican party. The condition of affairs in "bleeding Kansas," supplied the means of success. The anti-slavery people met in a "Freesoil" convention in Bloomington in 1856. To this convention Lincoln was chosen a delegate. It was to this convention he delivered his celebrated "lost" speech. It was called his "lost" speech because the reporters were so overwhelmed by its power and eloquence that they forgot to report it.

Joseph Medell commenced to report it for a Chicago paper, but after writing a few lines of the introduction, he laid aside his pencil and thought no more of the report until the conclusion of the speech. It was preserved in this way. A young lawyer with whom Lincoln had thoroughly discussed the matter of the speech before its delivery, took accurate and elaborate notes, by which he was afterwards enabled to reproduce it. I doubt whether any other speech, ever delivered on this continent, ever produced consequences so momentous. That speech formed and solidified the Republican party and made Lincoln its great leader. After the expiration of Davis' service in the Cabinet, he was returned to the United States Senate, from Mississippi, and became, by common consent, leader of the pro-slavery, States Rights sentiments of the South. Lincoln was elected President on an anti-slavery platform. Davis was the recognized champion of slavery and States rights, as guaranteed by the Constitution.

Lincoln and Davis were alike in some respects. They were each endowed with the highest order of mind. They were both thoroughly educated; Lincoln, self-educated by close, constant, laborious reading and patient and profound thought and extensive observation and experience. Davis' education, the best the foremost institutions of the country could give, was enlarged and perfected by reading, thinking, and official association with the first men of this and foreign lands, in the discharge of cabinet, senatorial and military duties. They were both perfectly familiar with the political history of the country. They belonged to opposite schools of constitutional construction and civic policy. Lincoln was elected President of the United States of America. The Southern States seceded, formed a new government, which they named "The Confederate States of America," and unanimously elected Davis, president. Thus, these two great men confronted each other. They stood like the disputing knights, looking upon opposite sides of the same shield. On Lincoln's side the device "Preservation of the Union;" on Davis' "The Sovereignity of the States, and the right of Self-Government." They were equally honest, conscientious, patriotic and determined, and compromise impossible, was inevitable, the fractricidal conflict came. No one knows and no one can tell, the burden of labor they endured, the torture of anxiety they suffered, and the anguish of grief they experienced, during the four years of slaughter and blood.

Lincoln and Davis were unlike in their personnel. Lincoln was tall in stature, six feet and two inches, raw-boned, with hands and feet large, and limbs long, ungraceful in movement and attitude; indifferent to dress and almost ludicrously uncouth on horse-back. The expression of his face was variable as the weather. In repose, it was indicative of profound thought. When telling an anecdote, in which he excelled, it kindled with the light of humor. At times, his face was shaded with the expression of mingled dignity and sorrow, with a "far-away look" that told of some tender emotion that silently stirred the depths of his great heart. Davis was five feet, ten inches in height, compactly built, with rather small hands and feet; a finely rounded and well-formed head; plainly but neatly dressed; talked in a low, calm voice; with manners the perfection of grace and elegance. He sat his horse like a Knight of the Crusaders. His step, with a very slight limp from a wound in the foot at Buena Vista, was the elastic tread of the trained soldier. They differed widely in their style of composition and elocution.

Lincoln expressed his thoughts mainly by the use of nouns, verbs and participles, using short, simple, Saxon words, many of them of one syllable, but well chosen, to express forcibly the idea. Like the miner, digging in the gravel for gold, he struggled by the shortest and simplest way, to reach the nuggets of truth his honest heart sought to find. He was sparing in the use of adjectives and adverbs. His sentences were sometimes rugged and disjointed. They lacked smoothness and completeness in roundness and rhythm, but went without ceremony or surplusage straight to the center, and presented his thought in unadorned purity. And yet occasionally, though rarely, he excelled all the great masters in the beauty, power and pathos of his style, as exemplified in his Gettysburg speech, his letter of condolence of Mrs. Bixby, and the incomparable sentences with which he closes his first inaugural. He said: "I am loathe to close. We are not enemies, but friends. We must not be enemies. Though passion may have strained it must not break, our bonds of affection. The mystic chords of memory, stretching from every battlefield and patriot grave, to every living heart and hearth-stone, all over this broad land, will yet swell the chorus of the Union, when again touched (as they surely will be), by the better angels of our nature."

Davis' style, like his character, was chaste and clean, his words aptly chosen, and so arranged into sentences as to evoke the precise thought, with mathematical accuracy. It was smooth, easy, graceful and clear as sunlight. It was cold, presented the thought intended without the slightest tint of coloring. Davis was precise but not pretentious. He seemed to be cold without being so. He believed in forms. It was constitutional with him. His training at West Point, his administration of the War Department, adding to his natural inclination in that direction, made him punctilious in the observance of forms. He was proud, but it was the soldiery pride of conscious honor and rectitude. He was brave; he never "stooped to conquer." He would have perished in flames at the stake sooner than bend the supple hinges of the knee, that thrift may follow fawning."

Davis closed his first inaugural in these eloquent words: "It is joyous, in the midst of these perilous times, to look around upon a people united in heart, where one purpose of high resolve animates and actuates the whole; where sacrifices to be made, are not weighed in the balance against honor and right, and liberty and equality. Obstacles may retard, but they can not prevent the progress of a movement, sanctified by its justice and sustained by a virtuous people. Reverently let us invoke the God of our fathers to guide and protect us in our efforts to perpetuate the principles which, by His blessing, they are able to vindicate, establish and transmit to their posterity. With the continuance of His favor, ever gratefully acknowledged, we may hopefully look forward to success, to peace, and to prosperity."

The attitude of these two great men may be summarized thus: Lincoln would destroy the "Constitution to serve the Union." Davis would dissolve the Union to serve the Constitution. During these stormy times, they had a similar personal and family bereavement; they each had a favorite boy. Tad Lincoln died in the "White House," at Washington; Joe Davis was killed by a fall from the veranda of the "Executive Mansion in Richmond." The heart of Lincoln had lavished all its wealth of affection on Tad. It was wrung with anguish at his death. I witnessed grief personified, in Davis, at the funeral of Joe. A feeling of deep sadness, stealthily steals over one, as he reflects upon the end of these two great men. Lincoln was the head of a government de jure; Davis, of a government de facto. They were respectively, the commanders-in-chief, of the armies and navies of their governments, in which three and a half millions of men were engaged—on land and sea—in a death grapple for national existence, and these were brothers of the same blood, identified in history, hopes and destiny. In the hour of exultant victory, Lincoln was basely assassinated by a citizen brought back into the Union he died and suffered so much to restore. Davis, in the mortification of defeat, was cruelly imprisoned, and disfranchised by a government, to the service of which he had given his best thought and blood, and died without a country.

It will be the wonder of those who come after us that a people with a history so glorious, resources so immense, progress so rapid, and a prosperity so universal, would rudely risk or wreck it all in a sectional Civil War. The reason they did is simple and obvious. It was because passion, avarice and ambition usurped the throne of reason, justice and patriotism.

CHAPTER XV.

Condition of the Southern People at the Close of the War.

There were three things which enabled unprincipled, ambitious demagogues, North and South, to madden the American people and create the conditions that made the Civil War possible, if not inevitable. They were, the conflict in Kansas, the assault of Brooks upon Sumner, in the Senate, and John Brown's raid upon Harper's Ferry. These facts appealed to passion, with a force that overcame the resistance of reason and patriotism. The deplorable assassination of Lincoln inflamed the victors into a frenzy of fury, put into the presidency the prince of ambitious demagogues, in whom neither party had the slightest confidence, and for whom neither had any respect, and thus entailed upon the vanquished the heritage of reconstruction. Had Lincoln survived, all the probabilities are, and all the indications show, that the States would have been allowed to readjust their relations to the Union, through their own voluntary civil action, without intervention of military despotism. And the butchery of Mrs. Surratt and Wirtz would not have disgraced the pages of American history. The Union would have been really restored and become stronger than ever before, in the affections of the American people.

Reconstruction was inaugurated and guided by a cyclone of malignant hate, upon a people who had bravely fought for their convictions until overwhelmed by resources and numbers. When the end came, their poverty was pitiable, their anguish pathetic, and their helplessness remediless, when this monstrous policy of despotism was imposed upon them. They were cut off from the world by the blockade on one side and by an army of immense numbers on the other. The boys and men between the ages of seventeen and fifty, were in the field. The four years of horrible war had absolutely exhausted all their resources of men and means. The glorious chivalry of the Confederacy filled unmarked graves—from the Susquehanna to the Rio Grande. Fields, orchards and gardens, had been trampled down. Dwellings had been abandoned or burned, towns and cities, sacked and consumed, people shot down and their homes "prowled." Churches and cemeteries had been desecrated and robbed. The people were practically without food and clothing, and absolutely destitute of money; schools were suspended, and services at the churches nearly so. The whole land was a scene of decadence, ashes and ruins; and every home filled with hearts breaking and bleeding with the agony of grief for dead loved ones. A few gray-headed men and matrons, many widows, some youths and children, and the maimed, shattered remnant of the world's bravest army, were left. Virtue, intelligence and patriotism were proscribed by law; and enfranchised, ignorant, illiterate, thieving negroes, were set to making organic laws—constitutions for the government of a people with the blood of Revolutionary sires flowing through their veins. This martyrdom continued in most of the Confederate States for seven years.

"Surely there is some chosen curse, some secret thunder, in the stores of Heaven, red with uncommon wrath, to blast the wretch who owes his greatness to his country's ruin." At the commencement of the war, planting was largely abandoned. It was a sort of social entertainment to cut and make neat uniforms for the boys; and pack, and ship to them, boxes of dainty viands. As the war progressed, the withdrawal of the labor of the field, reduced the production of supplies. The tax in kind claimed a large share for the support of the army; and the question of support soon began to be a serious one, for the non-producers—the women and children at home. It became impossible to obtain coffee; parched meal, corn and rye were substituted. When the supply of clothing was exhausted, the good women, resorted to the old-time spinning-wheel and loom,—both home-made. The State managed to distribute among the people a small number of pairs of cotton-cards; and the land became vocal with rasping, crashing cards, the hum of wheels and the banging-rattle of loom. Home-made apparel, dyed with maple and sweet-gum bark, ivy leaves, and the bark off walnut roots, constituted the wardrobe. It is surprising with what artistic skill the dear, good women mingled these colors into a "thing of beauty," and therefore, "a joy forever." They met necessities by improvising expedients. They exhibited resources of invention that entitles them to a lofty niche in the temple of genius.

It made but little difference that Confederate money constantly depreciated, because there was nothing to buy nor sell. What little trading was done was on credit; but the price agreed on was upon the basis of the face value of Confederate currency. The last purchase I made before the surrender, was a bushel of salt, for which I paid $1,000.00. There was much indebtness contracted before the war, existing at its close. At my suggestion a public mass-meeting of the people of Forsyth County was held, which unanimously adopted a resolution asking creditors and debtors to settle by compromise, the indebtedness, upon reasonable terms. Many of them did so. The people of Georgia, in the Convention of October 1865, passed an ordinance authorizing the courts and juries to adjust the equities between the parties to Confederate contracts, upon the basis of the value of the money and the value of the thing for which it was promised, as compared with gold, or par money. This was a happy solution of a perplexing problem.

The more enterprising class of the recently emancipated, ignorant, free negroes united with Yankee "Carpet-baggers," Confederate, boom-proof refugees, and conscript "dodgers," joined Congress, led by Steven Sumner, Butler and their partisan followers in the work of reconstruction. Another class of negroes, as soon as they were enabled to procure the desired outfit of a brass watch-chain, a cane, umbrella, eye-glasses, Prince Albert coat, standing collar and plug hat, joined the ministry. They engaged in soliciting contributions to build imaginary churches. The cash they thus obtained, which was not inconsiderable, never materialized into tangible buildings. The remaining class of the colored people, and by far the largest, entered with vigorous energy upon their favorite pursuits of running rabbits, burning rails, stealing chickens, attending frolics and funerals and reporting to the "Freedman's Bureau" complaints of contracts which they themselves had violated. They generally secured redress from this august tribunal, by imposing upon the employer a punishment for the negro's violation of his contract.

The true and faithful men, women and children, with broken-down army horses and mules, and such implements as they could improvise, went to work impelled by necessity and inspired by hope. Many a brave Confederate, with one arm or a wooden peg-leg, followed the plow in cheerful toil, to support the wife and children of his love. They nobly requited this devotion by generous aid in the field, and the faithful performance of the wifely domestic duties of the household. Rigid frugality, unremitting industry, and the blessings of the great God, who notes the sparrow's fall, and feeds the young ravens when they cry, rewarded their heroic efforts with signal success.

There was a saving factor in the preservation of order and the prevention of lawlessness in the institution and organization of the "Ku Klux Klan"—the report of the Congressional committee to the contrary, notwithstanding. It was the old patrol system of slavery times; with the addition of fantastic dress and hobgoblin masks, intended to restrain base negroes from crime and lawlessness, by appealing to their superstitious fears. It acted like a charm. I never heard of a case of outrage perpetrated by the "Klan," except through the report of the Congressional committee, based upon the testimony of men of the type of Titus Oates and Dangerfield, the vile emissaries of reconstruction, who would incite the black race to crime against the white.

The mind that conceived the "Klan" was a genius. He understood precisely the nature and weakness of the negro; and he discovered the means of making that weakness, instead of the instrument of crime, the element of safety to both races. It met an emergency of the gravest character with a remedy of the most absolute success. The triumphant defense finds expression in the legal maxim: "Salus populi, suprema est lex." Constant, patient, hopeful toil; with remunerative prices for the South's great staple, and the blessing of Divine Providence, the influx of capital and the immigration of sterling, energetic business men from the Northern and Northwestern States have within the brief space of four decades transformed the South from a plain of ashes and ruins, into a garden of bounty and beauty.

The promise and possibilities of the future have no horizon. All this was accomplished by a people, who, —like Job—were "chosen in the furnace of affliction." It is something to have lived in the age of such a people. It is more to have been a part of such a people.

It is due to the colored people to put on record (which I do with great pleasure,) their fidelity and devotion to their masters, their families and their interests during the war. They were reliable, faithful and true, until contact with the Federal army inspired them with treacherous hostility. Some—a few—have remained faithful to the attachment and friendships of their former relations—through all the vicissitudes that followed their changed condition. An aged slave of the brother of Jefferson Davis, who lived in Florida, was accustomed to send to the ex-President and his family, at "Beauvoir," choice fruits from his garden and orchard. And when the venerable old man heard that the President was dangerously sick—through great difficulties—he made his way to New Orleans to grasp, one time more, the hand of his friend and his idol. He reached the city the day after the death; and found the room containing the remains, closed to visitors. Mrs. Davis admitted him to the death-chamber. The humble African standing looking upon the dead President, with his aged, dim eyes streaming with the torrents of grief, and heart heaving with agony, presents a scene of anguish so deep, and love so pure that I drop the curtain and let God and angels only, look upon this "sanctum sanctorum" of devotion and love.

When Sherman's army reached Kennesaw, I found it necessary to fall back in imitation of the Fabian policy of General Joseph E. Johnston; and refugeed from Cumming to Jefferson, in July 1864. Being a member of the Confederate Congress was supposed to be a sufficient cause for my arrest and imprisonment, if not execution. The day after I left a squadron of Yankee cavalry made its appearance in town for that purpose; but after plundering the citizens, shooting at some boys and capturing a few horses, retired without accomplishing their high and patriotic purpose. I remained in Jefferson until October 1865. When I left I turned over my house, garden and orchard to a homeless shoemaker, to occupy, free of rent until called for. In October I came over to notify him that I had arranged to return home and wanted the house. To my amazement, he said he did not see how he could leave. He made various pretended excuses for not vacating, all of which I promptly removed, or answered. At last he said flatly that he would not leave, that the property was given him by the Yankees and was his. This exhausted the argument or reduced it to the argumentum ad hominem. It is scarcely necessary to add that he speedily found it eminently convenient to retire from the place.

It is strange how calamitous times develop the opposite phases of human character. While angels of mercy in human form, are helping the stricken and suffering in the Johnstown and Galveston floods,—incarnate fiends are cutting off the fingers of dead women to rob them of jewelry. This tenant at will would requite a favor with robbery. There is no form of conscience to which these degenerates can be remitted. The final assize, alone, can settle with them. From the surrender in April 1865, to the close of the year, I did not have a penny in money, in this world. My two former slaves, Adam, and Jane, his wife, remained with us during the year and aided us in moving back home. I supplied them with an outfit of household furniture; and each of them a neat, substantial suit of clothes (for which I went in debt); and furnished them a wagon and team, to move to their chosen home. Adam soon became prominent in religion and politics. About two years thereafter he came into my office—the shreds of the suit I had given him, dripping with water and his teeth chattering with cold,—to employ me to defend him for stealing meat. After all, emancipation is not an unmixed blessing!

From January 1866 to the last of December 1873, I was engaged in practicing law, in ten counties in "Blue Ridge" and adjoining circuits, with occasional cases in other counties and in the Supreme Court. During the course of my practice I have appeared in about sixty cases of murder, generally for the defense. I have had three clients executed, for one of them was assigned with Colonel C. D. Phillips, by the court. Among these clients were three women, two of them white, and one colored. But one white woman has been hanged in Georgia since I came to the bar. I never heard of but one other, a good record for the 'Empire State of the South.' These seven years were immediately succeeding the surrender and during the reconstruction period. The courts in the mountain counties were full of cases growing out of the war. This litigation was characterized by bitter and fierce passion. It is due to the bar to say, that the lawyers did much to allay personal hostility, and restore fraternity among the people. A circuit practice, among a rural people, was delightful to me. It is a fine school in which to study human nature. The ludicrous, the humorous and pathetic, all pass in kaleidoscopic panorama before the court.

CHAPTER XVI.

THE FORTY-THIRD CONGRESS AND PARTY LEADERS.

The Forty-third Congress met in December 1873. The representatives from Georgia were Morgan Rawls, Richard H. Whitely, Phillip Cook, Henry R. Harris, James H. Blount, James Freeman, Pierce M. B. Young, Ambrose R. Wright and Hiram P. Bell. General Wright died before Congress assembled; and Alexander H. Stephens was chosen to fill the vacancy. Morgan Rawls was unseated, upon a contest by Andrew Sloan, who took Rawls' seat. Three of these representatives were Republicans,—Whitely, Freeman and Sloan. The delegation took the modified oath. The Forty-third Congress was overwhelmingly Republican. James G. Blaine was re-elected speaker and Edward McPherson, clerk. The Congress was spotted with half a dozen or more, free negroes—three of whom were from the State of Calhoun, Preston, Lowndes and McDuffy. Three of the late Confederate States, South Carolina, Louisiana and Arkansas, were still struggling in the anarchical throes of the aftermath of reconstruction. The vital national questions before this Congress were: the silver question, the Force Bill, the Civil Rights Bill, repeal of the Salary Grab Act of the Forty-second Congress, etc. Much time was devoted to contested seats, occupied by Democrats, by defeated Republicans, who generally won upon party grounds. It was during this Congress that Kala Kawa, King of the Hawaiian Islands, visited Washington. He was accorded an official public reception by the House of Representatives. He was a dark, copper-colored negro, appearing to be about forty-five years old; six feet in height, squarely built with an avoirdupois of about 200. He wore a black "Prince Albert" coat, standing collar and plug hat. He took his stand in front of the Speaker of the House. Mr. Blaine received him in a formal, handsome speech of official palaver, to which the King's premier, Mr. Allen, a Massachusetts Yankee, responded with the same material, less handsomely. During this memorable State occasion, I happened to occupy a seat next to Hon. A. Herr Smith; a small, dry, hard, typical Pennsylvania Republican, and the successor of Thaddeus Stevens. Mr. Smith seemed to be enraptured and said to me, in a whisper, "Oh my! What a magnificent king!" I replied jocularly, "Yes, that negro would have brought $1,500.00 on the block in ante-bellum times." It so offended him that he did not wish to speak to me afterwards. President Grant gave to the King a State reception at the White House, and I had the honor of an introduction to the King, by the Hon. Hamilton Fish, Secretary of State, as the King stood by the side of the hero of Appomattox and President of the United States. How much all this may have had to do with afterwards obtaining the King's domain, I will not undertake to say. It was during colored radical regnancy that the radical leaders caused the South Carolina negro,—Elliott, to reply to the great Constitutional argument of Alexander H. Stephens against the Civil Rights Bill. The bill was passed. The scene in the House of Representatives attending this legislative folly, was a memorable and historic one. The bill was the offspring of malignant hate, intended to harrass and humiliate the white people of the South. It was unconstitutional, subversive of social order and mere brutum fulmen, when enacted into law. It emanated from the brain and heart of Benjamin F. Butler, of Massachusetts. On the day of its passage, the lobby and galleries were crowded and packed to their utmost capacity with excited, anxious spectators, who came to witness,—by a combination of Northern radicals, Southern renegades and free negroes, through the forms of law—the degradation of a section and a brave people that had given Washington, Henry, Jefferson, Madison, Monroe, Jackson, Clay and Calhoun, to national glory and history. As I surveyed from my seat, that crowd, Macaulay's magnificent description of the audience at the trial of Warren Hastings, pressed with vivid force, upon my thought and memory. There was this difference only. In the American audience, there was not, as in the English, the stars, garters and heraldic insignia of hereditary nobility. Butler made the closing speech. His personnel was not prepossessing. He was rather below medium height obese, heavy, full with flabby cheeks, shaggy eye-brows and cock-eyed. He was a man of decided ability and will power; in partisan politics, a free lance, but always for Butler. In speech his voice was harsh and his manner and attitudes ungraceful. His points in debate were sharp and vigorous. When under the influence of high passion in speech, he blew and spouted, like a harpooned whale. Senator Voorhees thought Thaddeus Stevens resembled Danton. Butler was the Marat in this attempted social revolution, to place the African upon an equality with the Caucasian. During his speech he made a statement involving racial chastity, concerning the people of Richmond, Va., whereupon the tall, handsome young Republican representative of the Richmond district arose, advanced a few steps down the center aisle, and fiercely and bitterly denounced the statement as a falsehood. The vote was taken, the bill passed, the infamy went on record—an Apple of Sodom presented to the negroes, which turned to ashes on their lips. The character, endowments and motives of the men in official life who lead the thought and make the laws for the government of the people, have always been the subject of interesting inquiry and considerations; and peculiarly so, in troublous and revolutionary times.

The writer is fully aware of the unconscious coloring which prejudice, arising from party affiliations, or opposing views, is likely to give in the estimate of those with whom we disagree. But he begs to assure the reader that in his estimate and criticism of the great public men with whom he deals, his sole desire is to present the truth, as it appears to him. Others, of course, may differ widely from him in opinion. But uniformity of opinion upon such a subject, is not attainable.

James G. Blaine was the unchallenged leader of the Republican party in the House of Representatives during the Forty-third Congress. He possessed many fine elements of successful leadership. A commanding figure, great personal magnetism, a good judge of men, an active, sprightly mind, a ready debater and a thorough parliamentarian, he found but little difficulty in controlling its policy, principles and legislation. And yet it seemed to me that he was lacking in the qualities of broad, comprehensive statesmanship. His public life impressed me as a play for the presidency. He was aided by able lieutenants—Dawes, Kelly and Garfield. These were men of great ability and large experience in public life. They were respectively at the head of the most important committees of the House. They were, while ardent partisans, fair debaters and patriotic legislators. They differed from Blaine in this: Blaine was a political leader; they were leaders in legislation and the practical duties connected with it. They were masters of its forms and procedures. They were all good speakers, none of them approximating the highest order of oratory.

Of the four, Blaine was the most pleasing speaker. Committee service in the House has a tendency to specialize the thoughts and efforts of members. Blaine's speciality was to keep his party properly in line, and ready for offense or defense. Kelly's specialties were: Currency, Manufacturers and Tariff. The thoughts of both Dawes and Garfield took in a wider range of legislation. Garfield was the most erudite of these famous men. He was not a successful party leader.

He was more of the scholar, philosopher and statesman. Blaine was the Knight whose plume the rank and file of the Republicans followed as their Oriflamme. The four great leaders of the Democratic minority of the House were Samuel J. Randall, James B. Beck, Samuel S. Cox, and L. Q. C. Lamar. They each differed from the others in qualifications, and each excelled the others in the different departments of parliamentary leadership. Randall was cool, quiet, of plain simple speech, always self-poised, knew exactly the precise status of the business, watchful as Argus, nothing escaped his notice and no advantage over the adversary was allowed by him to pass unimproved. He led the 60 successive hours, day and night, of fillibustering against the Civil Rights Bill. His mastery of the mystic mazes of the rules of the House, and the skill with which he unwound the knotty tangles of parliamentary puzzles, showed a genius of the highest order. The value of such a leader of the minority against a united majority, not troubled with scruples of conscience, is invaluable.

James B. Beck was a rugged, robust Scotchman. He represented the Ashland district, made famous by the representation of Henry Clay and John C. Breckenridge. When he first entered the House he was placed on the Committee on Reconstruction, as he said to me, for "the reason that the Republicans supposed *he* had no sense," and could give *them* no trouble.

But that appointment sowed dragon's teeth, the harvest of which the Republican party continued to reap as long as Beck lived. He was honest, bold, courageous, and irrepressible. As a speaker, he was not eloquent nor charming; his style was plain—all ornament was discarded. He was always equipped for debate. He was a gallant knight, in full armor, standing for the right and against the wrong. No vicious legislation escaped his exposure and denunciation; no wise measure ever lacked an advocate, and the people always found in him a fearless champion, and their enemies a dreaded antagonist. Barricaded in a fortress of facts and entrenched in authorities, he vanquished his assailants—in combination or detail—as they chose to attack him. In the opinion of the writer, he was the strongest debater and the wisest practical legislator in public life, during the period of his long service in Congress. He was precisely the man the exigencies of the times demanded in the halls of legislation.

Samuel Sullivan Cox, Representative in Congress from Ohio, for four terms, and from New York for ten and elected for the eleventh, in many respects stands alone in the Legislative history of the United States. Personally, he was, perhaps, the best beloved, and at his death, the most universally lamented of any man of his time. He was great from boyhood. Hereditary revolutionary blood flowed through his veins. Upon his graduation, at Brown University, he carried off the prizes in history, in poetic criticism and in political economy. He was a marvelous man. He had travelled in Europe, Asia, Africa and South America. He had drawn learning and inspiration from the temples and tombs of Athens, Rome and Jerusalem;

had stood in the shadow of the pyramids and studied the riddle of the Sphynx, and the dynastic history of the Pharoahs; mused among the ruins of Memphis; and breathed the fragrance of the roses at Damascus. He was an unabridged encyclopedia of learning; he seemed to me to know everythng—science, art, literature, history and political economy—in all their various departments—were as familiar as household words—and this knowledge included accuracy in the exact sciences.

The authorship of a most brilliant description of a sunset, after a storm, caused him to be dubbed with the sobriquet, "Sunset" Cox. This was a misnomer—it should have been "Sunshine" Cox. Sunset has no appropriateness to him, except in the eclipse of the grave. Sunshine is the proper symbol of his illustrious life and character.

In high social qualities he was without a peer. It was truly said of him that "he had friends everywhere; enemies nowhere." Malignity and hate had no place in his warm, generous heart. He was a living embodiment of the doctrine of the universal brotherhood of man. Armed with great learning and endowed with the highest social attributes, he stood on the floor of the American House of Representatives for twenty-eight years—the fearless, unyielding tribune of the common people, of a common country.

The Hon. Amos Cummings, in his funeral eulogy, says: "To the nation he was born here; it was here that his generous, genial, manly spirit had full play; here he displayed the patriotic fervor, the exquisite eloquence, the iridescent imagery, the peerless diction, the penetrating logic, the sparkling humor and the delightful disposition that endeared him to the nation."

Mr. Cox spoke often, and never without the closest and most respectful attention of all parties. His rising came to be regarded as the signal of a coming argument of power, adorned with gems of literature, sparkling wit, classical illustrations and spiced—as occasion might require—with bitter sarcasm, withering irony and burning invective. The House was never disappointed in expectation. He had the capacity, greater than any orator of ancient or modern times, of combining all these, in harmonious proportions, in a speech. And yet his spirit was so genial, and style so persuasive, that he never offended an antagonist. His resources of learning were so great, his knowledge of facts so accurate, his style so chaste, his wit and humor so bright and exuberant, and his patriotism so pure, that he never failed to conciliate the love and admiration of his auditors. For three decades his meteoric genius and learning made both hemispheres radiant with brightness and beauty, which still scintillated in the mellow glow of his books and his speeches.

He entered Congress at the early age of thirty-two, and continued a member for twenty-eight years—through the stormiest period of his country's history. In nine days after his entrance, he delivered the first speech made in the new hall of the House of Representatives. He witnessed the fight on the floor between Keith and Grow, when the belligerents of the opposing sectional parties, met in the *melee,* with Washburn, of Illinois, and Potter, of Wisconsin, leading one, and Barksdale and Lamar, of Mississippi, the other. Through all these years of strife and storm he stood, with a wealth of intellectual resources, unequalled; with passions under absolute control, in an armor of integrity more invulnerable than the shield of Achilles, the Ivanhoe of the American House of Representatives.

Lucius Q. C. Lamar was, by one year, the junior of Cox in age. They entered Congress at the same time—Lamar continuing a member for two terms—until the secession of Mississippi. He was a native Georgian and graduated at Emory College, under the presidency of that illustrious humorist, jurist and divine, Augustus B. Longstreet, whose charming daughter became his wife. Mr. Lamar removed to the State of Mississippi, was elected adjunct professor of mathematics and assistant of the celebrated Dr. A. T. Bledsoe, in the university of his adopted State. In 1866 he was elected professor of political economy and social science in the University of Mississippi, and in 1867 was transferred to the professorship of law. He was a member of the Forty-third and Forty-fourth Congresses, and elected to the United States Senate. He was less vigorous in debate than Beck, and less ready and versatile than Cox, but was a close student and an intense thinker. His range of thought was not so wide as that explored by Cox and many others, but it was exhaustive in its search for truth upon the subjects which it embraced. His style was severely chaste and clear—pruned of all surplusage, and in thought, odorous with the oil of the lamp. His professorship of mathematics, political economy, social science and law, together with his association with that metaphysician, Dr. Bledsoe, had doubtless been controlling factors in his mental operations and processes. If he did not, in debate, beat down an adversary into jelly, with the battle-axe of Richard—like Beck; or hack and slash him to pieces with the scimiter of "Saladin"—like Cox, he pierced his most vital part with no "Spear of Ithuriel," and left him the bleeding victim of defeat, as more than Roscoe Conkling ascertained. Lamar was less skilled in parliamentary tactics than Randall—less efficient in general practical legislation than Beck or Cox; but, cool, clear, cautious—the recognized representative and exponent of the chivalry of his section—he was dominant in the policies and councils of his party, and commanded the universal respect of the opposite party. He was full of resources in emergencies. When John Young Brown deliberately rose in his place in the House and uttered his terrific "Burking" denunciation of Butler (that fell as suddenly and startlingly as the shroud of Saladin, appeared at the banquet) it brought the Republican members to their feet, in a tempest of excitement; motion followed motion, and pandemonium reigned. Beck asked Lamar to take charge of the situation. Lamar arose and, with a dignity of manner, in a tone of voice and with an expression of face that exhibited regret, sorrow, sympathy and apology in combination, in a few suave, deprecating words, allayed the storm. The sequel was a mild reprimand of Brown by the Speaker.

There were many true and able Democrats in the Forty-third Congress, less prominent in leadership than Randall, Beck, Cox and Lamar. Among these was Alexander H. Stephens, whose famous history had, even then, been made up and placed on record, and who, like Chatham, came in his feebleness and on his crutches, to protest against the constitutionality of the supplemental Civil Rights Bill.

The iron-clad Republican party of the North, speckled with a scattering remnant of white renegades and free negroes from the South, had an overwhelming majority, with the conqueror of Appomattox President; and every subordinate office in the government, occupied by the creatures of bitter partisanship. This party sought, in the Forty-third Congress, to accomplish two things: to entrench itself in power by the passage of the Force Bill, and to insult and humiliate the white people of the South by the passage of the Supplemental Civil Rights Bill. It failed in both objects. The Force Bill was defeated and the Civil Rights Bill was paralyzed by the blows it received in the Senate and House. It not only proved "a barren sceptre in their grip," but it secured a Democratic majority in the House in the Forty-fourth Congress. The American people, in the language of Roosevelt, are for a "square deal." They were unwilling that that majority should say who should vote or when and how voting should be done. Nor were they willing to regulate their social life and relations by the standards or tastes of Benjamin F. Butler, around whose name, negro troops, the blood of Mumford, and insults to women gathered in mingled memory.

There were able men on both sides in the Senate. Among the Republicans appear Oliver P. Morton, John Sherman, George F. Edmunds, Matthew Carpenter, Henry M. Teller, Reuben E. Fenton, Roscoe Conkling, George S. Boutwell, William B. Allison and John J. Ingalls and many other men of decided ability. Charles Sumner died during the Forty-third Congress. The Democratic party presented in this Senate: Allen G. Thurman, Thomas F. Bayard, Eli Saulsbury, Joseph E. McDonald, John W. Stevenson, Matthew W. Ransom, William Pinckney Whyte, Thomas Randolph, Henry G. Davis, Thomas M. Norwood, John B. Gordon and Francis M. Cockerell. Two of the Republicans, Reuben E. Fenton and Henry M. Teller, were liberals of a very high order of ability and statesmanship. The debates in the Senate upon the vital party issues were elaborate and exhaustive. Thomas M. Norwood delivered a speech in the Senate against the Civil Rights Bill which attracted much attention, created great amusement and enlightened the judgment of the people throughout the country. About one-half of the speech, which was a long one, was devoted to the ridicule of the measure, in severe irony, ludicrous illustrations and blistering invectives; all presented, in an elegant, scholarly style. This greatly amused the American people. The remaining half of the speech was devoted to a masterly argument against its constitutionality, which Associate Justice Field, of the Supreme Court, pronounced to be the ablest constitutional argument made upon the subject. It will be remembered that in the House the party managers put forward a South Carolina negro to reply to Alexander H. Stephens' argument against the constitutionality of the bill; so in the Senate they put up to reply to Norwood an ignorant, slack-twisted, white reconstruction renegade, who posed as Republican Senator from Texas, whose name was *Flannagan.* He had been thrust into the Senate by the military influence that had put the negroes Revels and Bruce, into the Senate from the State of Davis, Prentiss, Sharkey and Lamar.

No minority ever served a country in legislative halls with more fidelity and profit than the Democratic phalanx in the Forty-third Congress served the people of these United States. Their gratitude found expression in returning to the House of Representatives of the Forty-fourth Congress a majority of Democratic members, and the election of Samuel J. Tilden to the Presidency. As soon as Tilden's election was ascertained and unguardedly conceded by Mr. Hayes, the Republican playwrights proceeded to put a *new* play on the political boards. This consisted in sending "visiting statesmen" to the States of Louisiana, Florida and South Carolina (overwhelming Democratic States), charged with the duty of working up and manufacturing charges of fraud in the election and suborning witnesses to sustain the charge by perjury. This was successfully accomplished. In vain did the Democratic House appoint committees "on the recent election in South Carolina, Florida and Louisiana," and in vain did these committees, or the Democratic majority ascertain and report the truth. The "visiting statesmen" had fixed things and completed their job. The election in these three States was so muddled in charges and counter-charges of fraud as to furnish a pretext for investigation. As the time approached for counting the electoral vote and declaring the result, President Grant was very quietly ordering troops from stations and garrisons to the vicinity of the Capitol. It was discovered that a partisan commission, with a Republican majority of one on the commission, was the proper authority to do the thing; that the Constitution declares the Congress shall do—count the vote and declare the result. And by a sort of unconstitutional legislative legerdemain the commission was created. The commission was composed as follows:

Associate Justices of the Supreme Court: Nathan Clifford, William Strong, Samuel F. Miller, Stephen J. Field, Joseph P. Bradley.

United States Senators: George F. Edmunds, Oliver P. Morton, Frederick T. Frelinghuysen, Allen G. Thurman, Thomas F. Bayard.

United States Representatives: Henry B. Payne, Eppa Hunton, Josiah G. Abbott, James A. Garfield, George F. Hoar.

This commission of able men was created by party jugglery and packed with a Republican majority of one, to perpetuate and consummate under the forms of law the most stupendous fraud of history. It put out of the office of President of the United States the candidate legally chosen by the people, and into it, the candidate rejected by them at the ballot-box. The determination of that packed tribunal was as well known before the investigation began, as it was after the decision was pronounced. The Democratic members stood for the truth. The Republican members committed the fraud. The evidence taken by the Potter Investigation Committee of the Forty-fifth Congress furnishes the proof of this statement. This transaction is remitted to future history for its impartial adjudication.

The Forty-fourth Congress seems to have been fruitful in transferring legislative functions to commissions. The silver question was referred to a commission consisting of John P. Jones, George S. Boutwell, Louis V. Bogy, Richard P. Bland, Randall L. Gibson, Geo. Willard, William S. Groesbeck and Francis P. Bowen.

The election in 1876 resulted in returning to the House of Representatives a decided Democratic majority. And the changes in the Senate had made the parties about equal in strength in that body. But the counting in by the commission of the defeated candidate, gave the President to the Republican party, and therefore, neither party had control of the policy of the government.

CHAPTER XVII.

The Forty-fifth Congress.

The Senators from Georgia in the Forty-fifth Congress, were John B. Gordon and Benjamin H. Hill. The Representatives were: Julian Hartridge, William E. Smith, Philip Cook, Henry R. Harris, Milton A. Candler, James H. Blount, William H. Felton, Alexander H. Stephens and Hiram P. Bell. Samuel J. Randall, of Pennsylvania, was elected Speaker, and George M. Adams, of Kentucky, Clerk. In the opinion of Alexander H. Stephens, this Congress, in the average ability of its members, outranked any previous one in the history of the government. There were men already famous, and others who afterwards became so, in this Congress. Beck, Lamar, Dawes, Blaine and George F. Hoar had been transferred to the Senate. In the House were: Alexander H. Stephens, Samuel J. Randall, Samuel S. Cox, John H. Reagan, Nathaniel P. Banks, James A. Garfield, William McKinley, Thomas B. Reed, Joseph W. Keifer, Roger Q. Mills, Proctor Knott, J. S. C. Blackburn, Clarkson N. Potter, William P. Frye, Eugene Hale and John Randolph Tucker. Of these, James A. Garfield and William McKinley became Presidents, and each met the sad fate of assassination while in office. Keifer and Reed became Speakers of the House. Reagan, Mills, Hale and Frye, distinguished Senators, the last-mentioned acting Vice-President after the death of Vice-President Hobart. In addition to these, there was a number of men of equal ability but less official notoriety, in the House. Of this class, the accomplished Randolph Tucker, John F. House and Thomas Ewing were typical examples.

Americans have been taught to believe that the "golden age" of the Senate was the times in which Webster and Choate, Clay and Crittenden, Calhoun and Preston, Forsyth and Berrien, Cass, Buchanan, Benton, Wright and Grundy crossed knightly lances in senatorial jousts. But it may be doubted whether that brilliant constellation was not fully equalled by the one formed in the Forty-fifth Congress. Conspicuous among the Republicans appeared George F. Edmunds, Roscoe Conkling, William B. Allison, Henry M. Teller, James Blaine, Matthew Carpenter, George F. Hoar, Henry L. Dawes and John J. Ingalls. And among the Democrats, Allen G. Thurman, Thomas F. Bayard, James B. Beck, John T. Morgan, Benjamin H. Hill, Matthew Ransom, John B. Gordon, L. Q. C. Lamar, and Augustus H. Garland. Zebulon Vance and George G. Vest entered the Senate later. Oliver P. Morton was dead, and John Sherman had entered the Cabinet, as Secretary of the Treasury. Among these great men, Allen G. Thurman stood, by common concession, primus inter alios, a jurist, publicist and statesman of the highest order and an ideal American Senator. Bayard was a very strong man, with a sublimated ethereal political purity, that sometimes lessened his value as a party ally. Conkling was richly endowed in mental power, a fluent, graceful speaker, of imposing personal appearance, tastefully dressed, and formidable in debate. His manner was characterized by a hauteur that was little less than repulsive. His step was the stride of Apollo, called by Blaine (in the spat between them in the House), "The strut of the turkey gobbler." His manner and bearing reminded me of Pollock's description of Byron: "He from above descending, stooped to touch the loftiest thought, and proudly stooped, as though it scarce deserved his verse;" and what Phillips said of Napoleon, "Grand, gloomy and peculiar, he sat upon the throne, a sceptered hermit wrapped in the solitude of his originality." He settled accounts with Blaine, when, in his response to the latter's request to make a few speeches in New York, in support of his candidacy for the Presidency, he stated: "That he had retired from the criminal practice." It was said that he declined the Chief-Justiceship of the Supreme Court, tendered to him by Grant. He was the friend of Grant; and led the 306 delegates, who supported Grant's nomination, for a third term. He broke with Garfield's administration, controlled by Blaine, and resigned his seat in the Senate, came to political grief, and soon met the fate of all the living. Carpenter was a first-class lawyer of splendid physique, bold, manly and able; a true type of the best product of the great West. Edmunds was the model Republican Senator. He was of medium height, thin, prematurely gray, with bald head, and very slightly stóoping shoulders. He was a charming speaker—his style, which was of the conversational order, pure as snow and clear as light. He went straight to the vital point of a question, cleared it of mists, and struck for the truth, as he understood it. He was a strong partisan; but a profound jurist, broad-minded statesman and faithful Senator.

Voorhees, "the tall sycamore of the Wabash," was the Ciceronian orator of the Senate, and of the country. His person, his voice, his taste and his talents—all conspired to make him the master of oratory in the sense of superb declamation, of fine thought in magnificently rounded sentences of peerless beauty. His appointment to speak was the signal for crowded galleries, and the guaranty of a delighted audience. Garland was a plain, quiet, steady man, who was the equal of the first constitutional lawyers of the country. Gordon, the most magnetic, in the senate or out, was a fluent speaker, ready, skirmishing debater and always eloquent. His chivalry and high social qualities made him a general favorite. Ransom was soldier, statesman, orator, and gentleman in harmonious proportions, and happy combination. Hoar, developed into one of the safest, purest, wisest Republican Senators New England ever gave the country. Ingalls was as bright and perhaps, erratic, as a comet. He was unique and picturesque in person, dress, style, manner—in everything. He was a brilliant speaker and a dangerous guerilla and free lance, in a general free-for-all senatorial intellectual combat.

Hill never ranked high for statesmanship, nor for

wisdom in party counsels, but he was a superior lawyer, a great orator and a matchless debater. Burke said of Fox, that "he was the greatest debater the world ever saw." But Hill had not then lived, and Burke had not heard him. As a debater, a disputant (in my opinion), history furnishes no account of his equal. He had in rich abundance all the powers of a successful orator and debater. His debate with Blaine, on the Amnesty Bill, in the House of Representatives, his Davis, Hall and Bush Arbor speeches in Atlanta, prove this statement. The writer heard him, in Concert Hall in Macon, in 1856, at night, deliver a speech in support of Fillmore for President, which lost, to at least two persons, the sleep of that night. This speech charmed, thrilled and electrified his audience. I happened to state to the late J. H. R. Washington that I could not sleep for a moment that night, after hearing the speech. He replied that his experience was precisely the same. I listened to him for four hours in the Supreme Court, in the "Choice murder case" in which he sought to reverse the conviction, in the lower court on the plea of insanity. He stated his legal propositions clearly, and argued them so masterfully that I could not see how he could possibly be wrong. But the court overruled every proposition upon which he insisted. He handled facts, existing, with a force that would admit of no answer; and improvised such facts as were necessary to his purpose with a skill that defied detection. The country will not soon forget the sportive cruelty with which he held Malone writhing in the agony of mental crucifixion in the Senate. Hill, at his best surpassed "Fox in debate, Brougham in invectives, Demosthenes in power, Cicero in style, and approached Prentiss in the highest realms of beauty and true eloquence." Beck, Blaine, Lamar and Dawes have been considered in another chapter. There were four members of this Senate now living, who, for thorough consecration to the public service, ardent patriotism, constant and laborious work, practical common sense, legislative wisdom and length of membership have already embalmed themselves in history as model statesmen and standard Senators. These are Jno. T. Morgan, William B. Allison, Henry M. Teller, and Francis M. Cockrell. In the Forty-fifth Congress, Georgia was represented on the most important committees of the House. Stephens was chairman of the Committee on Coinage, Weights and Measures, and a member of the Committee on Rules. Cook was chairman of the Committee on Public Buildings and Grounds, and on the Committee on Reform in the Civil Service; Harris, on Committee of Ways and Means, and on Expenditures in the Treasury Department. Blount was on the Committee of Appropriations. Bell was on the Committee on Banking and Currency, and on Education and Labor; Hartridge, on the Judiciary, and on Expenditures in the Department of Justice; Candler, on Privileges and Elections, and on Expenses in the War Department; Felton, on Commerce, and on Mines and Mining. W. E. Smith, was on Public Lands, on Patents, and on the Joint Committee, on the Census. The great questions before this Congress were the Tariff, Currency, Silver

Coinage, Repeal of the Specie Resumption Act, and the investigation of the Presidential Election Frauds. On the currency and silver questions, the discussion was protracted, able and exhaustive. Stephens, Harris, Felton and Bell participated in this discussion. The Free Coinage Silver Bill—known as the "Bland Bill"—was passed. Mr. Bland was a small, quiet, modest man. He had mined in Colorado and Utah. He farmed in Missouri, and was a plain, practical, sensible man, thinking much and speaking little. He fought courageously for years for the restoration of silver as a basic money of final redemption with gold, at 16 to 1, and finally won. His triumph was turned into defeat by the veto of President Hayes—dictated, doubtless, by his great secretary, John Sherman. The government was suffering with a virulent attack of the Ohio political "grippe." Ohio men filled the offices of President, General of the Army, Chief Justice of the Supreme Court, and Secretary of the Treasury. It has always been supposed that the sword, the purse and the law, were instruments of power in controlling the affairs of government. This instance does not explode that supposition. Mr. Hayes was an affable, accommodating gentleman of high moral character, nominated by accident, and counted in by fraud, with no expectation of a second term. Of mediocre ability, among the third class of statesmen, he turned over to his Secretary of the Treasury, who was looking to the success, the management of his administrative policy. Sherman was unquestionably the greatest master of finance in the country. He was said to be among those who made fortunes by its manipulations. He stood with the creditors of the government, and capitalists of the country for the "Wall" and Lombard streets, theories of finance, which was to change the government debt from a currency, to a coin debt, eliminate silver from coinage, destroying its debt-paying capacity, thus converting a currency into a gold debt; and, then, resume specie payments. The South and West were so clamorous for the double standard, and the nomination for the succession impending, that another bill of Mr. Bland for free coinage of silver,—which passed in the House—was amended in the Senate on the motion of Senator Allison; and finally passed both houses and became known as the "Bland-Allison Act." In general terms this act authorized the Secretary of the Treasury to purchase a limited amount of silver bullion, monthly, and coin the same at the ratio of sixteen of silver to one of gold. This act continued in force, with good results, until Cleveland's administration, under Wall street influence, secured its repeal, divided the Democratic party and entrenched the Republicans in power, indefinitely. The Republican National Convention met, and the great secretary failed to reach the guerdon so long, and so arduously sought and another Ohio man won. Ohio has been fruitful in great men. She has produced at least one woman who merits the highest niche in the Temple of Fame. In simple, plain elegance in dress and manners, in ardent devotion to the duties of wifehood, in the charmed circle of home-life, in dignity of bearing, in court life, in sympathetic response to appeals for help, and in thorough consecration to the pious duties of the religion of Christianity, Mrs. Lucy Hayes is the finest exemplar of the virtues of American womanhood that ever occupied the White House or illustrated the civilization of the nineteenth century. It is reassuring to recognize in her the typical representation of a very large majority of our countrywomen. There are perhaps, some blessings, in the control of the different departments of government, by opposite parties. If but little good legislation can be secured, much bad may be prevented, while such as is absolutely necessary may be assured. During this Congress there were many measures, some good, others bad, presented and pressed, which failed. A New York engraving and printing bank note company, had presented in the House, a bill to abolish the "Bureau of Engraving and Printing." It was referred to the committee on Banking and Currency. Geo. S. Boutwell, ex-Secretary of the Treasury, was employed by the company to represent it before the committee, which he did, in an elaborate argument. Upon my motion, Edward McPherson, the accomplished chief of the Bureau, was invited to reply; which he did in a masterly way. It was simply a job to destroy the Bureau and rob the government by a contract to do its engraving and printing. On my motion a private speculative job was defeated, in which, I have always, felt that I rendered the public some service. As a recognition of this service, the chairman of the committee appointed me the Congressional member of a committee of Treasury Experts raised to determine the relative merits of the work done by steam, and the hand-press. I presided over this committee and wrote its report. As chairman of a sub-committee, I reported favorably to the Committee on Education and Labor, a bill to distribute for education among the States, upon the basis of illiteracy, the proceeds of the sale of the public lands. This beneficent measure failed.

Nine members of the House had been members of the Confederate Congress. They were Alexander H. Stephens, John H. Reagan, Otho R. Singleton, Robert A. Hatcher, J. D. C. Adkins, John T. Goode, William E. Smith, Hiram P. Bell and Julian Hartridge. Hartridge died in Washington while a member, deeply lamented by Congress and the country. Stephens had been vice-president of the Confederacy, and Reagan postmaster-general of both the Provisional and permanent governments. Reagan and Ex-Gov. Lubbuck were with President Davis when he was captured. They had entered into a covenant to personally stand by him *to the last,* and share his fate whatever it might be; and nobly did these true and knightly men keep that agreement. In all the elements that go to make up a pure, noble, great man, John H. Reagan had few equals and no superior in the age in which he lived. The Texas delegation was a strong one—Reagan, Throckmorton, Culberson, Mills, Giddings, Willie and Shliecher. Shliecher died at his post during his term. I wish to emphasize the statement, that the legal maxim "*expressio unicus, exclusio alterius,*" has no application to my reference to men or my failure to refer to them. If conditions would allow, it would afford me great pleasure to put on record my appreciation of the ability of most of the Senators and Representatives of the

Forty-fifth Congress. They were, in the main, men of great ability, high moral character and unquestioned patriotism. Some of them became famous in history. Many of them have rendered valuable service to their country and their kind, and all of them did their duty as they understood it. A great number of them have crossed the silent river, and found what the survivors will never know until they rejoin them in another and a different state of existence. In the storm and conflict of opinion and policy of Congressional life, there is the sunshine of genial companionships, valued friendships and pleasant and tender memories.

There is one colossal figure of these times that especially claims consideration. Ulysses S. Grant was born in 1822 in the State of Ohio. He was educated at West Point, brevetted captain for gallantry in the Mexican War, and a few years after, resigned his commission in the Army. He engaged in farming in Missouri and later in the leather business in Illinois—in neither of which was he regarded as successful. He was a strong, quiet, modest, silent man who enjoyed a cigar, was fond of horses, of which he was an excellent judge, and was said to be a connoisseur in the qualities of whiskey. When the Civil War commenced, he organized a company of volunteers, of which he was elected captain. He was soon Brigadier General of volunteers; captured Fort Henry and Fort Donelson; won the second day's battle of Shiloh, after losing the first; captured Vicksburg; was appointed Major-General in the regular army and placed in command of the Mississippi Division. In March, 1864, he was appointed Lieutenant-General of the Armies of the United States. He engaged Lee in battle at the Wilderness; sought to flank Lee and reach Richmond; was defeated at Spottsylvania, North Anna and Cold Harbor. He crossed the James, finally surrounded Lee, and compelled his surrender, April 9th, 1865. In 1866, he was made General of the Armies of the United States. He was twice elected president, traveled around the world, the feted and flattered guest of kings and emperors. He lost his fortune in a commercial bubble, wrote his book and died 23d July, 1885. His countrymen gave him the grandest state funeral ever accorded to an American citizen. The meteoric splendor of this greatness in the world's popular judgment of human greatness, can only be accounted for upon the coincidence of two facts—the inherent qualities of the man and the opportunity his environments gave for their development. Grant's high qualities were common sense, equanimity of temper, constancy of purpose, force of will, fearlessness of consequences and magnanimity of spirit. His environments were exactly suited to their development, to the fullest extent. He had opened the Mississippi River and divided the Confederacy. He was at the head of the Union armies with the confidence of his government, supported by resources of men and means, without limit. Lee had successively defeated McClellan, Burnside, Pope and Hooker in pitched battles. Relying upon numbers, he encountered Lee at the "Wilderness." The result of this battle determined Grant's policy in conducting the war. This policy was the exhaustion of the Confederacy's resources of men and supplies. Grant knew that conscription had robbed the cradle and the grave—that when the last Confederate disappeared the Union would still have an army. Hence he defeated every effort to exchange prisoners: with him, every Confederate kept out of the army was as good as dead, and could not be replaced; while the Union could lose its prisoners and still its ranks be filled. There was little genius but much mathematics in this logic. Rivers of blood and hundreds of slain in battle, and the suffering and death of thousands in prison, did not count. This policy pursued by Grant for one year carried him from the defeat of the Wilderness to the victory of Appomattox. As president of the United States, he appointed his friends and kinfolks to office; communicated his views on public questions in clear, brief messages, and allowed his party in Congress to manage public affairs pretty much as it pleased. He gave all his personal and official influence to the pacification of a disturbed country. He closed his letter accepting the nomination for the presidency with the sententious sentence: "Let us have peace." His official, civil life was devoted to that end. He had mingled in enough strife. He showed his magnanimity of soul at the surrender, and in the promptness and spirit with which he rebuked the threatened indictment and arrest of Lee in violation of its terms.

CHAPTER XVIII.

Disappointed Ambition.

There were eight distinguished statesmen who paid the penalty of ambition in the disappointment of desire, and the mortification of defeat, in their aspirations for the presidency—Calhoun, Clay, Cass, Seward, Douglass, Chase, Blaine and Sherman. Calhoun's breach with Jackson and doctrine of nullification eliminated him from among the possibilities for that high office. Clay lost by the fatal blunder of opposition to the annexation of Texas. Cass' hopes perished in the blaze of Buena Vista; Lincoln's debate with Douglass side-tracked Seward; Appomattox put Grant between Chase and his goal; Kansas and Nebraska placed Douglass on the retired list. The ballot-box disposed of Blaine. Sherman could never reach the nomination station in the race. When the political angel stirred the waters of the pool, another stepped in. All these men had been representatives in the House, had won the Senatorial toga and with the exception of Douglass had been cabinet ministers. Several of them had been Governors of States; two of them Speaker of the House; one Vice-president, another Chief Justice of Supreme Court, and another foreign minister. All these men wore the highest honors, save the presidency, the people or the government could possibly bestow.

It would seem that all this ought to satisfy human ambition and fully fill the loftiest human aspiration. Yet these men, like the youth bearing the banner with the strange device, "Excelsior," sought to climb the

Alpine heights of power and only grasped a frozen shroud. They seem to have forgotten that there was but a step between the conquest of Gaul and the dagger of Brutus—the sun of Austerlitz and the eclipse of Waterloo. Whence this insatiable hungering and thirsting in the human soul—for honor, power and fame? Is it the silent assertion of its conscious immortality, wandering like the lost pleiad in search of its original center? Or, is it that the stain of sin has diverted its powers from the enjoyment of the spiritual and eternal, to the material and perishing things of the Universe? It dominates now, and has dominated men and women—to a greater or less degree in all ages, classes and conditions of the race, through all time. It is to be met and reckoned with in human affairs. And yet the history of the wisest, the richest and the most powerful of kings has put it on record, that "All is vanity and vexation of spirit." Webster desired the presidency, but did not seek it, and perhaps, entertained no hope of attaining it. Horace Greely both desired and sought it. It is amazing that he, for a moment, should have indulged the thought or entertained the slightest hope of defeating Grant. And yet the earnestness with which he prosecuted his campaign, shows the intensity of his desire and the hope of his success in securing the coveted prize. An eyewitness assures us that, returning to his office, certain of defeat, and finding scattered over it burlesque cartoons by "Nast" (ridiculing his candidacy) he put his face in his hands upon his desk, burst into tears and said in anguish, "Is this the reward of my life of labor?" and literally died of a broken heart, and was borne to the silence that stills the tumult of strife and withers the laurels of ambition. What these great men suffered in chagrin, disappointment and mortification at defeat, can not be known. How much of real joy and happiness they sacrificed can only be conjectured. It is a fact that most of them died comparatively young; Calhoun at 68; Sherman at 69; Chase at 65; Blaine at 63; Greely at 61; Douglass at 48. Only Cass, Clay and Seward lived beyond the "threescore and ten." There are at least two men in American history who attained the highest official honors without seeking them, and discharged their duties with an ability and fidelity that will make them famous through all the ages. These are George Washington and Jefferson Davis. They responded to emergency calls for public service; and unselfishly gave it. In the one case, success made a victor, in the other, defeat, a victim; in both, the best illustration of true greatness, the unselfish service of others.

Our theory of a double government, general and local, national and State, under a written constitution, defining and specifying the powers of each, is a beautiful—a Utopian theory. It assumes that those in control will exercise only constitutional powers, and will strictly observe constitutional limitations; that the people will subordinate personal to public interests. If this were true the government would be a Utopia. But in applying the theory in practice, it encounters the passions, selfishness, avarice and ambition of both those who govern and those who are governed with a diversity of interest and opinion, difficult to harmonize and reconcile. And hence, self-government will always continue an experiment. The fact that one generation has governed itself, does not prove that the next one will. "Eternal vigilance is the price of liberty." With all our progress, development and power —the first century of our experiment is not altogether reassuring. The Northern States were astonished that the Southern States would secede; the Southern people were surprised that the government would attempt to hold the States together by force. But the unexpected happened in both cases, and a stupendous war resulted. Three presidents have been assassinated. And the theory applied to existing conditions fails to materialize into the Utopia.

Ours is the best system of government ever devised by human wisdom. The National Government undertakes the regulation of our affairs and relations with foreign governments to protect and secure to the States their rights in the exercise and enjoyment of the right of self-government and home rule. But in a government, thus complex in its form and nature—with a domain so large, resources so vast, and a population so numerous,—differences of opinion, antagonism in interest and collisions of passion will inevitably exist. These conditions constantly present new questions of public policy for the solution of statesmanship. The sole instrument of power is the ballot. The success of this experiment of self-government depends upon the virtue, intelligence and patriotism of the electors, and the wisdom, capacity and faithfulness of public officials. The honors and emoluments of public office are open alike to all, and this is equality and therefore right. But while it invites aspiring patriots to desire office as a means of serving the public, it presents to the ambitious demagogues, the bane of republics, the temptation to seek office for selfish purposes. The danger is that the people do not always wisely discriminate between them. They do not appreciate the oft-repeated truth, that public office is a public trust, to be exercised alone for the public benefit. If all the people of this great country could or would properly appreciate a government that secures the inalienable rights of man, the proper limitations of liberty by law, the perfect equality of all before the law, the equal distribution of taxation and the duties of citizenship, and an open track for the race of life; they would consecrate themselves to its preservation and transmission, unimpaired, to posterity. The blessing of liberty and good government is the product of thousands of years of struggle, suffering, sacrifice and blood. And to maintain, preserve and perpetuate it, requires virtue, vigilance, wisdom and patriotism. The United States of America is the temple that holds the Ark of her Covenant, and shrine of her worship. Let her kneeling devotees forever keep her altar fires aflame.

CHAPTER XIX.

Social Problems.

There are certain social and economic problems now confronting the government and people of the United States which clamor for solution. Among the least of these is the race problem. The effort already made by law to solve it upon the basis of equality, is a demonstrated failure. The attempt now being made to dispose of it by literary education, will soon prove to be another. The proposition and practice of taxing the labor and property of the country to train free negroes in idleness and crime, and inspire them with an aspiration for equality they can never reach, will be abandoned when its folly and injustice become generally understood. Various theories have been propounded for the disposition of this question—such as their general distribution throughout the United States; their colonization in this country; their removal to Africa, etc. So far as the colored race is concerned, its duty and its interest is to earn a living by honest labor. Its capital consists in its muscle and knowledge of agriculture. That plan which puts the negro to work in the ground for his livelihood, solves at least, the materialistic branch of this problem. The race question as it relates to the African, has very much the characteristics of a tempest in a teapot. The Southern people may be relied on to take care of it. They principally have to deal with it. They understand it. They know how to manage it and will find ways to meet its emergencies in the future. There are questions of graver import than this, pressing for solution. Prominent among these is the divorce question. At last the country seems to have become aroused at the danger to social order arising from the numberless and shameless dissolutions of the sacred bonds of wedlock sanctioned by law. This is not surprising when it is remembered that marriage is the God-ordained method of propagating, preserving and perpetuating the race. The family is the primary and basic institution upon which society in all its forms and organizations rests. Marriage is the indispensable initiative of the family. Remove, impair or destroy this foundation and the superstructure must crumble and perish in ruins. The recklessness with which marriage is contracted and the facility with which it is dissolved has justly alarmed Christians, patriots and philanthropists. This is a question within the control of law. Indeed its evils result from bad law. Its remedy is simple. It only requires a change in the law of the grounds upon which, or the cause for which a divorce may be granted. Whatever difficulty may exist in securing the desired change in the law, will be found in harmonizing the public sentiments of the different States, upon the ground upon which it should be granted. To consider this question the governors of the several States have been invited to meet in consultation. Bar associations, legislatures, church councils and organized bodies of various other kinds, have given expression of their wish for the suppression of this evil, and the restoration of marriage to its proper purity and sanctity. There is one cause for which Christianity gives it sanction. It would seem that a Christian nation might agree upon that cause. It is impossible to secure exact statistics of the number of divorces granted each year in the United States. But judging from the best sources of information available, the number in proportion to the number of marriages is appalling. "Modern Women," August 1905, publishes the following table of marriages and divorces in thirteen cities of the United States in 1902:

	Marriages	Divorces	Proportion
New York,	33,447	817	1 in 40
Chicago,	16,684	1,808	1 iu 9
Boston,	6,312	446	1 iu 14
San Francisco,	3,656	847	1 in 4
Philadelphia,	9,912	492	1 in 20
St. Louis,	5,959	573	1 in 10
Cleveland,	3,199	454	1 in 7
Indianapolis,	2,608	471	1 in 5
Kansas City,	1,704	420	1 in 4
Los Angeles,	1,818	405	1 in 4
Seattle,	1,351	323	1 in 4
Dallas,	1,291	210	1 in 5
Chattanooga,	550	103	1 in 5

This proportion of divorces to marriages, applied to the entire United States, would give for one year in this country, 35,846 divorces. That this is below the true number, which, judging from the statements of the public press, seems to be rapidly increasing, there is but little reason to doubt, 35,846 divorces means that number of wrecked homes, and twice that number of ruined lives—to say nothing of the children and families who suffer in consequence of the sin. But this is the least evil. To weaken and destroy the sacredness and obligations of the marriage relation is to sap and subvert our social, civil and religious system and institutions, and paralyze and ultimately destroy our Christian civilization. It is the training of pure and happy homes, that makes good men and women, and great and prosperous nations. It is the home where reverence for law and obedience to its supremacy is taught and learned. If the wicked reign of passion and crime is to be controlled or prevented, its purity and sanctity must be preserved.

Another great problem with which the American government and people are now dealing is the conflict between capital and labor. That these two agents of all material progress which are the compliments of each other should paralyze their potentialities in a conflict which produces want, loss, bad feeling and bloodshed, instead of uniting and co-operating in serving the best results to both, is folly for which language has no adequate expression. It must be conceded that each is entitled to perfect equality in rights; that each is absolutely and equally indispensable to the other and to society. Then why not eliminate all antagonism and controversy between them and obviate the numerous evils that flow from their strife and conflict? Capital has the undoubted right to legal protection in the enjoyment of its legitimate profits,

Labor has precisely the same right to protection in the earnings and value of its toil. There is inherently no hostility between them, but on the contrary, an identity of interest that demands alliance and co-operation. Their relations and rights can be regulated by contract and enforced by law. When capital —formed into combinations to rob labor—and labor unions united to wrong capital—produce war between them, after both parties and the public suffer much (like they do in all wars) the military power of the government is invoked to suppress it. The frequency of this state of affairs in the United States, is a pessimistic prophecy. And the time has come, when the means of prevention should be found and applied.

Another problem pressing for attention and solution upon the American people is the question of immigration. The Puritans and Çavaliers and their descendants,—combining the best elements of both, settled this country, and framed and established its institutions. They have brought its progress and civilization to their present state, and they are the only safe conservators of these institutions. They hold them in sacred trust for posterity. Our example, like a Pharos, has guided France, Mexico and the South American Republics into the light of free representative systems of governments and liberalized the monarchial systems of Europe. Our distinguished racial capabilities and excellencies must be preserved from deterioration. Immigration should be restricted to those of good moral character, who are eligible to naturalization, and come to discharge the duties of good citizenship, as well as to enjoy the blessings of good government and who wish to assimilate with our people and institutions. We have neither room nor use for the Lazzaroni of the effete despotisms of Europe and Asia. The preservation of our system rests with the race that created it.

Among the problems engaging public attention none is more vital to the republic than the purification of the ballot. The ballot is the expression of the original inherent sovereignty of the people. It is the foundation of power. Corrupt the fountain and the stream necessarily becomes polluted. That the ballot has become in many places and under different circumstances an article of commerce—of bargain and sale,—must be admitted by all familiar with the facts of current history. By this means the popular choice of rulers has been defeated. Virtue, intelligence and patriotism ostracized and saloon rowdies manipulated by ward-heelers and county demagogues have chosen men to make and administer law, who barter the franchise, rights and interests of the people for bribes. It is astonishing that the American people continue so quiet under such wrongs, so fraught with destruction to their highest interests. This astonishment is increased when it is remembered that the remedy is so obvious and simple. There are many methods of purifying the ballot by law. It may be done by guards placed around the place of voting; by amending and enforcing the law, prescribing the qualifications of voters; by increasing and vigorously enforcing the penalties against the crime of illegal voting, even to the disfranchisement of the criminal. A concentrated public opinion can speedily secure this reform so imperiously demanded by the highest considerations of the public interest. Will the people rise to the height of the argument? Or, will they, by their apathy and indifference like "the base Judean, cast a pearl away, richer, than all his tribes?"

There is another problem before us, with which the government has undertaken to deal, and, which it is ardently hoped, it may be able to righteously solve in ultimate suppression. This is the combination of capital known as "Trusts," formed for the purpose of destroying competition, monopolizing the trade and fixing the price in certain articles of necessity to the public, in which they deal. In a word, it is a combination to dictate the price the people must pay for things indispensable to them. In all the essential elements of morals they stand upon the same basis of the highwayman and the train-wrecker. They force the people's money from them contrary to their will, and without compensation. These trusts are public robbers, and should be summarily placed under the ban of public opinion and of law. This insufferable greed and avarice diverts capital from its beneficence in the prosecution of legitimate enterprises, profitable to the owner, and useful to the public, and converts it into war upon commerce and plunder of the people. The President of the United States deserves the gratitude of the nation for his efforts to free it from this blood-sucking octopus. In a world of movement, change, activity, progress and retrograde, there will always be problems pressing for solution upon the race.

CHAPTER XX.

Woman in War.

(Address of H. P. Bell at the Confederate Reunion, at Marietta, Ga.)

Confederate Comrades, Ladies and Gentlemen:

The highest expression of patriotism is the offering of one's life upon the altar of his country, in the defense of its honor, its liberty and its flag. This expression every true Confederate soldier has freely and voluntarily given. Confederate soldiers had no agency in causing the late Civil War, not creating the conditions which made it inevitable. They dealt with it as an existing fact. When their country was invaded and volunteers were called for they responded promptly. They left home, farm, office, business, wife, children—all that was dear to them, and submitted their blood and life to the chance of battle. They endured heat and cold, hunger and thirst, fatigue and toil, sickness and suffering, danger and death; and all this without a murmur. They did their duty always and everywhere with unfaltering fidelity. For four long and bloody years, on more than five hundred battlefields, they held at bay more than thrice their number, and these stood, until overwhelming numbers and resources, depleted their ranks to a corporal's guard by exhaustion and death. They enriched the soil of their country with their blood, and its history with their valor. When surrender became inevitable, they acquiesced; and fought the more difficult conquest of self in overcoming hostility to their enemies. The sacred and shattered remnant of this glorious army returned to their despoiled homes to struggle with poverty, support their families, repair their fortunes and discharge the duties of good citizenship. Thus engaged they were confronted by an effort of the Federal government to subordinate them to the political domination of their recently emancipated slaves; and for a period of five years struggled against the monstrous crime of reconstruction. They finally succeeded in placing their State governments under white Democratic control; and defeated the nefarious scheme to destroy white supremacy in the South. In all the calamitous national vicissitudes, all the Confederate soldiers did their full duty, faithfully, nobly, heroically. But one duty remains to be performed by them. That duty is the erection, by them, of a monument to commemorate the patriotism of the glorious women of the Confederacy. It is a shame to us that this duty has been so long neglected. And we have but little time in which to perform it. It is upon us, a duty of the highest obligation.

If woman's hand first, "Forth reaching, plucked that forbidden fruit, whose mortal taste brought death into the world and all our woe," yet, nobly has she wrought and patiently has she suffered in atonement for the disaster that blighted the bloom of Eden. She has in every age of this world's history identified her potentialities for good with all human affairs, in all the departments of human endeavor, from the least interest of an individual to the highest concerns of the race. It was the genius of a woman that preserved in the frail craft of floating bulrushes, on the Nile, the world's greatest leader and lawgiver. It was the minstrelsy of a woman that celebrated that leader's triumph on the hither side of the sea. It was a brave woman, who, at the peril of her life, dared to approach the Persian throne in the absence of the outstretched scepter to secure the repeal of an unchangeable law, relieve a nation from the condemnation of death and bring to condign punishment the vilest criminal of history. It was the strategy of a beautiful widow that dispersed the Assyrian army, cast the bloody head of the commander at the feet of the despairing Sanhedrim, and saved from destruction the beleaguered capital. It was a Spartan mother, who, looking upon her son, pointed to his shield and said: "Come with it when the battle's won, or on it from the field." In the bloody butchery of Saragossa, the beautiful Agostina issued from the convent, clad in white, kissing her cross, and mounting the breach with lighted match, at which the last gunner had fallen, poured from his silent gun a storm of destruction upon the assailants, dictated the reply of Palafox, "war to the knife," to Leferre's demand for surrender and defeated the conquerors of Marengo and Austerlitz. When the commander of Carthage, against the protest of his wife, surrendered to Scipio, she cursed his treason, gathered her children into her arms and with them plunged into the burning temple and perished with her city, rather than witness the triumph of the Romans.

It was a gentle maiden, that poured the contents of the broken alabaster box upon the head of the weary Nazarene, made nineteen centuries fragrant with the odor of love, and embalmed in historic immortality the name of Mary of Bethany. It was a group of sorrow-stricken women who lingered latest at the Cross and appeared earliest at the sepulcher. It was a woman who caught at the empty tomb, from angelic lips, the thrilling whisper, "He is not here. He is risen," and first proclaimed the truth of the resurrection, that cables the broken heart of humanity to the cherished hope of immortality. It is thus seen that in all human affairs, the agency and influence of woman has been manifest. In civil government, in religious and social systems, in science, art and literature, and in the tragic events of the history of the race, she has appeared at the front and acted her part. And yet, her most potential activities have been exerted in quietude and silence, without the emblazonry of publications on the pages of history. This is eminently true of her relations to, and service in the late war between the States. With the united opposition of Southern women, defense against invasion would have been impossible. With their lukewarm support it would have been brief and feeble. But with their sympathy, their service, their sacrifice and their suffering, it was protracted, heroic, glorious, Upon these grounds their claims to monumental commemoration rest. These queens of love, regnant in the realm of home, surrendered all that was most dear to them, in their devotion to their country. The declaration of war was the signal to the women in city, town, and country to seek new fields of effort, industry and economy, in preparation for the impending struggle. They bore increased burdens of labor without a murmur, submitted to the loss of comforts, without repining, and performed duty with a fidelity that would admit no excuse. After providing for the management and support for the family at home, they found time to hasten to the side of sick, wounded and dying loved ones on distant battlefields; to accomplish which, they disregarded military orders, baffled the interference of guards and overcame the protests of conductors. They threaded the aisles of hospitals in ministrations of mercy, relief to the suffering and solace to the dying; and love and grief for both. They consecrated their souls and bodies, a living sacrifice of unselfish service to others with a devotion worthy of Eastern devotees. They suffered want without complaint and concealed their grief in silent tears.

"The maid who binds her warrior's sash,
And smiling, all her pain dissembles,
The while, beneath a drooping lash,
A starry tear-drop hangs and trembles,
Though Heaven alone, records the tear,
And fame may never know her story,
Her heart has shed a drop as dear,
As ever dewed the fields of glory.

The wife who girds her husband's sword
'Mid little ones, who weep and wonder,

Then bravely speaks the cheering word,
  Although her heart be rent asunder,
Doomed, in her nightly dreams to hear
  The bolts of war that round him rattle
Has shed as sacred blood as ere
  Was poured upon the plains of battle.

The mother who conceals her grief
  As to her heart, her son she presses
Then, speaks the few brave words and brief.
  Kissing the patriot brow she blesses;
With no one but her secret God,
  To know the grief that weighs upon her,
Sheds holy blood, as e'er the sod
  Received on freedom's field of honor."

The labors they performed, the privations they endured and the sacrifices they made, were trifles compared to the agony they suffered. This, speech has no power to express, and art, no skill to portray. Family circles broken, loved ones in unmarked graves on battlefields in distant States; and scarred and broken hearts bleeding in desolated homes; it seemed that they had exhausted their resources of labor and love. Not so. They were quick to discover and occupy new fields for the exhibition of their enterprise and affection. When they could no longer aid, still they could honor their dead heroes. This they did in their efforts to build monuments to their memory, of marble, and pay tribute to their graves, in flowers. And, descending from mother to daughter their work still goes on.

Once every year in the sweet spring-time, these pilgrims come to their Mecca with their offering, and dead valor reposes

> "Under the roses the blue,
> Under the lilies the gray."

Pagan and Christian alike, through all the ages have commemorated the virtues, services and achievements of their great men and women in monumental shafts, storied urn and magnificent mausoleums. The pencil, guided by genius; and the chisel, under the same mysterious force, have transmitted their features and forms in breathless beauty on marble and blushing colors on canvas to perpetuate their glory, challenge the admiration and stimulate to imitation the generations to come after them. I appeal this day to the gratitude, the honor and chivalry of Confederate heroes to discharge their only remaining duty; to build a monument to the memory of the glorious Confederate women who aided with their hands, encouraged with their smiles, comforted with their prayers and blessed them with their love. Our mothers, wives, sisters and sweethearts, of Confederate times won the bravest battle that ever was fought.

> The bravest battle that ever was fought,
> Shall I tell you where; and when;
> On the maps of the world, you will find it not
> 'Twas fought by the mother s of men.
>
> Nay, not with cannon nor battle-shot,
> With sword or nobler pen,

Nay not with eloquent word or thought
  From mouths of wonderful men.

But deep in a walled-up woman's heart
  Of woman that would not yield,
But bravely, silently bore her part.
  Lo! There was that battlefield.

No marshalling shout, no bivouac song,
  No banners to gleam and wave.
But oh! these battles they last so long
  From babyhood to the grave.

And faithful still, as a bridge of stars
  She fights in her walled-up-town;
Fight on and on, through the endless years,
  Then silent, unseen, goes down.

Oh ye, with banner and battle-shot
  And soldiers to shout and praise,
I tell you the kingliest battles fought,
  Are fought in these silent ways.

O, spotless woman, in a world of shame,
  With grand and splendid scorn
Go back to God as white as you came
  The kingliest warrior born."

The part taken by the women of the Confederacy in the war between the States is preserved only in fading memories and perishing hearts. These frail witnesses will soon fail to bear their testimony to the greatness of their character and the lesson of their lives. History and literature devote their attention mainly to the management of campaigns, the result of battles and the criticism of commanders. The great battle of the women at home has gone without a historian. The knightly chieftain of the Confederacy has honored himself in dedicating his great book: "The Rise and Fall of the Confederate States of America," to his countrywomen. But the wilderness of material furnished to the poet, the painter and the sculptor has remained unexplored by them. Four decades have elapsed since Appomattox rang down the curtain upon the bloody tragedy; and still the privilege of expressing our gratitude has been neglected and the consciousness of duty discharged lost. Many, perhaps, most of these noble women have crossed the silent river. Many of them who did their duty and blushed at fame, have gone from humble homes to unmarked graves, and rest from their labors but their works follow them. Their daughters trained, by their instruction, and inspired by their example, have taken up the work of sentiment and love which they inaugurated; and thus, their work is perpetuated. It may be well enough to honor maids of honor and sponsors in reunion parades, frolics and balls; but it is a poor tribute to the service, sorrow, sacrifice and sufferings of the heroines "chosen in the furnace of affliction" in the fiery ordeal of war. Can surviving veterans afford to blur their record with ingratitude so great? Are they willing to close the record of their lives without a lasting and permanent expression of admiration and love for the women who shed luster upon all the virtues of their self in the darkest hours of national calamity? Whatever reasons of poverty, misfortune or other things, may have hitherto been urged as an excuse for the neglect of this duty, can no longer be accepted. Prosperity universally abounds all over this Heaven-favored country. Then let the surviving veterans crown their claim to knighthood by erecting on the soil they sanctified with their blood, a monument to the memory of their countrywomen. When this shall have been done, their duty to country and kind will have been performed, and like Simeon, they will be ready to depart in peace. Let them build of the most enduring granite or purest marble; and let it rise to a height proportionate to the virtues it commemorates, which will make it the loftiest on the planet. Place upon its summit her faultless stature, molded in bronze by some Mills or Crawford or chiseled in marble by some modern Praxiteles or Canova. Plant her feet upon the conquered cross; and on her head the victor's crown. Morning's earliest blushes would kiss from her lips the sweetest dews of night, and twilight's last lingering rays would mingle with the charm of her smile until the stars of heaven mustered to stand nightly sentinel, around her beauty and her glory.

CHAPTER XXI.

Reminiscences of Some Famous Preachers.

The religion of a people is a force not to be ignored in the matter of government and civilization. And this is true, whether it is established by law, as in England, or prohibited from such establishment, as in the United States. In the former it is legal, in the latter it is moral force. The utterance, "My kingdom is not of this world," would seem to repudiate the alliance of church and state; and discountenance the union of the kingdom of Christ, with the kingdoms of the world. The ministers of the religion of Christianity are supposed to teach its doctrines correctly, illustrate, in their lives, its virtues truly and to advance its interests wisely. Diversity in the power and degree of gifts obtains, among them, as among other classes and professions. Some have received ten talents and some one. I have enjoyed the privilege of hearing some of the distinguished preachers of my time. Dr. Lovick Pierce said to the writer, that he never heard a poor sermon. I have enjoyed that high privilege, on more occasions than one. Most of these great and good men have passed away. Their biographies have never been written, published and spread. There are a few, the fragrance of whose memory still lingers in tradition only —whose life and work have not been written, why not, is unaccountable, to those familiar with their merits. Among these may be mentioned, William J. Parks, John W. Glenn, Jesse Boring, Samuel Anthony, Jackson P. Turner, Gadwell J. Pearce, and William M. Crumley. These men were all Northeast Georgians. A radius of fifty miles, from a common center, would include the section from which all sprung. They were contemporaries. They were all self-educated; not one of them had been in college. They were all brought up in the country and on the farm. All of them (except Jackson P. Turner, who died in middle life) lived to advanced age, and fell at last with armor on. This constellation planted the Methodist Church in North Georgia more than half a century ago. They differed widely in the personal elements of power. But they were a unit in the possession of power. Parks was a Franklin County farmer of small means and limited education and of unprepossessing personal appearance. He joined the South Carolina Conference in the first quarter of the nineteenth century, and soon became a distinguished leader in the Methodist Church. He owes this distinction to two qualities: integrity and common sense. Plain, practical and sensible, he treated and dealt with all questions in the concrete. At the General Conference at Nashville, the Presiding Bishop, forgetting or pretending to forget his name for the moment, referred to him as the "brother from Georgia, who always says something when he speaks."

John Walker Glenn was a Jackson County farmer. He had been a local preacher for some years when he joined the Georgia Conference. He at once took a high stand in this body of strong men. He was fearless, aggressive, able and eloquent. He was an ardent believer in the dogmas of American Theology and defended them with the skill of a master. At his funeral service at Griffin, at the Annual Conference in 1868, Dr. Lovick Pierce said: "John W. Glenn was the brightest star in the galaxy of the Georgia Conference." These two great men, more than any others—than all others—planted the Methodist Church in North Georgia. As soon as the Indians were removed, Cherokee, Georgia was formed into a Presiding Elders' District over which they were among the first to preside.

Jesse Boring (unlike Parks and Glenn) joined the Conference at Charleston, while Georgia was a part of the South Carolina Conference, when he was quite a young man. He was a native of Jackson County, Georgia, and, no doubt, a sheaf gathered from the sowing of Parks and Glenn. His first charge was a mission (I think Pensacola) distant from his home, 300 miles. Previous to his joining the Conference, Parks—being the pastor at the church of which my parents were members—put up Boring to preach, who, after announcing his text, stood awhile in great confusion, and said, finally, "Unless you all repent and believe, you will be damned." Parks had to come to the rescue and preach without expectation or the usual preparation. They dined that day at my father's house. At the table Parks said to Boring, "Young man, you will never catch me in such a trap again." Whatever criticism may be made of Boring's sermon, it must be admitted that it had the soul of wit, brevity, and that it compressed into very few words a vast amount of Gospel. This same young man lived to win a triumph of power and eloquence that has never been equalled on this continent. When Presiding Elder of the Mobile district, at a country campmeeting not far from the city, on Sunday, at 11 o'clock, he preached on the "Judgment," he captured the multitude at the commencement. As he argued its certainty, its necessity, and its finality, the people in the congregation began to rise to their feet, lean forward, listening in rapt attention with a stillness and awe that reacted upon the speaker and increased the tide of power he poured upon them. In his wonderful strain of overmastering eloquence when he reached the blast of the Judgment Trumpet, that called the quick and the dead from earth and sea, the vast multitude fled in every direction from the stand, as if it had been stricken by lightning and closed the service of that hour. Dr. Boring, though below the average size, was of impressive presence, his complexion dark and cadaverous, his nose Roman, his head massive and finely rounded and balanced. His figure, though thin, was erect. His movements were easy, graceful and dignified; his enunciation clear and distinct; his pronunciation accurately correct; his emphasis perfect. His conversation and public discourse had all the marks of punctuation properly placed. He was a master of logic and rhetoric. His voice, which was thoroughly cultivated, had a peculiar, weird tone, which increased its power. As a preacher in the sense of developing, explaining and enforcing the truth of a text, he was superior to any man I ever heard, and I have heard the most distinguished preachers of the Presbyterian, the Baptist, the Episcopal and the Methodist Churches. Dr. Boring graduated in the Science of Medicine, and held a professorship for some years in a medical college. He was many times a member of the General Conference; was a member in 1844, at New York, when the Church divided on the slavery question. He was a missionary to California in the early fifties. His greatest work was securing the establishment of the orphans' home as an institution of the Methodist Episcopal Church South. This measure he originated and carried through the Conference at Memphis in 1868 against both indifference and opposition. He undertook to raise, by voluntary contribution, the funds for the Georgia home at a time when the people were in great poverty, and harassed with reconstruction troubles. His appeals in behalf of the orphans of dead Confederates—never surpassed in pathos, power and eloquence—bore fruit, in the prosperous orphans' homes in the various Conferences of the Southern Methodist Church, to say nothing of similar homes it incited other great churches to provide. He lived for more than fourscore years and devoted his splendid talents during his life to the service of religion and humanity. And a great church, full of fine writers with an immense publishing house has never put on permanent record, the achievements of his great life and service for the benefit of others, but left them to fade out in traditional memories.

Jackson P. Turner was born in Gwinnett County of poor parentage; joined the Georgia Conference without education, in 1842; served the Dahlonega Circuit as junior preacher and in less than two years became the Presiding Elder of the district, a thorough scholar, and took his place among the ablest preachers in the State. He died a young man. His death eclipsed the hopes of a most useful and splendid career.

William M. Crumley was a native of Habersham County. Like Turner, he was brought up in poverty and without educational advantages. He joined the Conference in early life and devoted himself unreservedly to the Christian ministry. He was in many respects a marvelous man, though never attained distinction in scholarship. His gentleness of spirit, suavity of manner, brilliancy of imagination and refinement of sentiment, added to his knowledge of the Scriptures and his power of simple illustration, gave to his sermons a power and pathos of persuasive eloquence rarely equalled, that was fruitful of trophies for the Cross. No congregation ever became weary under his sermons, and no charge he served, ever desired a change of pastors.

Gadwell J. Pearce was a Gwinnett County man, not distinguished for piety in early life, but for high powers of intellect. He was bright, fearless and aggressive. After his conversion he was licensed to preach, joined the Conference and rose rapidly to usefulness and distinction. He was Presiding Elder, filled various agencies, and represented his Conference in the General Conference. He was of fine personal presence and bearing. As a speaker, he was distinguished for his originality and style, as well as for the force and uniqueness of his illustrations.

Samuel Anthony, another Gwinnett County man, has been justly embalmed in historic fame by the facile pen of Bishop Fitzgerald, in his "Centennial Cameos." An attempt to add to the Bishop's tribute would only mar its beauty and detract from its force.

There were two other men in North Georgia in the forties, for a few years, who left a deep and lasting impression upon the public mind from their power in the pulpit. These were Robert J. Cowart and Russell Reneau. Cowart was a middle Georgian. He joined the Conference when a young man with an inferior education. In 1843, at the age of 29, he was appointed preacher in charge of the Marietta Circuit, with W. H. Evans as Junior, and Peyton P. Smith Presiding Elder. This Circuit embraced the counties of Cobb, Cherokee, Milton and the Southern portion of Forsyth. This was before the Church changed its policy and abolished week-day preaching. There were twenty-five or thirty churches in the charge and preaching at each church once in every two weeks, so that each preacher made the round of his Circuit once a month. It so happened that Cowart's appointment was at a near-by church on the day of the plantation fire referred to in a former chapter. After preaching a magnificent sermon, he came in the afternoon to the aid of the writer in fighting fire. A few years after, we were associated in the defense of Musgrove, a Baptist preacher, charged with stealing a negro, in Forsyth superior court. (It is due to the memory of Musgrove and to the

Baptist Church, to say he was acquitted.) Physically, intellectually and socially, he was a magnificent specimen of manhood; six feet and two inches in height, with an avoirdupois of two hundred and twenty, and intellectual endowments in harmonious proportion. Approaching middle life, full of vigor, with constant reading and speaking every day, his great gifts developed rapidly into a masterful control of the thoughts, passions and emotions of his auditors. His mind was rapid in its operations; his perception quick; his vocabulary aesthetic and extensive; his emotions sympathetic, and his power of description unrivalled. He was a powerful, eloquent and charming preacher. The Conference appointed him for the following year, to Jacksonville, Fla. He declined to go; located and read law under direction of the late Gov. Joseph E. Brown. He was admitted to the bar and soon after was appointed by Governor Johnson, attorney for the Western and Atlantic Railway. He was afterward judge of the City Court of Atlanta. Most of his friends thought he made a mistake in leaving the Conference and retiring from the active ministry.

Russell Reneau came from the Holstein to the Georgia Conference, and was appointed Presiding Elder of the Cherokee District in 1845. This district included nearly all of North Georgia. He had been early in life a school teacher, preacher and Presiding Elder in the Holstein Conference. He was, in person, below medium height, inclined to obesity in middle life, and in the full maturity of his intellectual power. He was a writer of power and author of an unpublished

English Grammar. He was a thoroughly trained debater; a fine English scholar and deeply read in polemic theology. He had been brought up in the pure atmosphere and surrounded by the magnificent scenery of East Tennessee, at the time and in the section so stirred by the theological controversies between Brownlow, Posey and Ross. He published a very able book on the much-discussed and hackneyed subject of baptism. He kept his glove in the arena, on all the dogmas in dispute, between the Armenians and Calvinists. When he came to the Cherokee District the county was new; had been settled but a few years, and settled mainly by members of the Baptist and Methodist, whose adherents were approximately equal in numbers. There was less intelligence and liberality in sentimen then than now. Each party was anxious to recruit its ranks; and the pulpit dealt largely in polemics. Sometimes the more ardent champions of the respective creeds would meet in debate, with the result always that each side claimed the victory. These conditions were precisely such as put him upon his metal and at his best, in the display of his Napoleonic power, in theological debate. His discussion was absolutely free from sectarian malignity. His mother was a Baptist, and often in the midst of an overwhelming argument against Calvinism, he would allude to it, and pay her piety and love a tribute of affection that would melt his congregation to tears. With him it was a conscientious duty to discuss, explain and defend the doctrines of polity of his church. His reason for indulging so largely in controversy was the necessity of instructing his people in the doctrines of Christianity and impressing them with the importance of seeking for the truth. It must not be inferred that his pulpit efforts always dealt with or in theological polemics. He was a masterful preacher of the Gospel. He had, in a more eminent degree than any man I ever heard, the power of compressing a whole discourse into a single expression or sentence. In this power he resembled and transcended Napoleon. His speech was in short, clear, strong, sententious sentences —never of dubious meaning; his voice of great volume, finely trained and controlled, was occasionally startling as a bugle blast. It was my fortune to hear the last sermon (I think) he preached in Georgia. It was at 11 o'clock on Sunday, at a campmeeting on the ground now occupied by the town of Alpharetta, Milton County, in the early fifties. His text was Psalm XXIII. It was his last appearance before a large concourse of his personal friends and admirers, as the year was fading into autumn, and death. The environments stirred the emotions of speaker and audience. His lips had been touched with a live coal from off the altar. His sermon was an orderly, lucid exposition of the Psalm. Towards the conclusion in a voice clear as crystal, and tremulous with emotion, with great tears dripping from his cheeks, he drew a contrast between the value of matter and spirit, the perishable and immortal, in a tide of eloquence that was perhaps never equalled, certainly never surpassed. Soon after this he went to the West. I heard that he died after preaching for six hours consecutively, at Fort Smith, Arkansas.

The lives of none of these great men, so far as I am advised, have ever been written and published. It is singular that they have not been. Two other great Georgia preachers have fared better at the hands of their contemporaries. The great lives and labors of Dr. Lovick Pierce and Bishop George F. Pierce have been preserved in biography—as was most meet—and transmitted in permanent form, to all future time.

Lumpkin camp-ground, located in Dawson County, on the road connecting Cumming and Dahlonega and nearly equi-distant between them, and easily accessible from Gainesville and Dawsonville, has been for more than fifty years perhaps, the largest and most popular camp-ground in the State. The people from the four towns named, and from the surrounding densely settled sections, annually tented in great numbers. The multitudes attending, especially on Sunday, would number four or five thousand. In 1867 or 1868, Bishop Pierce attended the meeting and preached on Sunday, to a vast concourse. His text was a verse from the 6th chapter of John. His theme was: "Christ the Bread of Life." He was at his best, in vigorous health and in the perfect maturity and strength of his marvelous powers. The surroundings were inspiring, the crowd from town and country immense. In the open air, with weather conditions delightful, the inspiration of the Holy Sabbath was upon the thoughts and hearts of the people. I occupied a seat between Ex.-Gov. Joseph E. Brown and Maj. Raymond Sanford—both ardent Baptists— in an eligible position for seeing and hearing the preacher. For one hour and a half he held the enthralled attention of thousands in a quietness as still as death, during such a sermon as he only could preach. When he concluded, Governor Brown turned to me with great tears rolling down his cheeks, and said, "that is the grandest man on this continent." Major Sanford concurred with him. To those who never heard the Bishop under similar circumstances, I can convey no adequate description; to those who have, it is unnecessary to try.

The contribution made to progress, civilization and Christianity by these men, and those of their class elsewhere, can never be measured, and will never be appreciated. The boys, college-called to the ministry in these days, may part their hair in the middle more artistically, perform gymnastic gyrations more gracefully, pitch, kick and catch balls more skillfully and talk more learnedly of teams, innings, and umpires than these great men; but it is gravely doubted whether they approach more closely the Throne of Mercy above or the hearts of the people below.

CHAPTER XXII.

Russo-Japanese War—President Roosevelt—Peace.

In 1904 Russia and Japan engaged in war. It continued for eighteen months. Russia put into her army and navy 840,000 men of which she lost 375,000—at a cost in money and property of $1,075,000,000. This includes sixty-eight ships of war. The army and navy of Japan mustered 700,000 men, of which number 250,000 were lost, with a loss in money and property, including twenty-four warships, of $475,000,000. The total number engaged was 1,540,000 men. The total cost was $1,550,000,000. This was a prodigal expenditure of men and means for an eighteen months' war. This vast sum does not include the incidental losses of the belligerents. Both parties distinctly announced that they did not desire the advice or interference of other powers; that they would settle the controversy in their own way and to suit themselves. Early in the summer of 1905, nearly a million of men in Manchuria confronted each other, in strongly fortified lines, from the hills of which frowned heavy guns numbered by the thousands. Battalions, brigades and divisions were manœuvering for advantage in position, under the eye of able and skillful leaders, preparatory for a decisive battle. The powers, the press and the people of Christendom were watching and listening with anxious solicitude, for news of the impending shock. In the fearful stillness, presaging the storm, one great man has the courage, the capacity, the patriotism and the humanity to step to the front with the olive branch of peace—Theodore Roosevelt, President of the United States—ten thousand miles from the scene of strife, addresses a similar note to each of the belligerents, suggesting to them an effort to secure peace by negotiation. He addressed a note at the same time to the great powers of Europe, informing them of what he had done, his desire for peace and invoking their co-operation with him in his effort to secure it. The belligerents, after manifesting diplomatic indifference (but both extremely anxious to get out of their trouble) finally agreed to advance far enough to make an effort to ascertain upon what terms it would be proposed and consented to appoint commissioners for that purpose. Some difficulty arose as to the place of the meeting. Each party objected to the nominations of the other. Washington City, United States, was finally selected as the place for the meeting. To promote the comfort and quiet of the plenipotentiaries, the President arranged for the meeting at Portsmouth, N. H., he spending the summer in his cottage at Sagamore Hill, in easy communication with the plenipotentiaries. M. DeWitte, on the part of Russia, and Baron Komura, with their respective suites and proper credentials, promptly met and earnestly entered upon the business in hand. They were each in daily communication with their respective governments, and in frequent separate correspondence with President Roosevelt, who was in constant communication through his embassadors, with the Emperors of Russia and Japan. All the effort made, and the labor bestowed, and the anxiety by the President in untangling knots, suggesting concessions and harmonizing conflicts, will perhaps remain unknown to all but himself. At last, on the 5th day of September, 1905, the treaty was signed and the civilized world drew one long, free, full breath of relief.

That President Roosevelt alone achieved this victory of peace will never be questioned. Emperors, Kings, Presidents, statesmen, diplomats and publicists throughout the world have honored and congratulated him for it, and the great heart of the great common people responded,

"Blessed are the peacemakers."

After the complete destruction of the Russian navy in the battle of the Straits, while each party had a powerful army in hostile array, each claiming the certainty of triumph, but trembling with the apprehension of defeat, the quick intuitive perception of President Roosevelt and the promptness in action for which he is so distinguished, discovered the opportune and critical moment for his interposition and the suggestion of negotiation for peace. It was a bold and tactful display of statesmanship that closed at once the bloodiest and most destructive war of modern times, save one, and placed the United States government, of which he was the head, in the van of the great powers of the world in power and influence in the control of international affairs. It made him the first man of the age, and glorified his country in the annals of humanity.

CHAPTER XXIII.

Legislatures of 1898 and 1900. In the House and in the Senate.

Legislation is a high function. It is the exercise of the supreme power of the State. Its dignity, gravity and importance are not always properly estimated. To a capable, conscientious legislator, it involves the drudgery of labor, constancy and clearness of thought, and honesty and integrity of purpose. Those men who regard it a frolic in which they may have a good time are wholly unworthy of the high trust. Contrary to expectations and he, may add, to his desire, the writer found himself a member of the House of Representatives in 1898 and 1899; and of the Senate in 1900 and 1901. John D. Little of Muscogee County was elected speaker and John T. Boifeuillet of Bibb, clerk of the House in 1898. These gentlemen possessed high qualifications for the offices to which they were chosen. There was a large number of the members above the average in ability; many of them of superior practical wisdom in statesmanship. I am restrained from expressing my opinion of them by name for two reasons. First, it might be misconstrued into disparagement of other worthy men. Second, since the example of Adam, Iscariot and Arnold, I believe in the possibility of falling from grace, and that it is better to crown the victor when he reaches the goal at the end of the race. Let it suffice to say, that association with these able and partiotic gentlemen resulted in forming warm personal friendships, the tender memory of which will end only with life. The routine of tax and appropriation bills engaged, mainly, the attention of this Legislature. There was no great question of overshadowing magnitude, enlisting popular attention before it. The nearest approach to it was the Willingham prohibition bill. This bill was thoroughly and ably debated. In the discussion, licensed saloons, blind tigers, local option, dispensaries, etc., came in for a large share of consideration. The bill passed in the House but was defeated in the Senate. Some questions of importance in the direction of reforms were raised and considered; but few measures of much public interest were finally enacted into law. An interesting episode in the history of this legislature was the visit of President McKinley to the capital of Georgia. He was accompanied by Generals Chaffee, Lawton, Wheeler, Lieutenant Hobson and others. He was formally received by the General Assembly in the representative hall. It was in his speech on this occasion that he captured the South, by saying that the "time had come for the government to take charge of the preservation of Confederate soldiers' graves." He held a public reception in the rotunda of the Capitol and made a most favorable impression upon the vast throngs that saw and heard him; and who little dreamed of the deplorable fate that awaited him at Buffalo.

In 1900 I was returned as the senator from the Thirty-ninth district, of which I was the first senator after its organization forty years previous. Of this Senate Clark Howell was chosen president, and Charles Northen, both of Fulton, secretary; and both without opposition. These gentlemen were popular, able and efficient officers. I was chairman of the committee on constitutional amendments and chairman of a special joint-committee of both Houses, appointed to consider and report on constitutional amendments generally. A bill was pending providing for calling a constitutional convention. This joint-committee was raised to secure such amendments as were deemed desirable, and thus avoid the expense of a convention. After much consideration and labor the committee reported a bill providing for ten vital amendments, which, if adopted, would have made the government of Georgia the best State government in the Union. Eight of them were adopted by the Senate. The bill failed in the House. All great reforms in peaceful times come slowly. The bane of legislation is that there is too much immature and local legislation. It has always seemed to me that this should be suggested by wisdom and necessity resulting from the experience of society. Our constitution undertakes to secure uniformity in general legislation. It is the vast amount of local legislation and the looseness and inaccuracy in the language in which bills are written, as well as frequent change by amendment, with different judicial constructions, that creates confusion and uncertainty in our law. This legislature re-elected Augustus O. Bacon to the United States Senate. And it was during its session that Admiral Winfield S. Schley visited the Capital. He was received by the Legislature in joint session in the Representative Hall. Fresh from the victory of Santiago and the idol of the popular heart the public affection for him was augmented by the effort of the Republican party to pluck his laurels for the brow of Admiral Sampson. He made an admirable speech, saying among other things "that there was glory enough in Santiago for all; and that men who stood behind the guns and in front of furnaces were entitled to their full share." That gallant Georgian, Lieutenant Thomas Brumby, who stood by Dewey's side on the bridge of the Olympia in the battle of Manila, was of Schley's party. A short time thereafter his remains were brought to Atlanta; and Georgia gave to Brumby a magnificent State funeral. "The paths of glory lead but to the grave."

In compliance with the joint resolutions of the two Houses, I delivered the address on the Secession Convention of Georgia, which appears in this volume. With this Legislature closed my very humble public service.

CHAPTER XXIV.

LIFE, SERVICE AND CHARACTER OF JAMES EDWARD OGLETHORPE, THE FOUNDER OF GEORGIA.

True greatness consists in the unselfish service of others. Tried by this test, James Edward Oglethorpe was truly a great man. He was born in 1696, and matriculated at Corpus Christi College, Oxford, in 1714, at the age of 18. The same year upon the recommendation of Marlborough, he was appointed aide de camp to Prince Eugene of Savoy, under whom he greatly distinguished himself for military skill and personal courage in the siege of Belgrade in the war with the Turks. His training under such captains as Marlborough and Eugene, made him an accomplished military officer at the age of twenty-one years. In 1722, at the age of twenty-six, he was elected a member of Parliament. He was one of the very few young men who enter public life with the sole purpose of rendering public service instead of promoting personal ambitions.

Of high family connections, a large endowment of intellectual powers, and inheriting from a deceased brother an ample fortune, the blandishments, splendors, and allurements of court-life on the one hand, and labor, anxiety, sacrifice and suffering for the unfortunate of his race, on the other, were before him. He chose the latter like another Moses. Impressed with the inhumanity of the British laws, which inflicted hopeless imprisonment upon helpless insolvents, and the brutal oppression of British jailors, he determined, if possible, to secure the reformation of the former and the punishment of the latter. He was appointed chairman of a committee raised by the House of Commons, to visit the prisons, to examine into the condition of the inmates and suggest means of reform. This committee in three separate reports, disclosed a condition of injustice, oppression and suffering that aroused the public indignation for the outrage against humanity and civilization. Honest, unfortunate men, who had failed in business of various kinds, possessing tender sensibilities, refined sentiments and high character, were crowded into filthy and loathsome dungeons with criminals of the lowest and vilest type, surrounded with stench and vermin to languish out a miserable existence of horrible cruelty and suffering. The English law then made no provision for the relief of insolvents from perpetual imprisonment. To Oglethorpe belongs the credit of its reformation. He conceived the scheme of compromising the debts, securing to the creditors such amounts as the friends of the debtors could be induced to raise; and the release of the debtors from prison on the condition that they would emigrate to America and plant a colony. After much effort and anxiety on the part of Oglethorpe, this wise plan was adopted. On the 9th day of June, 1732, King George II., granted to certain trustees, of whom Oglethorpe was one, a charter to the tract of land situated between the Savannah and Altamaha rivers. The proprietary of South Carolina having surrendered all claim to it, for the reason that the new colony would be a protection to South Carolina against incursions from hostile Indians, this place was selected for the colony. To promote this enterprise Parliament donated £10,000, and institutions and individuals contributed liberally. The emigrants spent their last Sabbath in England at Milton, on the Thames. They attended divine service in a body. On the 17th day of November, 1732, the galley Anne, of 200-tons burden, commanded by Captain Thomas Oglethorpe with about one hunlred and thirty persons, sailed to seek a home in the wilderness. This frail craft bore across the waves the fortunes of empire. The youngest son of Richard Cannon, aged eight months, and the youngest son of Robert Clark, died on the passage and found a grave at the bottom of the sea. The pathos of their burial at sea is too deep and intense for expression. On the 13th of January, 1733, the Anne dropped her anchor outside the bar at Charleston harbor. On their arrival, the first thing they did was to assemble the immigrants and engage in devout thanksgiving to Almighty God for their preservation and protection in the passage. They were most hospitably received at Charleston. After spending a few restful days they sailed, touching at Port Royal for Yamma-craw bluff on the Savannah River, which Oglethorpe, assisted by Col. William Bull, had previously marked out for their future home, where they landed early in February, 1733 and laid the foundation of the beautiful city of Savannah, and the great State of Georgia. Here, under a charter securing to them the rights of

British subjects, in a wilderness filled with savage Indians and wild beasts, these noble and heroic spirits recommenced the battle of life which they had fought and lost in the old world. In their early struggles they seem to have been marvelously protected against the triple bane of colonies—famine, pestilence and massacre. For this exemption they were doubtless indebted to the gracious providence of God and the wise leadership of Oglethorpe. Oglethorpe's policy of justice and fair dealing conciliated the confidence anl secured the friendship of the Indians. Caution, exercise and temperance preserved the health; and a genial climate, fertile soil and active industry supplied the wants of the colonists. No colonists were ever animated by a loftier purpose or followed a wiser leader. The device, "Non sibi sed alliis," indicates the object of this enterprise and the character and purpose of Oglethorpe. The duties of his position were grave, complex, numerous, onerous and responsible. An accurate account of his transactions was to be made to the trustees. The improvements of the settlement were to be conducted under his supervision. Disagreements and disputes among the colonists were to be adjusted by him; complaints of the Indians for inflicted wrongs by the whites were to be heard and the wrongs redressed; the health and morals of the people to be conserved; the boundary between the grant in the charter and Florida to be clearly ascertained; the movements of the ever malignant, treacherous and avaricious Spaniards to be constantly watched. All these duties were discharged by him with an ability and fidelity that illustrates his character and establishes his claim to a high place in the list of unselfish philanthropists. These duties were performed at the right time and in the best way, with the utmost order and system. In his first letter to the trustees, after reaching his destination, among other things he said, "I am so taken up in looking after a hundred necessary things that I write now, short, but shall give you a more particular account hereafter." A gentleman from South Carolina visiting him, writes as follows: "Mr. Oglethorpe is indefatigable; takes a vast deal of pains; his fare is indifferent—having little else at present, but the simplest provisions. He is extremely well beloved by all his people. The general title they give him is "Father.' If any of them are sick he immediately visits them and takes a great deal of care of them. If any difference arises he is the person that decides it. Thus this great man, with the "attention and affection of a patriarch, watches over and takes care of his people." Oglethorpe soon concluded articles of friendship and commerce with the Indians. His policy in dealing with the Indians is characterized by wisdom, humanity and statesmanship. The venerable and able Mico Tomo Chi Chi, wise in council, courageous in action and faithful in friendship, co-operated heartily and efficiently with him in his policy of justice and friendship in their dealings and relations. These relations being satisfactorily settled, he next addresses himself to the extension and protection of the settlement. He planted different settlements at eligible places and constructed fortifications to secure their safety. The population was increased by the accession of small numbers of

Hebrews, Italians and Germans at different times. At the end of fifteen months, this great enterprise was successfully inaugurated. Oglethorpe returned to England, taking with him Tomo Chi Chi, the Mico, his wife, son and a few chiefs. The colonists were greatly affected at his departure, following him to the ship on which he sailed, weeping. In the language of Mr. Von Reck, "They could not restrain their tears when they saw him go, who was their benefactor and their father; who had carefully watched over them as a good shepherd does over his flock; and who had so tender a care of them, both by day and by night." The Indians were presented at court and received by the King on his throne. They were feted, flattered and wondered at to their delight and amazement during their stay in England. Oglethorpe resumed temporarily his seat in Parliament. He availed himself of the interest which the presence of the Indians crèated in the public mind to solicit contributions of books, for the religious and literary instruction of both the colonists and the Indians. The importation of African slaves and arms into the colony was prohibited.

On the 10th of December, 1735, he sailed from England with two ships, the "Symond" and the "London Merchant" of 200-tons burden each, convoyed by H. M. sloop of war "Hawk," with two hundred and two persons on board. Elaborate preparation had been made for Oglethorpe's passage on the "Hawk" but he chose to deny himself these comforts and take a cabin on the "Symond," where he could be in personal association with the emigrants. These ships bore to the colonies supplies of provisions, agricultural implements, arms, ammunition, etc. Among the passengers were John Wesley, as missionary, and Charles Wesley, his brother, as secretary of the Indian affairs for the colony of Georgia. While they each practically failed in Georgia they both became famous, John, as the founder of a great Protestant church and Charles as the peerless, sacred poet of history. The theology of the one and the songs of the other, have thrilled and solaced the heart of humanity around the planet.

Oglethorpe placed Causton in charge of affairs in the colony. His management was unwise and injudicious, resulting in discontent among the people and financial embarrassment to the colony. Upon his return he brought over something more than two hundred immigrants for whose settlement he immediately provided. He settled Augusta about this time. He also discovered the true line between Georgia and Florida and secured the adoption of a treaty or arrangement by which the dispute with the Spanish was harmonized and adjusted which, however, was rudely repudiated by the Spanish authorities. He was alert in strengthening the defenses of the coast to meet the impending invasion. The distance from England, the delay and difficulty in obtaining assistance and his inadequacy of men and munitions of war placed him and the fortunes of the colony in the utmost peril. But they developed in him the highest qualities of the true soldier and statesman. His defense of St. Simons, against a vastly superior force was characterized by the rarest courage and military skill and strategy, of which a fitting memorial is the name of the "Bloody Marsh." The retreating Spaniards were followed subsequently by Oglethorpe to St. Augustine and the failure to capture this stronghold resulted only from the weakness of Oglethorpe's force.

Causton had been deposed and the mischief his conduct had inflicted upon the colonists in the main repaired. The negro insurrection in South Carolina suppressed and the Spanish invasion repelled, Oglethorpe now provided for the future security of the colony by thoroughly repairing the fortifications upon which its protection depended. This accomplished, the colonists with a career of prosperity opening up before them, after ten years of arduous toil, deep anxiety and self-sacrifice, he left Georgia for England, July 23, 1743. It would seem that this pioneer knight of humanity, after having done, suffered, sacrificed and accomplished so much for the service and happiness of others, would escape the wrongs of misrepresentation, calumny and persecution. Yet such was not the case. Ambition, avarice, malignity and meanness have characterized every age of this world's history. These contemptible vices put in their appearance among the colonists. A mutinous soldier attempted to assassinate Oglethorpe. Others with higher pretensions but equally base spirit, by vile slander, would paralyze his influence and blast his fame. One, Col. Cooke was conspicuous for his assaults upon the character and conduct of his general. A British court-martial branded the charges as false; and dismissed him from the service with infamy. The contrast of these low vices with his illustrious virtues only added brilliancy to their splendor. In the brief period of a decade this loyal subject of the crown and faithful servant of the trustees—equally a master in the conception of the grandest schemes and the execution of the smallest details, perfectly familiar with the caprices of human nature, and largely endowed with the power to control men, disregarding difficulties and overcoming obstacles, pursued his purpose with a step as steady as time, planted a colony in the wilderness, conciliated the friendship of the Indians, humbled the pride of the Spanish and thus laid upon the granite foundations of justice, truth and virtue, the corner-stone of the great Empire State of Georgia, which stands and will forever stand—the imperishable memorial of his greatness. Upon his return to England he submitted his report to the trustees and received their sincere thanks for the ability, fidelity and success with which he had discharged the trust.

The king appoved his conduct, recognized his ability and the value of his services, and promoted him to the rank of Lieutenant-General, Major-General and finally, General of the British Army. Artists, scholars, poets, orators, statesmen and philosophers sought his society and friendship. He retained his seat in Parliament until 1754, and was recognized as the Governor of the Colony of Georgia until the surrender of the charter of the trustees to the crown in 1752. He lived to witness the dismemberment of the empire he had done, suffered and spent so much to extend and glorify. He held an interview with Mr. John Adams, the first plenipotentiary from the young republic to the court of St. James. He lived to the advanced age of ninety-seven years, nearly one-third of a century longer than the allotted span. He died with the serene tranquility of a philosopher in the sublime faith of a Christian.

The analysis of Oglethorpe's life and character develops a rare and bright constellation of high qualities and shining virtues. If he had ambition it was not that reprehensible sort which seeks power, wealth and fame for self-aggrandizement, but rather that laudable kind which seeks to be remembered for the good done for others. A wise, practical legislator and statesman, he knew how to discover and apply remedies for existing evils. A brave and skillful commander, he knew when and where to protect the weak. Recognizing his duty to his God and his race, his heart trembled with sympathy to the appeals of sorrow and his strong hand was outstretched for the relief of suffering. He exchanged ease, comfort, pleasure and security for toil, anxiety, hardship and danger. He devoted time, talents and fortune upon the altar of philanthrophy to minister to the help of others; and stands the foremost Englishman of his age; and next to Washington, the finest character in history. Marlborough and Blenheim, Wellington and Waterloo, Nelson and Trafalgar, pale and fade in comparison with Oglethorpe and Georgia. If it be true, as an American poetess has sweetly sung

> "That parted friends of whom we say
> 'In beds of clay they rest,'
> Bend meekly down from glory's sphere
> And, with an angel's smile or tear
> Allure us to the blest;"

then the spirit of Oglethorpe must woo, with solicitude the prosperous, happy millions of Georgians, to the practice of virtues, his own life so gloriously illustrated.

CHAPTER XXV.

The Religion of Christianity.

The soul of man has thirsted and panted in all climes through all the ages for the solution of the mysterious problems of life and death. Divine revelation as contained in the sacred Scriptures alone furnishes it. The religious element or instinct of the race has found expression in vague theories and speculations and the establishment of monstrous and revolting systems of idolatry to propitiate the unknown and unknowable cause or author of being, of its origin and destiny.

The book of nature, open to all the world, has suggested to reason and philosophy the invisible things of Him from the foundation of the world, which are clearly seen, being understood by the things that are made even His eternal power and God-head." But reason and philosophy could never find out the institution and administration of a moral government involving law, prescribing death as the punishment of its violation, nor the stupendous scheme of merciful salvation, which infinite Goodness ordained for the pardon of sin and rescue from death. Divine revelation alone reveals this truth; hence its necessity and value. It opens with a brief historic summary of the Creation, communicated by God, through inspiration to Moses.

It shows that the first pair were created male and female, free from sin, endowed with volition, put in a pleasant place, assigned to agreeable employment and subjected to law. This was the law of faith and obedience, the cardinal and constitutional law of the Divine administration, unchanged and unchangeable. They disbelieved, disobeyed, and thus brought death into the world with all our woe;" and thus raised the great problem with which the religion of Christianity deals,—the maintenance of the integrity of an unchangeable law that condemns to death and yet saves the criminal under its condemnation. After the disaster of the fall, the law of faith and obedience was presented in another form—in the form of promise. "The seed of the woman shall bruise the serpent's head." This promise was vague but Abel caught its import of atonement and pardon and evidenced his faith by his offering of the symbol in sacrifice of the lamb slain from before the foundation of the world. The revelation of God, of Himself and His government was slow, gradual and progressive with salient points and crises which served as keynotes in the music of the march. Such were the translation of Enoch, the call of Abraham, and the giving of the law to Moses. Enoch walked with God; by which is meant he believed and obeyed Him. He was translated as the sign and proof to the patriarchial age of the final resurrection. Abraham was chosen the head and founder of the family through which the promise was to be fulfilled, and deliverance was to come. His selection was made after subjecting his faith and obedience to the severest test that Infinite wisdom and goodness could devise. The Decalogue, written by God on tablets of stone, was delivered to Moses as the basic rules and principles for all time, by which the race should regulate its conduct and relations with the Creator and each other. It vindicates the majesty of the sovereign and provides for the protection of every right and interest of the subject. The worship of the Tabernacle with its symbolic ritualism was the shadow of good things to come. "Our schoolmaster to bring us to Christ." Obedience to the ceremonial law was the test of faith in the promise. It was in a sense spectacular, appealing to the thought through the senses. The prophetic succeeded the patriarchal age. The promise had been repeated with increasing clearness and emphasis. The Temple superseded the Tabernacle.

Elijah's fiery flight had illustrated to the prophetic age the glorious truth of the final resurrection. Job knew that his Redeemer liveth, and that after his skin, worms destroyed his body, yet in his flesh he should see God. Daniel saw a kingdom set up which shall never be destroyed. Isaiah, whose lips were touched with a live coal from off the altar from the loftiest summit of prophetic vision, witnessed the final sacrificial scene, which he described with historical accuracy and announced the truth before the event that "with His stripes we are healed."

Zachariah saw in the twilight of the dispensation of law a prophecy, "a fountain flowing out from the House of David, and from Jerusalem, half of it towards the former sea and half of it towards the hinder sea; and in winter and summer shall it be." The multitudes of the former sea slaked their thirst for immortality by faith in the promise, those of the hinder sea by faith in its fulfillment. In the fullness of time there was a rumor at Jerusalem that a new king of the Jews was born.

A strange star had appeared and guided wise men to Bethlehem to offer him their fealty and worship. The shepherd told a strange story of a new song "Glory to God in the Highest; Peace on Earth—Good Will to Men." Herod became alarmed for his throne and massacred the children of Bethlehem in the hope of destroying the new king. But his parents, being warned in a dream of danger, fled with the young child into Egypt where they remained until Herod's death.

These events seem to have passed out of the public thought, except the memory of Herod's cruelty and of the grief of the sorrow-stricken mothers of Bethlehem. Thirty years thereafter a bold, fearless and earnest ascetic emerged from the wilderness and startled the country by boldly proclaiming that "the Kingdom of Heaven was at hand" and preaching the doctrine of "baptism and repentance for the remission of sins," as the necessary preparation for the reception of the King. The seed of the woman appeared on the banks of the Jordan, whom when John saw, he exclaimed to the multitude "Behold the Lamb of God that taketh away the sin of the world!" Startling announcement!

Annealed by the baptism of water and the Spirit for His mission, which was "to seek and to save that which was lost," He selected His Disciples and entered upon His offices—of prophet to teach, priest to atone, and king, to rule. His advent was in the fullness of time. The highest tides of Grecian, Roman and Hebrew intellect and learning met at the Jewish Capital. The nations were at peace. Judaism, power and paganism were at their best to examine the pretentions and contest the claims of the Carpenter of Nazareth to the Messiahship. "And seeing the multitudes, He went up into a mountain, and when He was set, His disciples came unto Him. And he opened his mouth and taught them, saying "what?"—stating the necessary conditions of spirit in the process of transition from condemnation to pardon, from pollution to purity, from death to life, viz:

Humility, repentance, submission, sincerity, forgiveness, purity. These eternal truths he utters in the sweet persuasive form of blessings. "Blessed are the poor in spirit, for theirs is the Kingdom of Heaven." "Blessed are they that mourn, for they shall be comforted." "Blessed are the meek for they shall inherit the earth." "Blessed are they who hunger and thirst after righteousness for they shall be filled." "Blessed are the merciful, for they shall obtain mercy." "Blessed are the pure in heart, for they shall see God." "Blessed are the peacemakers, for they shall be called the children of God." This is the culmination, purity of heart and peace with God. The Master in this discourse is dealing with the questions of life and death in a kingdom of law and love. He asserts the supremacy and duration of the Decalogue; and proceeds to interpret it according to its true spirit and meaning, and to explode its perversion by false teachers. He proceeds with His instruction in the application of the provisions of law, and principles of love in the conduct of life, in terms so simple, with illustrations so clear, that the weakest mind could not misunderstand; and with wisdom so profound that the shrewdest malignant could not assail until He reached the climax: "Be ye therefore perfect, even as your Father which is in heaven is perfect." After this, He returned to the line of instruction, asserting the true and assailing the false in motive and method. He emphasized the importance of sincerity and rebuked the shame of hypocrisy in professed worship. He guards all the coming generations against the ignorance, weakness, selfishness and hypocrisy in prayer by instructing how, and for what to pray. "After this manner therefore, pray ye: 'Our Father which art in heaven, hallowed be Thy name.'" Not your Father nor mine, but Our Father in the plural, so that each one prays for himself and all others—thus recognizing the relationship of family—father and children with all the tender sentiments of affection which the relationship implies and in precise conformity to the law.

"Thou shalt not take the name of the Lord thy God in vain." Hallowed, honored, revered and glorified be Thy name. Thy kingdom of truth, love and law—to all hearts the expression of hungering and thirsting after righteousness. "Thy will be done on earth as it is in heaven." The unconditional surrender, submission and obedience of the human to the divine will "Give us this day our daily bread." Christ is the bread of life, of which if a man eat, he shall never die. This invocation calls for the spiritual life of Christ as the daily banquet of the hungry soul, and also the material which nourishes the physical body. "Forgive us our debts, as we forgive our debtors." This recognizes the absolute equality of rights and obligations; and that no one can claim forgiveness who refuses to concede it.

"And lead us not into temptation, but deliver us from evil." This has been called the wisest utterance that ever fell from lips—human or divine. It seeks certain safety by avoiding all risks. The Teacher knew that temptation had wrecked the race. He had felt and struggled with its power. He knew the weakness of men. He knew whence deliverance comes; and graciously ordains this invocation as the means of securing safety. The spirit that utters this prayer truly will not fail to realize that God's is "the kingdom, the power and the glory forever." Following this prayer, are lessons of truth simply stated and beautifully illustrated, dealing with the providence of God and the hearts and life of men, in their relations to Him, and to each other—uniting the authority of the law, the prophets and the gospel in support of the infinite wisdom and absolute perfection of the rule, "In all things whatsoever ye would that men should do to you, do ye even so to them."

The people were astonished at His doctrine, for "He taught them as one having authority and was not as the Scribes." What blessing and a joy it would have been to Socrates, Seneca and Plato to have heard this most wonderful discourse!

Truth is unchangeable. The great Teacher never modified these truths, but as occasion required, elaborated, emphasized and intensified them, in simile, parable and story, and exemplified them in his life. The Epistles continue their explanation and seek to secure their adoption in faith and practice. All available resources were exhausted to suppress them, and discredit the Teacher. As these efforts increased in magnitude and malignity, He assumed a bolder attitude; and interposed higher claims for their authorship and authority; and overwhelmed his assailants with dismay, chagrin and discomfiture. The common people heard Him gladly. The scribes and elders rejected Him. But a Greek woman and a Roman captain believed, and were blessed by Him. The scepter was departing from Judah, in the presence of the Lion of his Tribe.

For about three years the Messiah toiled and traveled over Palestine and preached the gospel of the Kingdom of Heaven on mountain and in plain, in cities and solitudes and on land and lake. He hungered and thirsted and was without home and shelter. Great multitudes followed Him always and everywhere and pressed upon and crowded around to hear Him. For "He spake as never man spake." He healed the sick, restored the blind, cured the lame, cleansed the lepers, cast out devils, gave speech to the dumb, fed the hungry, stilled the storm, and calmed the sea, raised the dead, pardoned penitents and preached the gospel to the poor. While thus engaged malignity having met him at the cradle with an edict for His death—

pursued Him without intermission, until it secured it on the cross. As He approached the end, He announced to His disciples plainly that His enemies would kill him, and that He should arise the third day. A few days thereafter, taking Peter, James and John with him into a mountain He was transfigured before them. Moses, representative of law and Elijah, of prophecy, appeared and talked with him of his approaching decease at Jerusalem, and witnessed the glorious light of the gospel, the gospel of salvation as symbolized in the transfigured face of its author. Moses received the tablets of the law in the terrors of cloud, thunder and lightning on Mount Sinai. Elijah overthrew the prophets of Baal with consuming fire from heaven upon Mount Carmel. But on the radiant brow of Mount Tabor, in the calm sweetness of light and love, the light of the world in His transfiguration, indicated the fulfillment of promise, prophecy and ceremonial law as well as His glorification after His resurrection, receiving from His Father, from the bright cloud which overshadowed Him, the message to all the world, for all time, "This is my beloved son in whom I am well pleased, hear Him." The end was approaching. The last authoritative celebration of the Passover was held, at the conclusion of which a new memorial was instituted; the banquet of faith in the broken body and shed blood of the world's Redeemer in the symbol of bread and wine and the monumental lesson of service and humility taught in washing the disciples' feet.

The awful tragedy of the betrayal, mock trial and Crucifixion immediately followed; succeeded by the Resurrection, the delivery of the commission to preach the gospel to all the world, the Ascension and the Pentecost. The three principal figures in the condemnation and Crucifixion scene—Judas, Caiaphas and Pilate—each sought refuge from despair in suicide. The Jews, at their Capital, through their constituted authorities murdered the Son of God. His response to that crime is read in the overthrow of the Capital by the Romans under Titus and the subsequent history of the Jews. The gospel of the Son of God and the agency of the Holy Spirit are the powers now engaged for the world's salvation. The sacred Scriptures revealed God as an eternally self-existing Spirit, in unity with the Lord Jesus Christ, His Son, and the Holy Ghost, proceeding from the Father, forming the one, only true and living triune God—the Creator and author of all things. He is absolutely infinite, in wisdom, in power, in righteousness, in knowledge, in justice, in truth, in mercy, and in love. They reveal further the establishment of a moral government, based upon law, faith and obedience—designed to glorify Himself and promote the happiness of His creatures. When unbelief resulting in disobedience brought death upon the race as the penalty for sin, He graciously provided for atonement and satisfaction for sin, by the death of His Son; and secured to the race upon the simple conditions of a repentance, faith and obedience to law, salvation and eternal life. "For God so loved the world that He gave His only begotten Son that whosoever believeth in Him, should not perish but have everlasting life."

"Let all the world fall down and know,
That none but God, such love can show."

The Kingdom of Heaven is not of this world. The religion of Christianity deals with the heart, soul and conduct of dying men and women during probation; and seeks by regeneration to translate them from the dominion of the law of "sin and death" to the law of the spirit of life in Christ Jesus, which makes us free from the law of "sin and death." The result is conformity to the divine will, spiritual life, hid with Christ in God and eternal life in the end. The kingdom of heaven is a kingdom of light, truth, love and life, that makes men and women pure and happy.

To prove the difference between the true and the false it is only necessary to contrast it with all other systems of religion. It has blessed the race with the establishment of hospitals, asylums, sanitariums for the afflicted, clothed the naked, fed the hungry, ministered to the sick, helped the poor, solaced the sorrowing, educated the ignorant, reformed the vicious, pardoned the penitent, purified the sinful; and lifted humanity to its present plane of civilization, hope, light and character. It has contested every inch of its progress with the innumerable powers of darkness and evil. It has steadily advanced through storms of persecutions—illustrated by the faith of confessors and sanctified in the blood of the martyrs.

What have Paganism, Buddhism, Tauism, Confucianism, Shintoism, Islamism, Mormonism and all the other 'isms done to bless the world? Echo answer, "What?" And yet, at the recent Chicago World's Exposition it was gravely proposed to compare, consider and discuss the relative merits of these monstrous systems, with the peerless truth of Christianity. All of the grand facts involved in the divine plan of administration of this world's affairs have now transpired and become historic, except two, the resurrection of the dead and the final judgment—awarding rewards to the righteous and punishment to the wicked. These are both assured by promise and prophecy. Indeed they constitute the keystone in the arch of time and probation.

Eternal life is the reward of faith and obedience; and eternal death the punishment of unbelief and disobedience. The one glorifies His grace, the other vindicates His justice.

Is the revelation contained in the sacred Scriptures true? If not, hopeless despair only remains.

The arguments demonstrating its proof have long since been exhausted and have remained; and will forever continue unanswered. To recapitulate them in brief: the mysterious system of the universe is known to exist. It could not and did not exist without a cause. No effect can exist without a cause. The Pagan world is proof that unaided human thought could never find out the cause. Hence the necessity of a divine revelation of the author and object of its creation. The great open book of nature which can not otherwise be understood, is read of all men, and fully explained in the light of revelation. Every star that sparkles in the crown of night, twinkles its silent testimony to the infinite wisdom, power and righteousness of its author. The unity of purpose, design, plan and object of the Creation as disclosed in the sacred writings, recorded by inspired men in different and distant ages, dissimilar in mental endowments, personal environments and under different social and civil systems, supply the strongest internal evidence of their truth. Another and an infallible test of truth, is found in the exact and precise fulfillment in their minutest circumstantial details of prophecies, cries uttered hundreds and thousands of years before the events, by inspiration. This seems to me absolute demonstration of the truth of this revelation.

God's revelation of Himself, His creation and His moral government and spiritual kingdom have been in all the ages, evidenced by the sanction of miracles. No human power can raise the dead. The Galilean startled and confounded His enemies and amazed the multitude by the miracles He wrought in their presence, to which He appealed as the proof of His unity with the Father, the omnipotence of His power, and the divinity of His mission. The final proof is the conscious conviction and experience of the human soul, directly witnessed by the Holy Spirit. Howbeit when He, the Spirit of truth is come, he will guide you into all the truth; for he shall not speak of himself; but whatsoever he shall hear, that shall he speak; and he will shew you things to come.

"He shall glorify me, for He shall receive of mine, and shall shew it unto you." The only sin that shall not be forgiven is the sin against this witness. The religion of Christianity transfers the dog-licked beggar from the rich man's gate to Abraham's bosom; and the penitent thief from the cross to Paradise with Christ.

Agnosticism removes Ingersoll from the triumphs of the platform and forum to a cupful of urned ashes. Reader, which do you prefer? Which? The Scriptures disclose Christianity as a kingdom of law and love, faith and obedience, light and life. "Thy Kingdom come."

CHAPTER XXVI.

The Miracles Coincident with the Crucifixion.

By H. P. B.

"Now when the centurion, and they that were with him watching Jesus, saw the earthquake and those things that were done, they feared greatly, saying: 'Truly, this was the Son of God." St. Matthew'

The Crucifixion of Jesus Christ was the most important event in the history of the world. The Cross is the grand focal center of the moral universe, to which the faith and hopes of a guilty race have gravitated in every clime and in all ages. It is the concave mirror that gathers from heaven all its rays of light and life, and the convex speculum that scatters them in every direction over the earth. Involving, as it does, the highest interests of humanity, as well as the great principles of the Divine administration, every incident connected with the Crucifixion is to be regarded as of significant import. This is certainly true of the co-incident miracles. I do not share in the opinion commonly entertained that they were intended as the mere attestations of the Divine displeasure at the cruelty exhibited in the execution of the Redeemer. This seems to have been the opinion of the guard detailed to watch him while on the Cross.

Darkness and earthquakes have certainly been used as the instruments of Divine punishment; but that they were not so used on this occasion is abundantly demonstrated in the fact that no one was destroyed or punished by them. That these miracles all occurred precisely at the time and place they did, and that they never occurred before nor since clearly establishes, as I think, the truth of two propositions: First, that they did not result from natural causes—from the ordinary operation of the laws of nature—and, therefore, were not accidental co-incidences; but that they were the immediate result of a supernatural, a divine agency, and for this reason, properly miracles; and second, that they were the representatives of great and vital ideas, involved in the divine administration, respecting the economy of human salvation.

Assuming this view to be the true one, and I apprehend none can controvert it successfully, the inquiry arises what are the ideas they were intended to represent? What are we to understand them to signify?

This article proposes to answer these inquiries, and present the solution of their import. They were four in number: 1. The darkness. 2. The earthquake. 3. The rending of the veil. 4. The resurrection of the saints; and will be considered in the order named.

These miracles all speak the language of symbol. In relation to the first, the simple statement of the Divine record is, that there was darkness over all the land from the sixth to the ninth hour.

Darkness is the symbol of despair. This miracle was the first in the order of time. So the first condition of humanity, affected by the atonement then in process of consummation, was one of the hopeless despair, of which the darkness was the terrific sign or symbol.

The language of the law was: "In the day thou eatest thereof, thou shalt surely die."

The immutable truth of the Almighty Lawgiver was pledged to the enforcement of the penalty upon the infraction of the prohibition. Adam's disobedience made himself and his offspring obnoxious to this penalty.

In the absence of the atonement outside of Christ crucified, the destiny of the race was precisely that of the "angels who kept not their first estate," and who were "reserved in everlasting chains, under darkness to the judgment of the great day"—a destiny of hopeless despair and eternal death. This was the thing of which the darkness was the sign.

It was a fit emblem of man's condition after the fall, aside from the provision made for his recovery. Ostracized from Eden, cherubims brandishing the flaming sword of wrath along every avenue that approached the Tree of Life, a ruined and wretched race moved in melancholy procession from the cradle to the grave, and from the grave to hell.

There was no eye to pity, no arm to save. It was the impending doom of despair and death that was sublimely signified in the darkness that overshadowed the scene of Crucifixion.

What consternation that vast multitude of scoffing spectators upon Cavalry must have felt, when, without any premonition, the eye of Heaven was put out to show them their ruin without the Savior they were engaged in crucifying! How they strained their aching eyes to peer through this noon of night! Oh! how their bosoms heaved with anxiety, and their hearts throbbed with fear, in that hour of dreadful stillness, as they listened to the blood-drops as they fell at the foot of the Cross from the Redeemer's bleeding side!

The next miracle in the order of consideration is the earthquake.

An earthquake is the symbol of revolution—the overthrow of dominion.

The idea presented or represented by this sign is the overthrow of the empire of sin and death—the conquest of the Cross of Christ.

"The Son of Man came to seek and to save that which was lost." The world was lost. "Sold under sin," taken by the Devil captive at his will, "Condemned already," "there were none righteous," "Judgment came upon all unto condemnation," mankind were the servants of sin and the subjects of Satan. The mission of the Son of God was one of invasion and conquest. He came to

> "Break the power of cancelled sin
> And set the prisoner free."

Paradoxical as it may appear, yet it is true, that the grandest declaration of war to which the world ever listened was the thrilling pean that swelled from the heavenly hosts of "glory to God in the highest, peace on earth, good will toward men." It announced the opening of the campaign that was to vanquish death and hell and result in the rescue and salvation of sinners. The Devil understood well its import. He knew with what antagonist he must measure arms. He opened the conflict by the same strategy that wrought our ruin in Paradise. He endeavored to subsidize the allegiance of his adversary by the temptation in the wilderness, but he was vanquished on this first field.

Everything that Jesus said, and everything that He did, was in hostility to the kingdom of Satan—was a blow aimed at his supremacy over the human soul—was an effort to break the slavish chains of sin in which he held the world in thralldom—to overthrow the spiritual darkness that reigned like the "starless night of desolation around its heart and hopes."

This conflict was to culminate in the fulfillment of the promise made in the Garden amid the scenes of our disaster, that "the seed of the woman shall bruise the serpent's head, and thou shalt bruise his heel."

Its crisis was the hour of Crucifixion. As the final conflict approached, Jesus was betrayed by one disciple, denied by another and abandoned by the rest. He encountered alone the trinity of hell—the world, the flesh and the Devil.

When crushed by the superincumbent burden of "sins not his own," He pressed His sacred face to the chilly ground of Gethsemane, and mingled the accents of His dying prayer with the midnight murmurings of Kedron. There was no arm bared in His defense, no teardrop to melt with His sorrow, and no heart to throb in unison with His anguish. It is true He was strengthened by an angel, but there was not a pang alleviated, nor a drop taken from the cup that pressed His quivering lips.

When he exclaimed, "It is finished," He dealt the final blow upon the head of Satan that broke his grasp upon the human soul, and sent him reeling back to his home in hell. And Heaven announced in the symbol of an earthquake, the redemption of the world from the dominion of death, as Jesus

"Conquered when he fell."

The veil of the temple was a curtain that separated the holy place where the priest ministered from the sanctum sanctorum, into which the high priest alone entered, once a year, to make expiation for the sins of the people. "And the veil of the temple was rent in twain from the top to the bottom."

When the veil of the temple was rent, or split, it disclosed to the public view the Mercy Seat, and opened access to it to all alike, priest and people, Jew and Gentile—signifying, symbolizing the great truth that Jesus, the Great High Priest of the new covenant, who, "through the eternal spirit, offered himself without spot to God," had "consecrated for us, through the veil—that is to say, His flesh—a new and living way" to the Mercy Seat above, of which that in the temple was the figure; where, "after he had offered one sacrifice for sins," "He forever sat down on the right hand of God." The whole ceremonial economy of the temple service was a system of symbolism—"a shadow of good things to come." The atonement offered by Jesus Christ, the Great High Priest, "once for all," was the substance. The rending of the veil as Jesus expired on the cross, proclaimed the fulfillment of the types and the shadows of the ceremonial system, in the new and living way opened up to the Throne of Grace—the Mercy Seat in Heaven, by a crucified, risen, ascended and continually interceding High Priest.

The intervention of priestcraft and the intercession of saints were exploded when the veil was rent. Salvation was purchased for all alike, Jew and Gentile, through the merits of the atonement, upon the simple conditions of repentance towards God, and faith in our Lord Jesus Christ. The hearthstone, church altar, the closet and grave, become shrines upon which penitent sinners and believing saints could offer, through the blood of atonement, the incense of an acceptable worship. And thus the "grace of God that bringeth salvation appeared unto all men."

"And the graves were opened; and many bodies of the saints which slept arose, and came out of the grave after his resurrection, and went into the holy city and appeared unto many."

The resurrection of the saints was the fourth and last miracle coincident with the Crucifixion. Many inquiries have arisen, and much speculation has been indulged upon this subject. The questions who were these saints, and what became of them may not probably be answered satisfactorily. The history of the transaction is certainly silent upon the subject.

But the question under consideration, and the one it is proposed to discuss is, what was the design of the miracle? What does it teach? What is the thing which it signifies? It is the sign or symbol of the general resurrection of the human body at the end of time—at the final judgment. The disobedience of Adam involved his race in the doom of spiritual, physical and eternal death. "The wages of sin is death." The atonement presents a sublime system or plan of recovering mercy, precisely adequate to human exigency in this condition. It justifies from Adamic transgression, relieves from the judgment of condemnation to which his disobedience exposed him. It grants a new trial, and places man back on probation. It secures the quickening efficacy of the Holy Spirit, which sufficiently restores spiritual life to enable him to exercise faith in Christ, which it substitutes for obedience to the law as the test of our probationary state; and offers pardon for actual transgression on the condition of repentance and faith, and thus saves from eternal death.

As we have already seen, the condition of the race after the fall was symbolized by the darkness, the overthrow of hell's dominion over it by the earthquake, and access to the Mercy Seat in Heaven by the rending of the veil.

But there is one consequence of original sin yet to be removed. This is physical death, the death of the human body. That exemption from this was not secured by the atonement of Jesus Christ is demonstrated by the broken hearts, graveyards and funeral crowds of earth. The inquiry then arises how did the atonement meet this difficulty, or relieve from this doom? The answer is not by exempting the body from death, but by restoring it to life after it died. This it does in the general resurrection at the last day.

"The hour is coming, and now is, in which they that are in their graves shall hear his voice, and shall come forth; they that have done good unto the resurrection of life, and they that have done evil unto the resurrection of damnation." This is the mode by which "our Savior Jesus Christ abolished death." This is the closing scene in the world's great drama, and was gloriously symbolized by the closing miracle in the scene of Crucifixion. The doctrine of the resurrection is the keystone in the arch of the Christian's faith; withdraw it, and the whole superstructure of Christianity tumbles into ruins, and leaves the world in the eternal embrace of relentless death. But while

"An angel's arm can't snatch us from the grave,
Legions of angels can't confine us there."

While humanity shudders at the gloom of the grave, the Christian looks upon its darkness, when spanned by the rainbow of hope, reflected from the blood-drops of Calvary and sings,

"Yet in this lowly bed was laid
The Savior's form divine,
And death's unbreathing cell became,
Salvation's living shrine."

The four great cardinal truths or facts in the history and destiny of the human race—the fall—the restoration—the salvation secured to all—and the resurrection of the body—were signified by these miracles that passed in symbolic panorama before the gazing world, on the bloody brow of Calvary when the son of man

"Closed his eyes to show us God."

Oh, what eternal interests cluster around the cross!

It threw back upon the symbolic blood of patriarchial altars, the light of a coming Savior. It poured its kindling splendors along the pathway of prophecy, the beacon star of kings and seers. It mingled its beams of hope with the sacrificial blood of the Temple, and pointed adoring priests to the lamb for sinners slain. It flashes upon earth's teeming and coming millions salvation from the power of sin and the thrall of death.

CHAPTER XXVII.

St. Paul.

The circumstances under which St. Paul makes his first appearance on the stage of history, indicate the decided and important part he is destined to act in its drama. The Prince of Peace had announced, before the crucifixion, that His kingdom was not of this world; and that those whom He had selected to establish it, should indeed drink the bitter cup that the world had pressed to His reluctant lips. The powers of earth and hell resisted, at the threshold, the establishment of His spiritual kingdom. Stephen was awarded the honor of wearing the first Christian martyr's crown. At his execution, St. Paul, although a young man, was more than a disinterested spectator. He was not only a witness, but a party to the transaction. His presence on this occasion, the interest he took in it, his age considered, and the consequences likely to result from it, evince, at once, a decided character, as well as an inclination to impress that character upon the history of his race by identifying himself prominently with its most important events. Nature was prodigal in the bestowment of her favors upon him. He possessed a mind of surpassing comprehension, clearness and power. His moral attributes were all in profusion. His aspirations were elevated, his prejudices high, his impulses strong, his affections ardent, and his will invincible. He was by lineage, a Jew, and by profession, a Pharisee. He was born and reared amid the culminating splendors of the Augustan age—the most intellectual, perhaps, of the world, the present excepted. At Athens, Hesiod and Thucydides had written, Demosthenes and Pericles had spoken, Pindar and Homer had sung. The marble was breathing under the polishing touches of Phidias and Praxiteles. Apelles had mingled the light of immortality with the colors of his pencil, and the canvass blushed in the trophies of his genius.

At Rome, great names illustrated the annals of painting and statuary, poetry and eloquence. Rome was the proud mistress of the world—there was none to dispute her empire or measure arms with her prowess. The wisdom of Gamaliel was the exponent of Rabbinical learning at Jerusalem. Mythology had enrolled her multitudinous divinities in the Pantheon, until every interest, secular and sacred, was under the protection of its peculiar deity. The greater portion of the intellect of this highly intellectual age was devoted to religion and the arts and sciences. The claims of rival systems of philosophy was the subject of constant disputation among the schoolmen. Vice and virtue, good and evil, the character and attributes of the human soul—all claimed their full share of consideration. In all these systems of philosophy, cultivated intellect was struggling with its own weakness; and the human soul was attesting its own immortality, and gasping for that light which divine revelation alone sheds upon its hope and destiny. The Gentiles were idolaters—were heathens. The Jews were the custodians of the Sacred Oracles of the true God, but had subordinated the mightier matters of the law—judgment and mercy—to the tithing of anise and mint; and had substituted for the doctrines of Revelation the commandments of men. St. Paul,—equal to any, and surpassed by none in his natural endowments, and these developed and embellished by every contribution that could be levied upon Roman, Grecian, Chaldean, and Hebrew literature,—burned with restless ambition to win a name and the honors and emoluments which merit confers on position. Brought up at the feet of her mightiest master, he was profoundly learned and deeply skilled in the abstrusities of the Mosaic Law, both as it was truly written and as it was perverted by the traditions of the scribes and elders.

Entering into the schemes and identifying himself with the fortunes of the Pharisees, he sought to distinguish himself in the effort to crush and strangle the infant Church. Hence, soon after the martyrdom of Stephen, he is found on his way to Damascus, breathing threatenings and slaughter, with a warrant from the High Priest, authorizing him to arrest and carry bound to Jerusalem, any disciples of either sex that might be found in that city. On his way to accomplish this mission of persecution and blood, he was converted by a miracle. With characteristic promptitude he inquires, "Lord, what wilt thou have me to do?" Notified that he was called to turn the Gentiles from darkness to light, and from the power of Satan to the power of God—receiving the royal investiture—he rose, mailed from

Heaven's armory; and bounded into the arena of moral gladiatorship with the world, a true knight of the Cross, floating a flag and bearing a shield emblazoned with Jesus and the Resurrection. The wealth and power, passion and prejudice of the world, were in hostile array against the religion whose championship he assumed. Its founder, humanly speaking, was an obscure Galilean, who had been crucified for alleged sedition against the great and powerful government of Rome. Some of his few and scattered disciples had fallen victims to the malice of the Jews, while the remainder were fugitives from their cruelty.

In addition to the opposition before him, and the difficulties around him, he must encounter the odium that treason attaches to party. But Paul's was not the spirit to flinch at difficulties, or quail at opposition. His was a spirit that panted for glorious strife, and rejoiced in foemen worthy of his steel.

His moral nature changed; his learning and great powers of logic and eloquence, sanctified by the power of the Holy Ghost; his whole conduct, brought under the disciplinary control of the Gospel; his heart burning and melting with sympathy for his ruined race, and burdened with the value of immortal souls, and a commission bearing the signet of the King of Kings, he enters upon a glorious career of trial and triumph, that presents him as the grandest character of all time and history.

The idolatry of the Gentiles, taught in the schools, practiced in the temples, patronized by the multitudes, and protected by the State, was to be assailed on the one hand. On the other, degenerate Judaism, with its exclusive claims to Divine favor, its boasted heraldry, its hereditary prejudices, its formulary of types and shadows, priests and blood, altar and victim—the fossil remains of an antiquated and exploded system—consecrated, however, by the hopes and faith of generation after generation, and hoary with the seal of ages, but perverted by apostates to the purposes of pride and partyism. The religion of Christianity was opposed to both of these, and proposed to recruit its army from them; hence its movements were aggressive and its object conquest. Vicissitude, temptation, trial, persecution, and suffering in all its forms were to be met and endured by those who embraced its faith, raised its standard and supported its cause. Paul was advised of all this. To use a favorite figure of his own, he knew that he was to enter upon a "fight." But he was undismayed at the prospect before him. He was prepared for any and for every emergency. As might have been expected, from his first entrance upon his high embassy, he was assailed from every quarter, from Jewish synagogue and heathen temple, from fierce rabble and cruel power.

Persecutions dogged his footsteps from city to city, from kingdom to kingdom, from country to country. Like a personified ubiquity, it met him at every step. It had gorged its hellish appetite with the blood of the incarnate Master, yet it panted with peculiar thirst for that of His greatest apostle. Bonds, imprisonments, stonings and scourgings, were the responses he received for his messages of love and peace. Humanity weeps at his own simple recital of his sufferings. Nor did he ever repine at the probable honors he sacrificed as a Roman Proconsul or a member of the Sanhedrim, in embracing the religion of the despised Nazarene. He never complained at the hardness of his lot, the burden of his labors, the severity of his afflictions, the intensity of his sufferings. He never faltered in his purpose. If he exclaimed in reference to the magnitude of the duties before him, "Who is sufficient for these things?" the reply was, "I can do all things through Christ strengthening me." He conferred not with flesh and blood. In the midst of affliction, suffering, trial and persecution, he gloried in tribulation, and felt, in response to a sublime faith, that "this light affliction, which was but for a moment, would work out for him a far more exceeding and eternal weight of glory." Greatness is developed either in doing or suffering. Paul displays it in both. These two grand achievements of virtue are exemplified in every act and circumstance of his Christian life. What a grand and glorious conception he had of the philosophy of the religion of Christ, when he exclaimed, "I take pleasure in persecutions, in reproaches, in necessities, in distresses for Christ's sake, for when I am weak then I am strong." Adversity shows the moral manhood that is in us. It is not difficult to be great in prosperity, brave in the absence of the enemy, and fearless when we are out of danger. It is the fire that discovers the pure gold. If he had been a mere time-server, he would have cowered before the insane yell of the maddened devotees of Diana at Ephesus, the clamorous rabble at Jerusalem, and the infuriated mob at Thessalonica. But thoroughly imbued with the spirit of his mission, and the importance of his message, he is, everywhere and under all circumstances, the same peerless herald of the Cross. He vindicates the claims of his Master to the Messiahship, from the authority of the prophets, upon the steps of the castle at Jerusalem, to the confusion of the Jews, and in the judgment hall at Cæsarea, to the astonishment of Festus. He proclaimed to the Areopagus in the midst of Mars' Hill, at Athens, the unknown God whom the Athenians ignorantly worshipped. He stood in the shadow of the Pantheon, upon the scenes of the triumphs of Demosthenes; and with the arm of Hercules, hurled the thunderbolts of a greater than Jupiter against the idolatry of the Gentiles. And yet with the humility of a servant, he gathered sticks at Melita to warm his shipwrecked companions. He unrolled the flag of the Cross by the Fane of Venus, at Corinth, totius Greciæ lumen, among her thronging thousands, and yet he plied the lowly trade of the humble tent-maker around the quiet fireside of Aquila and Priscilla. He could wish himself accursed from Christ for the salvation of the Jews, and yet he pronounced the bitter malison: "God shall smite thee, thou whited wall," upon Ananias, their high priest. He was not a whit behind the very chiefest of the apostles, and yet he was less than the least of the saints. He was the storm-god of the tempest, and the genius of the zephyrs. These antitheses were not antagonisms, were not contradictions, but the extremes of a perfect character, at once, both unique and harmonious. They doubtless conspired to impress the multitude with widely different views respecting this remarkable man. Regarded as the tutelary divinity of eloquence at Lystra, he was denounced as a babbler at Athens. Supposed by the barbarians on the Island to be a murderer, when the viper fastened its fangs in his hand, they thought him a god when he shook it unharmed into the fire.

He was as abundant in labors as he was patient in suffering. His travels, sermons, debates, defenses, speeches and writings are the everlasting monuments of his labors. Every Sabbath bell proclaims, and every church spire attests throughout Christendom, the glorious results of his life and labors. We look through the dust and moss of eighteen centuries and behold him in the closing scene of his life. The wisdom of the Senate had rejected the suggestion of Caesar to enroll the name of Jesus among the divinities of the Pantheon. Still the banner of the Cross floated by his eagles even in Rome. But its bravest knight, although a victor, was a captive. Contemplate him in this his last hour of conflict and of triumph; in chains and in prison, condemned to die and awaiting the hour of his execution; sitting upon the straw of his dungeon, with the meagre remnants of his stationery lying upon the stone, on which he had just written his last letter. There he sits, of diminutive stature and slightly deformed person, scarred with the terrible conflicts of life's great battle; his brow calm, his countenance placid, the Christian's deathless hope sparkling from his eye and the martyr's smile of triumph playing upon his lip. He is uninterested in the high debates of the Senate, the inflammatory harangues of the forum, or the wild shouts of the populace as they welcome the returning victor, who bears to the feet of Caesar the crowns of subjugated kingdoms. He surveyed the present, forecast the future, and retrospected the past. In looking over the fields of his conflicts and triumphs, he beheld no trampled vineyards, no desolated gardens, no sacked cities, no burnt villages, no smouldering ruins nor blood-dyed battlefields. He heard no widow's wail nor orphan's cry, nor shriek of violated virtue. Oh! no, none of these for the weapons of his warfare were not carnal; but every field was strown with the scattered wreck of decaying Judaism, and piled with the ruins of the Empire of Sin. The dismantled fortress of Idolatry had disgorged its captive thousands, to breathe the air of truth with which Christ made them free indeed. Joy and peace, and hope, and light, and life and love were the monuments that marked the spots where his victories were won.

He bequeathed to his race this magnificent autobiography, unapproached and unapproachable by anything in history, sacred or profane.

"For I am now ready to be offered, and the time of my departure is at hand. I have fought a good fight, I have finished my course, I have kept the faith. Henceforth there is laid up for me a crown of righteousness, which the Lord, the Righteous Judge, shall give me at that day."

The trial is past, the fight is ended, and the guerdon won.

He sealed his discipleship with the blood of martyrdom, and dying, left a name that, like the gorgeous splendors of a summer's sunset, pours up the horizon of history a stream of posthumous glory, that makes the world radiant with the light of a deathless hero.

CHAPTER XXVIII.

BISHOP A. G. HAYGOOD.

So much has been said and written, and so well and tenderly said, and written of the dead Bishop, that it would seem to be superfluous to add more. But these beautiful tributes have come through the mist of tears; and from tongues and pens tremulous with the emotions of grief. His great life deserves contemplation and analysis in the calm light of history and philosophy.

Like Alexander Hamilton and the younger Pitt, Haygood was great from the beginning. Hamilton was an orator and statesman at the age of seventeen; the trusted military counsellor of Washington at twenty; led the last charge of Continentals for liberty at Yorktown at twenty-five; suggested a written constitution for the government of the people—whose independence his sword had done so much to achieve—and stood at the head of the American bar before he was thirty; was secretary of the treasury at thirty-four; at the touch of his magic genius a stream of prosperity fertilized a dessert of bankruptcy and made it blossom as the rose.

William Pitt was a member of parliament at twenty-one; British premier at twenty-five, holding the high office at the request of the king—in defiance of all precedent against the adverse vote of the commons—allied nations against the ambitious schemes of the Man of

Destiny, and, at the age of thirty, stood alone, the peerless statesman of Europe.

They each died young, and at the same age—forty-seven; Hamilton, the first thinker, writer, constitutional lawyer and financier of a hemisphere; and Pitt, the most accomplished orator, statesman and diplomat of Europe; the one, wept by a continent; the other mourned by a kingdom.

Haygood, at the age of twenty-one, commenced his life work on a totally different, less famous, but more important line; junior preacher on the Watkinsville circuit; rapidly rising to the charge of a circuit, thence to stations, army chaplain, conference secretary, presiding elder, delegate to the General Conference, Sunday-school secretary, author, college president, editor of the church paper, elected to (but declined) the Episcopate, fraternal delegate to the General Conference of the Methodist Episcopal Church, agent of the Slater fund, elected bishop the second time, which office was accepted—excelling in each and all of these high positions. Stricken at fifty-seven with the shaft of death, in the full-orbed splendor of his moral, intellectual and spiritual meridian; he passed in a blaze of glory, from the field of conflict to the crown of martyrdom, his death sending a thrill of sorrow round the world. How blessings brighten in their flight!

The value of such a life and character to the world will never be known until revealed in the "final consummation." His great gifts, powers, and services were not duly estimated by all while he lived. He was misunderstood by some, misjudged by others, and misrepresented by a few. This annoyed and grieved him, Indifferent as Mansfield to the applause of the multitude, he enjoyed, like Canning, the approval of the wise and good. Some of his eulogists have intimated that he was not an orator, others that he was not a scholar. This needs explanation. They doubtless mean that he was not an orator after the type and style of Pierce and Prentiss. And who living or dead ever was? His was not the rounded, sonorous, pompous style of Cicero. He did not speak to the gallery nor play to the grandstand; nor did he scatter bouquets of dainty flowers sprinkled with rose water upon his audience; to the delectation of esthetic imbeciles or sentimental enthusiasts. Yet he was an orator of the very highest order of a particular school of this divine art. Graceful in attitude and action, distinct in enunciation, always emphasizing the right word, using precisely the proper word and the fewest possible in number, to give the thought the greatest force, severe in invective, and melting in pathos, with a voice as clear as a clarion, and a soul all aglow with light from on high; he sent from pulpit and platform—to the heart and consciences of men and women, great, concrete truths—burdened with the responsibilities of time and pregnant with the destinies of eternity, with a power that few men in this or any age ever equalled. Those, who, at a country campmeeting, at eleven o'clock on Sunday, at the close of the war—heard him arraign and denounce the dominant sins of the times, upon the text: "Because iniquity abounds the love of many shall wax cold," had the privilege of witnessing the exhibition of a power of invective that Brougham never equalled. And those who have heard him upon the Master's touch of the leper, heard a depth of pathos sounded that Summerfield never reached.

His style was suggestive. He expressed the controlling central thought of a subject; but in such logical and harmonious connection as to keep an intelligent hearer busy, filling in those that were suggested. And, usually, there was more thought suggested by him, that was expressed by others who were esteemed good preachers or speakers. So, of his writings. There is more pure thought scattered along to be read between the lines than most writers express in the lines. He never failed either to convince, or enlighten, or edify his auditors—always interested, and often charmed them.

But it has been intimated that he was not an accurate scholar. Those who make this intimation, mean, I suppose, that he was not a scholar in the sense of wandering about among lizzards, in the ruins of Babylon, searching for a scratch or a mark on a brickbat to prove who was the principal workman, in building Babel; or how many bricks it would take to complete the job. Nor of the enthusiast who would spend one-half of a life-time, with a pick and shovel, digging through strata of forgotten ages, after the dead root of a Greek verb, that was obsolete before Homer sung or Troy fell; and when he thought he had found it, spend the other half in defending his opinion of its meaning. If to know God and men, books and things, if to understand the laws and truths of the kingdom of truth and grace—

as disclosed in revelation, and the kingdom of nature as revealed in science, if to understand thoroughly, the greatest living, and read fluently, two of the greatest dead languages of the earth; if to understand himself and be able to teach the mental and logical process by which the truth is discovered; if to know all the great events of history—ancient and modern—that have shaped the course of civilization and controlled the destinies of nations; and if to know the obligation of duty in all the relations of life, and how to discharge it,—constitute scholarship,—then, he was a scholar of rare attainments. He was an orator, scholar, theologian, statesman, philosopher, philanthropist, patriot and Christian. Some may deny to him statesmanship. Let us see if his claims to this distinction are well founded. At the close of the war, the Southern people—chagrined with the humiliation of defeat and appalled at the outrages of destruction—stood aghast at the magnitude of the race problem with which they were confronted. Intelligence, patriotism and virtue were disfranchised and ostracized; while ignorant negroes from the cotton fields were ordaining State constitutions. How were the races to live together? What was to be done with the negroes? No greater social and political problem ever appealed to statesmanship for solution. Haygood solved it in four words, and three of them monosyllables. These words were the title of a book—"Our Brother in Black." Their uniqueness arrested public attention. Their wisdom appealed to the public sense of justice, and their philanthropy secured the support of the wise and the patriotic. This title, by implication, epitomizes the book—justice in dealing with the negro —his education in letters, in morals—and especially in the industrial arts. This unpretentious book, more than a decade in advance of public sentiment, has done more to disarm sectional and promote national fraternity, than all the frothy speeches made at banquets or in congress, during the last thirty years. Accepting the agency of the Slater fund, he illustrated by his work, what he taught in his book. But is his solution a success? Let the speech of Booker Washington, and the colored exhibit at the late Atlanta Exposition answer. The fame of Bishop Haygood does not rest upon the evidence of brass bands, processions and the newspaper puffs of paid correspondents. It rests on the granite foundation of what he was and what he did. The measure of true greatness is the amount and extent of service rendered to others. This infallible test has been established by an authority, from which there is no appeal.

"Whosoever of you will be the chiefest, shall be servant of all." Great, as he unquestionably was, in his gifts and attainments, his chief claim will forever stand upon the entire, unselfish and unremitting consecration of all that he had, and all that he was, to the service of the Lord and to his kind. This service explored every part of his Master's vineyard and permeated every interest of humanity. Whether he was the official head of a particular department of Church work, he was always a leader, if not the leader in it; and this is true of all the departments and enterprises of his Church. He was undismayed by opposition. Neither elated with success nor discouraged by defeat. "Instant in season and out of season;" always ready to aggressively advance or heroically defend the truth, in pulpit or council, on platform or hustings—meeting bishops, boards, committees, traveling through rain and sun, in heat and cold, in day and night, always and everywhere in full armor—another veritable Knight of the Leopard, ready for combat with any Saracen who opposed the claims of his Master, or assailed the interest of his kingdom. No summer vacation, nor pleasure trip to Europe ever allured him from the dust and strife of the field, where the battle raged for God and humanity. It is impossible in a paper like this, to even summarize a tithe of the great things he has done. All he did and all he thought was great. He lived in a realm and dwelt on a plain of faith and thought, occupied by few men of this world. His great head, heart and hand, all through his life, scattered the seeds of a harvest that will be gathered all along the coming ages. He was the incarnate genius of work; and all his work was for others. There was a felicity in his death; he had done enough. He needed rest. With him "To live was Christ, to die was gain." He fell with his armor on, and his face to the foe—combining the integrity of Soule, the intellect of Doggett, the saintliness of Marvin, the spirit of Pierce, with the toil of Asbury and McKendree—he goes to history, among the foremost men in the illustrious roll of American Methodism.

CHAPTER XXIX.

Causes of Crime and the Best Method of Prevention.

The primal cause of crime is the hereditary taint of sin in human nature. The remedy, regeneration, belongs to the realm of the spiritual. "Ye must be born again." The exciting cause is the presence of temptation. The remedy for this is avoidance and resistance. There is infinite wisdom in the utterance, "Lead us not into temptation, but deliver us from evil."

Crimes may be classified into two divisions, namely, those that flow from sensualism, and those that spring from the intellectual side of our being. In both cases it is the prostitution of powers designed by divine wisdom to promote human happiness. The question is, what is the cause of crime and how can it be prevented? In every age of this world's history, there has raged a conflict between the opposing forces of good and evil. This conflict is perhaps more intense now than at any former period. One great cause of the increase of crime is the almost total abdication of the parental duty of properly training children in the home circle. The home is society in embryo. It is the State in incipiency. It is the granite foundation upon which the church rests. The selection of Abraham as founder of the Jewish commonwealth and church was based on the fact that he governed his house. "Train up a child in the way he should go, and when he is old he will not depart from it," is the inspired truth of Revelation. The experience and observation of the ages have crystalized this truth into the aphorism, "As the twig is bent the tree is inclined." The careful training of children in the home, God's ordained institution, in the provisions of the Decalogue as matter of law, and in the doctrines of the Sermon on the Mount as the expression of love, will form the highest type of virtuous character, and present the surest guarantee against crime. The Sunday-school with its perfunctionary performance and the common school with its routine of daily lessons, while they may aid, they can not possibly substitute the constant, watchful, patient parental training of the home. It is this training that forms good character; it is its neglect that makes criminals. The moral lessons of the pulpit come in the cold abstract, and do not reach children. The principal cause of all the crimes resulting from sensualism comes from two institutions, namely, the tolerated brothel and the licensed saloon. This truth is so manifestly self-evident that it would be worse than a waste of words to argue it. Nor is it necessary to list the long catalogue of horrible crimes of debauchery, slaughter and suicide, with their train of wretchedness, blight and ruin that flows from their bitter and poisoned fountain. To suppress these by moral suasion is about as practicable as to arrest a cyclone with a feather. The only successful means of suppression is the imperial edict of the law, vigorously and rigidly enforced. It is less difficult to make a good man or woman by proper training in childhood, than by reformation after they become confirmed in crime in manhood and womanhood. The worship of gentleness, culture, purity and love, around the sacred altar of home, in which duty is the daily sacrifice, is the surest way to prevent it in the future. To remove the temptation as far as practicable, and to punish the hardened criminals with absolute certainty, is the most effectual method of protecting individuals and society. That class of crimes which spring from the intellectual side of the human nature is the offspring of the vices of idleness and pride, and the passion of avarice. Too lazy to work, and too impatient to wait, the get-rich-quick demon seizes them, and a long list of frauds, thefts and robberies, ranging in turpitude and magnitude, from the snatching of a dime purse on the street by a negro footpad, to the plunder of Bengal by Warren Hastings, is inflicted upon society.

This dark catalogue includes every variety in amount of booty, and every grade in type of villiany. It draws its recruits from those who should be of the highest classes of society, who ought to promote its interests and exemplify its virtues. It includes both sexes, as witness Senators Mitchell and Burton, Madame Humbert and Cassie Chadwick. Young men of promise, middle-aged men of culture, and old men of wealth, rob widows and orphans, impoverish stockholders and depositors. Another class of criminals, pickpockets, rob stores, blow open safes, wreck trains and assassinate the aged and infirm, for the pittance their toil and self-sacrifice had laid up for a rainy day. These crimes seem to be increasing in frequency and tragic horror. A prophecy of evil portent to our civilization, is found in the popular, and legal disregard of the sanctity of the institution of marriage, the impunity with which its dissolution is sought, and the facility with which it is obtained. Against the social and civic evils of divorce Christian people have protested in vain. This evil has grown so rapidly and been so destructive of the joys of home life as at last to arouse the public conscience to some appreciation of its magnitude. The antidote for this evil is the repeal of the law that provides for divorce, or to reduce the grounds upon which it may be granted, to the single one authorized in the New Testament. The number and character of the grounds upon which it may be granted, in conservative Georgia, have reduced the cable of wedlock to the weakness of a cobweb. The unwise, not to say wicked, divorce law is the fruitful source of numberless debasing crimes that sap and undermine the foundations of our social system. To thoroughly arrest this downward social and moral gravitation, only requires a short, simple act of the legislature. The legislature has provided, by long and elaborate laws, when birds may be killed, doves baited and fish caught. But small matters, like the sacredness of marriage, the purity of the home, and the preservation of our social system seem to have escaped its attention. There is another crime of great moral turpitude committed with unblushing audacity, amazing frequency, and practical impunity. This is the crime of perjury. This crime assails the very citadel of truth itself. It endangers every human right and interest. The law has attempted to prevent and punish it, but it has blundered in the technicality and complexity of its definition; so that, though constantly committed, it is seldom punished. This definition should be revised and simplified so as to facilitate conviction, and secure its punishment.

There are but two forces available in preventing crime, one moral, the other legal. There are other auxiliary forces that may aid or retard these, but they are adventitious and may, or may not, operate. It seems to me that philanthropists and humanitarians have exhausted their resources of invention and activity in their varied and multiplied efforts to reform criminals and prevent crime. Such small success as they may have achieved, has been confined mainly to small boys and girls floating like driftwood on its muddy current. But these isolated cases, worthy and Christianlike as the work is, do not meet the exigency of the case. It is society in its individual and aggregate relations with which sociology is dealing. Crime is war upon society. It attacks the absolute rights of life, liberty and property. In the defense of these rights, society, like Scipio, should carry the war into Africa. Our Penal Code needs some amendments. All forms and degrees of larceny, robbery, burglary, and embezzlement should be punished with life imprisonment. Safe-blowing, train-wrecking, and the kidnapping and holding a person for ransom, should be punished with death. This change would eliminate from society the professional and incorrigible criminals, relieve its fears, secure its peace and protect its property. It may be urged that such rigor would be too severe for young offenders, and in cases where small amounts were involved. The reply is that the constitution clothes the executive with the power to pardon or commute. The exercise of this power would meet such exceptional cases, if they should arise. It may be insisted that this change would be extreme and radical; but it must be remembered that desperate diseases require heroic treatment.

Some observation, and the best thought that I have been able to bestow upon the question under consideration, brings me to the conclusion that reform is needed in the following particulars: In the home training of the children of the State; in the repeal or reformation of our divorce laws; in the absolute prohibition of brothels and licensed saloons; in increasing the punishment of certain crimes, and the vigorous prosecution and punishment of all crimes. It is not supposed that the accomplishment of these reforms would exterminate crime, but that it would greatly diminish it there can be no reasonable doubt. The sources of crime are perennial. The conflict between right and wrong will continue as long as time shall last.

> "Vice is a creature of such hideous mien,
> To be hated, needs but to be seen,
> But seen too oft, familiar with its face,
> We first abhor, then pity, then embrace."

All that human agency can do, is to give the right its best support with all the means at command. To succeed with these reforms requires the concentrated sentiment, and united effort of all the good people of the State. If in harmonious co-operation with the leaders, the powerful daily press would devote the space in their columns filled with the nauseating details of police court proceedings, and bridal trousseaus, to the discussion of these vital questions; if the pulpit would substitute for its dull platitudes and hazy, scientific speculations, the vital truths of Revelation, in thoughts that breathe and words that burn; if legislators, instead of planning for higher honors and maneuvering for party advantage would raise these questions in the halls of legislation and discuss them like statesmen; and if parents would appreciate their momentous responsibility to their children and train them in the paths of rectitude, public sentiment would be aroused and united, these and other reforms secured, crimes diminished, society safeguarded and civilization advanced.

The late Civil War, directly or indirectly, contributed immensely to the increase of crime. Four years of indulgence in hate and the practice of plunder and slaughter, scattered the seeds of harvest which we are now reaping. Before emancipation, the home life, constant employment and discipline of owner, overseer and patrol, made the negro practically an unknown factor in the commission of crime. The withdrawal of these restraints by his emancipation made him its greatest quantity. Before the war executions were seldom, now they are frequent. Then we had no stockade nor chain-gangs, now the State is dotted with them. Then our jails and penitentiary were comparatively empty, now they are crowded to overflowing. Then the crime, nameless here, was scarcely known, except by its definition in the Penal Code, now it is almost of daily occurrence.

The genius who discovers a preventive for this crime will outrank Columbus as a benefactor. Other crimes are punished by ordinary legal methods, but outraged public opinion falls back on the higher law of "Salus populi suprema est lex," and punishes this without the expense and tedium of judicial procedure.

To recapitulate: The primal causes of crime are, 1st, The hereditary moral weakness of human nature; 2nd, The existence and presence of temptation; 3rd, The adoption of wrong principles and practice of bad habits in childhood. The best methods of prevention are, 1st, The proper moral training of children by the parents in the home; 2nd, The removal of temptation by all means possible; 3rd, Its speedy, certain and severe punishment.

April 12th, 1906.

CHAPTER XXX.

Literary Address Delivered at the Commencement of Madison Female College.

Ladies and Gentlemen:

The nineteenth century is distinquished for its progress and development; its inventions in art, and its discoveries in science. This progress has exploded cherished theories; and induced the abandonment of old methods. In nothing is the advancement of civilization more strikingly exemplified, than in the inauguration of female colleges, and the recognition of woman's equality in capabilities of intellect, and her claims to superiority in the realms of sentiment.

It is a star in the diadem of Georgia that she established the first female college in the world, and thus led the van of the nations in the endeavor to give the widest range, and the fullest development to the powers of the female mind. This recognition so long withheld, of equality in powers and privileges, has resulted in the discovery of new fields of legitimate operation for woman's enterprise and avocation; and assigned to her, her true position, in the domestic, social, moral and intellectual relations of life.

The future historian of the annals of the race, will record, as the grandest discovery of the century—so full of the marvelous conquests of mind—the true position and high destiny of woman. Sculpture has exhausted the resources of its genius in moulding the graces of her form. Painting has mingled the hues of the rose and lily, to heighten the blushes of her beauty. Poetry has festooned her with garlands, woven from the wild flowers of fancy, to sublimate and etherealize her charms, and chivalry has apotheosized her among the divinities of its worship, and bowed with devotion at the shrine of its idol. But sculpture, painting, poetry, and chivalry, have never comprehended the mysteries of her being, the magnitude of her labors, nor the grandeur of her destiny. Divine Revelation—source of all truth, presents her, as a being of flesh and blood, soul and spirit, sinning in Eden, and weeping on Calvary, help-meet for man; the joy of the home life, the charm of the social circle and the ornament of the Christian church. She unites in blended harmony, with the gentle graces of manner and the bewitching smiles of love, the high qualities of patience, endurance and courage. Every age of the world, every form of civil government, every system of religion, and every type of civilization finds her rising to an equality with great emergencies, and displaying rare powers for sacrifice and achievement.

I invoke your attention, as not inappropriate to this occasion, to the consideration of Woman's patriotism.

No merely secular interest is of equal importance with civil government, which defines and protects human rights, public and private, absolute and relative. Patriotism—unselfish sacrifice for the public weal, deep solicitude for the common interest, faithful discharge of public duties,—has always held a high place in the catalogue of public virtues. "Render unto Cæsar the things that are Cæsar's," was the utterance of high authority. Woman's love is the inspiration of patriotism in men. If there were no homes made happy by the love of devoted wives, there would be no country worth defending. If there were no mothers nor sisters to protect, there would be no incentive to discharge the obligations patriotism imposes.

This inspiration is a perennial influence, controlling the conduct of men in the minor duties of citizenship, in the unobtrusive walks of peaceful life as well as in nerving the arm of valor for the defense of home and country, "Where the front of battle lowers."

It was this subtle, silent power that moved the heart of French chivalry, and swelled the song of British valor, on the night before the storming of the Malakoff. A soldier guarding the outer trenches cried out to his comrades "give us a song!"

"They lay along the batteries' side,
Below the smoking cannon,
Brave hearts from Severn, and from Clyde,
And from the banks of Shannon.

They sang of love, and not of fame,
Forgot was Brittain's glory,
Each heart recalled a different name,
But all sang: "Annie Laurie."

Voice after voice caught up the song,
Until its tender passion,

Rose like an anthem, rich and strong,
  Their battle eve confession.

Dear girl, her name he dare not speak,
  Yet as the song grew louder,
Something upon the soldier's cheek
  Washed off the stains of powder.

Beyond the darkening ocean, burned,
  The bloody sunset's embers,
While the Crimean Vallies burned,
  How English love remembers.

An Irish Nora's eyes are dim,
  For a singer dumb and gory.
An English Mary mourns for him,
  Who sang of "Annie Laurie."

The memory of loved ones at home was the inspiration of those heroes in life, and their solace in death. The world will never know how many a soldier boy has breathed to his breaking heart with his dying breath, the name of its idol.

But it is not so much, of the patriotism which women inspire in men, as that which they exhibit in themselves, that I am to speak. I do not seek illustration of my theme, in the example of the world-renowned women, whose triumphs in founding empires, conducting wars and commanding armies, constitute the romance of history. Women like Margaret of Anjou and the maid of Orleans. But the thrilling story of Esther combines so many of the true elements of patriotism, that I will be pardoned for allusion to it. It presents the high resolve to save her kindred and her nation. Womanly strategy in devising the methods to accomplish her purpose, heroic daring in approaching the King to ask the abrogation of a law of the Medes and Persians, sublime faith in the success of her enterprise, the self-sacrifice that periled life upon the issue of the undertaking; success vindicated the wisdom of her strategy, the claim of her courage and the confidence of her faith.

It is said that women do not reason, that they substitute impulse for logic. There is no greater mistake; they may not, and do not,—like cautious, politic men,—toil through the labyrinthine mazes of major and minor propositions, syllogisms and sequences, nor do they bewilder themselves with the complex substitues of metaphysics. But give them the data, the facts, and mind and heart-faith and feeling conduct them at once, to the correct conclusion. And from the judgment thus formed, who dares enter an appeal? Cæsar disregarded the remonstrances of his wife, went to the Senate and fell at the hands of assassins. The world furnished but one, who had the judgment to discover the innocence, and the courage to interpose for the life of the rejected Nazarene. "Have thou nothing to do with that just man," said the wife of Pilate to the Governor. So long as these two transactions,—one recorded in sacred, and the other profane history remain, husbands at least, may well tremble to disregard the deliberate judgment of their wives, founded in wisdom and announced in love. Whatever the process may be,—intuition, inspiration or reason,—the fact is shown to be true, by observation, experience and history, that a womans' conclusions are seldom wrong. There is so much love—of hope and heart,—of faith and feeling, in her patriotism, that it is difficult to discover its source, define its extent, or measure its value. It is neither confined to periods nor occasions; it is an attribute of the sex,—distinguishing them always and everywhere. Its manifestations are multiform. They embrace her smiles and tears, her notes of warning and words of encouragement, and a thousand acts, undefined and undefinable, ranging, from the administration of cordial to a dying soldier, to the founding of an empire for the government of millions. It crops out in the material example and precept, in the family, the formation of communities, States and society; in its sympathy for the sorrowful and its ministrations to the suffering. History has embalmed in immortality, the name of Florence Nightingale; and yet thousands of American women, unknown to song, story and fame, have done all that she did. They have breathed the poison of hospitals and braved the slaughters of ensanguined fields to mitigate the pain of the wounded, and soothe the anguish of the dying.

The late war furnished a severe test of women's capabilities for doing. The resignation with which she submitted to privations, the cheerfulness with which she endured labor and the faith with which she offered her oblations, are testimonies of her patriotism. But her ministries did not cease with the war. Her liberality commemorates valor in monuments; and her affection, in the annual tribute of flowers and tears. The severest, the crucial test is found in what she suffers—what she bears. History records the deeds of men, the results of battles, the fame of heroes; and throws a glamour over the horrors of slaughter, and in their wild excitement they forget their fallen comrades; time mitigates their grief, and business engages their attention. But it is not so with the mothers of the land. Like those of "Cornelia" their sons were their jewels; and though they sent them with the heroism that immortalizes the Spartan Matron, yet the wounds are unhealed in the hearts from which they were torn; and in sorrow and silence they bear their grief and never complain.

The wives made widows by the war, have struggled on, toiling for bread to appease the hunger of helpless orphans; committing them in faith and in tears, to Him who hears the young ravens when they cry; and no history records their trials, and no one ever dreams that each moment wrings a burning blood-drop from a broken heart.

The maiden whose only love fills an unmarked soldier's grave, gently smiles in the festive throng, but the subdued sorrow of a languid eye, and the slightest palor of a sweet lip tell a story of anguish that would make the angels weep.

During the war our country-women passed around guards, against orders, crossed the lines without passports, and periled life without fear, to reach the objects of their love, and the recipients of their benefactions. No disappointments discouraged their efforts, no defeat chilled their ardor and no despair clouded their faith.

On a bright May day at Malmaison, the Empress of France and Queen of Italy, passed away. Whispering with her last breath, "Isle of Elba-Napoleon." A few years later by a singular felicity, the "man of Destiny" murmured back from the ocean-girded rock, his last words in response: "Head of the army, France-Josephine!"

Home—Country—Love!—the trinity that inspires patriotism in men and women living, and shrives them with sacred ministries, dying.

A gallant Admiral responded to the question, "Which is the most exciting moment of battle?" "the moment in which the deck is sprinkled with sand to catch the blood."

This college sends out, each year, her class of graduates, to enter upon the struggles of duty in the cruise of life; and these commencement ceremonies sprinkle the deck of the ship upon which they sail, with sand to catch the blood shed in the strife.

Young ladies of the college, and especially of the graduating class, allow me to congratulate you upon the completion of your college course, and upon your advent into society; and to say that your new relations involve important duties and grave responsibilities. Duty is the grandest word in the language of earth. It will levy its contributions upon your patience, courage, faith and hope. Its pathway leads to success, honor and happiness. It subdues enemies, overcomes temptations, triumphs in trial, and wins the guerdon at last. Your education is not completed; it is only commenced. The foundation is laid; it remains for you to erect and adorn the superstructure. I apprehend that no student ever left college a thorough scholar. All that the best institution proposes to do, is to develop and discipline the powers of the mind, train it in the proper methods of thought, and supply it the elementary principles and ascertained facts of science; and thus enable the student to complete the work of education.

Again allow me to remind you that an ardent attachment for kindred and race, for the institutions of home and country, does not meet the behests of your being and destiny. You remember the beautiful story of "Paradise and the Peri." The Angel who kept the gate of light, beheld the Peri weeping.

> "Nymph of a fair but erring line,
> He gently said, 'One hope is thine.'
> 'Tis written in the book of fate,
> The Peri yet may be forgiven,
> Who brings to Heaven's eternal gate,
> The gift that is most dear to Heaven.
> Go seek it, and redeem thy sin,
> 'Tis sweet to let the pardoned in."

Her first offering was liberty's last libation—a drop of patriot blood. This offering was rejected. Her next was the lover's dying sigh, but this moved not the crystal bar. She then presented the repentant sinner's tear and the gates moved ajar.

"And well the enraptured Peri knew,
Twas a bright smile the Angel threw,
From Heaven's gate to hail that tear,
Her harbinger of glory near."

The claims of religion are not met in love or patriotism; they can not be ignored with impunity, nor supplied by substitutes. Poetry regards woman an Angel, and Revelation represents her as fallen. Believing the truth of the one, and adopting the fancy of the other, I declare her, though fallen, an Angel still.

H. P. Bell.

CHAPTER XXXI.

Semi-Centennial Address.

DELIVERED AT THE COLLEGE CHAPEL, CUMMING, GA., SATURDAY EVENING, JULY 18TH, 1902, AT 7 O'CLOCK P. M.

Ladies and Gentlemen and My Brethren of LaFayette Lodge:

It has been characteristic of the human mind, in all the ages to mark by some expression of commemoration its appreciation of important events. At the National Capitol the highest shaft in the world honors the greatest man of history. We celebrate the birth of Constitutional Liberty by appropriate ceremonies on the Fourth of July, its natal day. We commemorate the great fact of the resurrection and the cherished truth of immortality by the festivities and worship, annually, of Easter.

In conformity with this custom of civilized people, LaFayette Lodge No. 44, of Free and Accepted Masonry, have thought proper by this occasion and these festivities to celebrate the semi-centennial of its existence. In my opinion it is wise to thus pause in life's pilgrimage, and retrospect the past, survey the present, and forecast, as far as practicable, the future.

In addition to this, the Worshipful Master has announced that this occasion of the commemoration of the fiftieth anniversary of the lodge's life, is intended as a personal compliment and expression of goodwill to your speaker, and a recognition of the length of his membership in the lodge, and his character and services in the community in which that fifty years have been spent.

Allow me, my dear brethren, to say to you that for this expression of your esteem and endorsement of my humble character and services, I give to you in return, the gratitude—the profoundest gratitude—of a heart that loves every one of you. I state the truth when I say that I would not exchange this expression of the love and confidence of my brethren, friends and neighbors

> "For all the wealth of every urn,
> In which unnumbered rubies burn."

I may be pardoned here for a personal reference. There is not a living soul in this town who was here when I came. There is not a living member of La-Fayette Lodge who belonged to it when I joined—not one. When I recur to the people of Cumming, old and young, fifty years ago, and remember with mournful pleasure the delightful associations of young life, the friendships formed in school, the festal joys of social life, and the sweet thrill of love's first young dream, and realize that the friends of those days—

> "Are all scattered like roses in bloom,
> Few to the bridal most to the toomb,

I feel like one who treads alone,
Some banquet hall deserted;
Whose beauty fled, whose garlands dead,
And all but me departed."

Fifty years—nearly twice the age of a generation. What changes! What momentous changes have been wrought in the last fifty years. What memories of joys and sorrows, of festal throngs and funeral crowds! Then, the graves were scattered over yonder on the hill, but now, they are as thick as" autumn leaves that strew the brook of Vallombrosa." Think of the changes affecting humanity in all departments of life, of human thought and endeavor, in the last fifty years. That dark continent of Africa has been explored and gone to Geography. That stupendous crime against humanity, the African Slave Trade, has been suppressed. The Empire of the Bourbons and Bonapartes has passed into the Republic of France. The South African Government has passed under the British Crown. The great Empire of Chas. V., which four hundred years ago dominated the earth, has surrendered its last inch of ground on the Western Hemisphere. The Iron Gate of the Orient has been unbolted, and Japan and China taken into the companionship of the mystic meshes of the telephone and telegraph, and the people of different and distant nations talk to each other as members of a family circle.

Engineering skill and enterprise has bored the granite base of the Alps, and scaled the dizzy heights of the Rockies, and the restless tides of trade and travel pour their rushing current under the one and over the other. The engine screams across the earth from Quebec to the Vancouvers and from St. Petersburg to Port Arthur, so that the globe is girded with railways and the ocean planted with telegraphs. Koch has discovered the microbe theory of human disease, and Pasteur a remedy for rabies, and Beatty, a Georgian, has achieved one of the most wonderful triumphs of surgery. The X-Ray makes visible the most opaque of solid bodies, and the genius of Edison has subjected electricity to the servitude of vision and machinery. All these in the last fifty years! And to these must be added a war engaging in arms three millions that reddened the earth and ocean in the blood of fratricidal strife, and struck the shackles from four millions of African slaves.

This is a world of transformation, of transmutation, of change, as well as progress. It is said that the human body changes every seven years, and that in each period of seven years an entirely new body is substituted. Change is constantly progressing in the human institutions, and in the form of the physical globe. Mountains sink and lakes appear on the land. Islands rise, and the waters recede into the ocean. But, my brethren, there are some things that do not change—never change. Truth never changes. Truth is as unchangeable as the God who ordained it. Unchangeable truth is found and taught in the symbols of Free Masonry. These truths are revealed by the Author of truth, and find expression in His word and law. The plumb teaches us precisely in accord with the Divine Revelation the obligation upon us to walk uprightly before God and man. "Mark the perfect man, and behold the upright, for the end of that man is peace." "Lord, who shall abide in thy tabernacle? Who shall dwell in thy holy hill? He that walketh uprightly, and worketh righteousness and speaketh the truth in his heart."

The level teaches us the natural equality of the race, its identity in the incidents to a common pilgrimage, from the cradle to the grave, that we are passing upon the same level to a common home and final assize.

The square is the emblem of virtue, and teaches us to measure with mechanical precision, our motives and actions by the rules of rectitude as prescribed by the provisions of law. The gavel admonishes us to break off from our conduct and character, the moral obliquities which impair moral symmetry and puts us out of harmony with moral rectitude. In practical or operative architecture, when the materials for a structure have been prepared and adjusted by the proper applications of the plumb, level, square and gavel, the trowel spreads the cement which unites the different parts into a whole, into strength and solidity, so that the building rises a thing of strength, symmetry and beauty. These simple, familiar implements are indispensable in practical or literal masonry. The simple, yet sublime, truths taught by them symbolically, are equally indispensable in adjusting and constructing human character. Contemplate the history of the race, marred and blurred by its record of wrongs, frauds, treacheries, injustice, oppression and slaughter—"in which man's inhumanity to man, makes countless thousands mourn"—

and contrast it with the ideal character of absolute perfection, illustrated and exemplified in the sinless life of the crucified Galilean, and say whether human nature and conduct do not need a vigorous application of all the tools that divest them of vices and polish them as fit stones for the everlasting temple.

"Poor ruined race, said the pitying spirit,
Dearly ye pay for the primal fall,
Some flowers of Eden ye still may inherit,
But the trail of the serpent is over them all."

Have men no passions to be subdued? No appetite to be controlled, no habits to be reformed, no hate to be overcome? No change or reformation of life to be made? Hate is hell, and hell is hate. Have we no favors to requite? No wrongs to forgive, no sorrows to solace, no assistance to render, no help to extend? If not, then we do not need the polishing of moral masonry.

Leigh Hunt, in his beautiful legend of Abou ben Adhem, illustrates this power of love so earnestly urged and strikingly symbolized in the trowel. An angel with a book appeared to ben Adhem, who asked what it contained. The angel replied, "The names of those who love God." "Is my name in the book," said ben Adhem. "It is not," replied the angel. "Then write my name as one who loves his brother," said ben Adhem. The next day the angel showed him the book, and lo! ben Adhem's name led all the rest.

My brethren, we do not know and do not appreciate

the privileges and value of that life which finds expression in helpfulness to others. True greatness consists in the unselfish service to others—

"He that hath soothed a widow's woe,
Or dried an orphan's tear, doth know—
There is something here of Heaven."

In this world of chance and change, of joy and sorrow, of trial and triumph, of strength and weakness, we have vast opportunities to do others good, with an infinitely small outlay of effort. And just in the proportion that we serve and help others, do we approximate the ideal type of real true life. The great God has so affiliated duty and pleasure, that the highest reward for helping others is the consciousness of having bestowed it, and with this consciousness is connected fearlessness to meet the adjudication of the final trial.

Every mason is confronted in his lodge with these symbols of truth, and upon the altar, with an open Bible containing God's revealed will and eternal law. Free masonry urges in all her teachings, conformity to that will and obedience to that law. Perfect and absolute compliance with the lessons of free masonry makes of a man all that can be made, except one thing. "By the deeds of the law no man can be justified." He is annealed in justification only in the blood of the crucified Nazarene, upon the condition of faith.

LaFayette Lodge has made up her record of half a

century. How does the record stand? If all right, it will stand forever. Have her members met all their obligations? Have her members lived up to her doctrines? Have they strengthened the weak, solaced the sorrowing, admonished the erring, visited the sick, fed the hungry, clothed the naked and buried the dead? If so, we have made the world better, and may claim the approval of Him who said: "Inasmuch as ye did it unto one of the least of these my brethren, ye did it unto me." If our record does not stand, if duties have been neglected, obligations violated, wrongs perpetrated, then the record is wrong and there is but one solution of it: Repentance for the past and improvement in the future.

No ken nor seer can lift the veil that conceals the next fifty years. It is safe to assume that there will be no member of LaFayette Lodge, now present, in life fifty years hence. Our pilgrimage will have ended, our privileges and opportunities to help others will have passed away, and our account and record will have been made up to confront us at the final Bar. Let these solemn truths incite us to aspirations for a higher plane of personal and masonic life, and vitalize us for redoubled effort in the faithful discharge of duty in all the relations of life.

Let us—each one—so live that when his feet shall brush the dews of Jordan's brink, he may gather "the drapery of his couch around him and lie down to pleasant dreams."

Appendix

In Second Confederate Congress.

Speech of the Hon. H. P. Bell, of Georgia, Delivered in the House of Representatives, in Secret Session, January 24, 1865, Against the Tax Bill Reported by the Chairman of the Committee of Ways and Means.

This bill proposed to continue in force the existing legislation imposing taxes, and to increase the amount of taxation one hundred per cent.

The House being in Committee of the whole, Mr. Sexton in the chair, Mr. Bell said:

Mr. Chairman: If I were to consult my own inclination, I should content myself with giving a silent vote against the bill now under consideration, but I do not feel that I could remain silent without a gross dereliction of duty to those who have confided to me the sacred trust of representing their views, their feelings and their interests upon this floor. The framers of the old Constitution denominated the taxing power, the vital part of the Constitution. The subject of taxation, always an important one, is now especially of vital concernment to the government, of difficult solution by Congress, and of deep and absorbing interest to the people. They have granted no right with more reluctance than the right to impose upon them the burdens of taxation, and have confined its exercise exclusively to agents or representatives of their own selection. The bill before the committee proposes to continue in force the existing legislation imposing taxes, and to increase the amount of the taxes one hundred per cent. upon all subjects of taxation, except upon agricultural products; but while it does not double the tithe, it repeals the law allowing the farmer or agriculturist to credit the tax upon property employed in agriculture with his tithe. The discussion, therefore, of this bill involves the consideration of our whole scheme of taxation as now established by law. And to the tax laws, as they now stand and as this bill proposes to continue them, I am invincibly opposed. And I mention as the first ground of my objection their *complexity.* It is not singular that the various acts upon this subject are of difficult comprehension, when we reflect upon the manner and circumstances under which they have been passed. Tax bills have originated with the Committee of Ways and Means: the views of different members of the committee have been various and conflicting; they have been modified and changed so as to harmonize them in order that a majority might be able to agree upon some sort of measure to be reported back to the House, where it encountered at the threshold, a greater contrariety of opinion and a multiplied number of amendments, involving increased antagonisms and incongruities; each member in the House proposes an amendment to carry out important views, which are often, not thoroughly digested, clearly defined, nor felicitously expressed; some are adopted; others rejected, and, ultimately, a sort of armistice is agreed on between belligerent opinions and rival propositions, and such a compromise, concluded as will harmonize a majority and secure the passage of a measure which, at last, entirely commands the approval of no one. Having thus passed the House, it is sent to the Senate, referred to the Finance Committee, reported back, where it passes through a similar process, and is subjected to the same legislative ordeal, resulting in the adoption by the Senate, of sundry amendments, in which the House refuses to concur, and finally becomes the subject-matter of discussion and settlement by a Conference Committee, where the same routine of conflict, amendment, agreement and compromise transpires, the result of which is a conglomerated jumble of legislative nonsense and folly. Enacted under these auspices, it is not remarkable that those who witnessed and participated in the throes of statesmanship in which our tax legislation had its birth do not understand the offspring of their own genius, and hence it becomes necessary to pass a multitude of explanatory statutes, and every additional act but increases the obscurity of the one it was intended to explain; it is but adding a deeper tint to the darkness of midnight. The tax laws thus originally incomprehensible and still more mystified by explanatory acts, pass from the laboratory of legislation into the crucible of construction; and if those who make the law do not know what it means, it is difficult to conceive how any one else can comprehend its meaning. If Congress, therefore, does not understand it, it can not reasonably be expected that the Secretary of the Treasury or the Commissioner of Taxes will be able to correctly construe and expound it. And although Mr. Memminger is an astute and able lawyer and Col. Allen both an able and faithful public officer, still the contradictory and absurd constructions of the

Treasury Department demonstrates that neither of these high and able functionaries knows what it means. To illustrate what I mean and prove the truth of what I say, it will be recollected that it was decided that under the Act of February 17, 1864, the tax of ten per cent. on profits had to be collected on merchandise bought *before* the first of January, 1863. Here is a solemn adjudication, an express official construction of the law. Subordinates acted in conformity to this decision, collected the people's money, and afterwards, the construction was overruled and the money collected under it had to be refunded. In one instance as much as twenty thousand dollars improperly collected, or rather collected under what was afterward held to be an erroneous interpretation, had to be paid back to the citizen by the collector. Again, it was decided that profits on produce made prior to 1863, but sold in 1863, was income of 1863. Here a distinct construction upon an important question involving the rights of the people, was deliberately made. Subsequent investigation satisfied the authorities that the law did not warrant the interpretation given, did not mean what they had held it to mean; the decision was reversed and it was declared that the profits were not liable to be taxed at all. It would seem that Mr. Memminger has either become bewildered in the arcana of this legislation or else he determined to depart from the usual and ordinary methods of ascertaining the meaning of the law, viz.: by exploring the intention of the legislator, etc., and draw upon the revellings of a disordered fancy and the inspirations of an erratic imagination to aid him in construing it. Under the Act of June 14, 1864, he construes the word family to include carriage, horses and to exclude a large class of slaves—and we have actually passed an act at the present session, gravely and wisely declaring that horses are *not* members of the family. And what is equally ludicrous, he held that shucks and straw, under another provision of the law, meant fodder. Shades of all the lexicographers! Who ever dreamed before that horses, under the magic of construction and the jugglery of departmental legerdemain could be transformed into members of the domestic circle. The expositions of these laws have increased their mystery and multiplied the difficulties of applying them; they have piled "Pelion upon Ossa," and made "confusion worse confounded," and as they now stand enacted by the legislature and expounded by the department, they defy the genius of interpretation. A compound subtlety in the abstrusities of metaphysics is the perfection of clearness and simplicity compared to their hidden enigmas; a blind man without a guide, in the gloom of midnight in the Mammoth Cave of Kentucky is surrounded with floods of noonday light, compared with the "unlucky wight" who undertakes to explore their labyrinthian mazes.

Sir, is it possible that Congress can not frame a law that can be understood? Or do you desire to keep the people in ignorance of the law by virtues of which the government thrusts its hands into their pockets and takes their money? I can hardly think that this legislation is the result of design; it is an illegitimate abortion of chance, the deformed progeny of a dwarfed statesmanship, and it ought not to be allowed to remain longer upon the statute book.

Mr. Chairman: This scheme of taxation is obnoxious to a still more formidable objection; this objection is based upon the inequality of its provisions, and therefore, the injustice of its operations. This inequality results mainly from the adoption of different bases of valuation for different species of property. Some property is estimated at the value of 1860, and therefore, estimated upon the specie value; other property is estimated at its value in currency at the time of assessment. Land and negroes are assessed at the value of 1860, which is the gold standard, and gold and foreign exchange are estimated in Confederate currency, and its value has been settled by the Treasury Department to be eighteen dollars in currency for one in gold or foreign exchange; therefore, the owners of gold and foreign exchange are taxed eighteen times as much as the owners of land and negroes. The injustice of this discrimination is too manifest to require serious argument to expose it.

Again, property purchased since 1862 is assessed upon neither the value in 1860, nor upon the value at the time of assessment, but upon the amount of the purchase-price. Why this basis has been adopted, ignoring the value of 1860, and the value at the time of assessment, simply because the property has changed ownership, I confess my inability to comprehend. The value of property in 1862 was probably double what it was in 1860, and perhaps half what it was in 1864 or 1865. If by adopting this mode of assessment it was intended to increase the taxes as a sort of punishment for purchasing it, it is simply an outrage. At all events, this mode of valuation is wholly indefensible upon any ground of sound logic or recognized political economy.

In further illustration of this ground of objection, it will be seen that railroad bonds and stocks, and Confederate bonds are taxed upon the amount due on their face. Here still another and different basis of assessment is adopted, and one that entirely ignores the question of value altogether. This principle of valuation is unequal and unjust for the reason that the railroad bonds are worth three or four times as much as the Confederate bonds; while the tax is assessed upon the amount specified in their face without regard to their value, the owner of the Confederate bonds pays three or four times as much up the *value* of his property as the holder of the railroad bonds.

The great difficulty upon this subject arises from the adoption of the value of 1860 as the basis of assessment. The value of property is constantly fluctuating in a revolution. In estimating it, time, place and circumstances, situation, etc., exert a controlling influence in regulating it. The value of the same kind and description of property is increased in one place while it is diminished in another. The proximity and depredations of the public enemy may have rendered it useless, and for this reason greatly diminished its value since 1860, while on the other hand many circumstances may have conspired to largely increase its value since 1860, and still the tax, under this arbitrary rule, is imposed upon the value of 1860, discarding the existing value at the time of assessment; when it is notorious that in one case the owner pays upon a value that does not exist and in the other he does not pay upon a value that does exist: or in other words, he pays precisely the same amount of taxes upon the diminished that he does upon the increased value. In the one case he pays too much, in the other he pays too little. When we survey the extent of country overrun by the enemy, and look at the amount of property that has thereby been diminished in value, while the property in those sections of the country not overrun has been largely increased in value, the monstrosity of this basis of assessment becomes apparent. What reason can exist for the perpetuation of a law, so palpably and manifestly unjust and inequitable in its operations? The people will apothesize among the tutelary divinities of their household worship the wisdom of that legislator who relieves them from the incubus of this wild and reckless legislation.

All the objections to the present scheme of taxation can be easily obviated by passing a bill predicated upon the ad valorem principle, simple in its terms, just in its provisions and equal in its operations. Such a measure shall receive my cordial support; under no circumstances will I vote for one of a different kind. I will neither share the glory nor divide the responsibility of those who adopt a burdensome, unequal and unjust system.

Again, I oppose the scheme of which the bill under consideration forms a part, on the grounds that it has been arraigned before the bar of an enlightened public opinion and received judgment of condemnation. The verdict of the people has been pronounced against it. I recognize the distinction drawn by Lord Mansfield between the voice of a virtuous and enlightened people and the clamor of a mob; and while I discard and contemn the latter, I yield implicit obedience to the behests of the former. The people want a plain, simple, equitable system of taxation, one that distributes its burdens equally and operates alike upon all classes of society. This is equality, and this they have a right to demand, and with nothing less, in my judgment will they be satisfied.

While I am satisfied that it is not true, yet it would seem that the government had exhausted its ingenuity in devising a system of measures to irritate, override and defy the popular sentiment of the country.

Sir, this government belongs to the people, they created it, and they are pouring out their blood and treasure with the profusion of a prodigal to establish and sustain it, and they have a right to shape its policy and control its legislation. The genius of our system of all representative government—is, that the government derives its just powers from the consent of the governed. You can not administer it upon principles antagonistic to the popular will in a time of peace, much less in the midst of a revolution inaugurated to establish and vindicate popular rights. The public will must have expression through the forms of law, or it will find it over the head of authority and in defiance of law. Our statesmanship has failed to comprehend the philosophy of the revolution. The government can not control public opinion in a free State nor in any form of government in a revolution; it can only guide and direct it. You may mount the phæton, seize the reins and guide the coursers, but you can do nothing more. It was the popular breath that bore Charles I. from the throne to the scaffold; it was the same irresistible power that carried Charles II. from exile to the throne. Cromwell did not create the revolution—the revolution created Cromwell, but he had the capacity and genius to guide it. And if you persist in forcing upon the people a line of policy and a system of measures to which they are hostile, you will drive them from the support of the government, and the revolution will result in disaster and failure. The bill now before the committee and our whole legislation upon the subject of taxation, is but a link in a chain of measures, the tendency of which is to alienate the affections of the people, destroy their interest and abate their enthusiasm in this struggle. They engaged in this war to secure and vindicate rights. They expected the protection of personal liberty, and received the suspension of the writ of habeas corpus; they looked for the preservation of personal security, and the country is filled with rapine and murder; they ask for the enjoyment of the rights of private property, and the land is ravaged with robbers and impressing officers, who sweep over the country like locusts, leaving poverty, want and desolation in their wake. They have "asked bread and you have given them a stone." The result of this policy is seen in the thinned ranks of your gallant army that desertion has depleted, and in the waning hopes and broken spirit of the noblest people on the earth.

Sir, you may pass this monstrous bill, but you will find it one thing to pass it and another to enforce it. The people are patient and patriotic, but they are now groaning under the burdens of heavy taxation, and I announce to you to-day that they can not and will not pay the amount imposed by this bill. It will remain a dead letter upon the statute book. They do not expect to get through the war without the payment of heavy taxes; this they are perfectly willing to do; but I have misconceived their character if they submit cheerfully to the wholesale robbery of this iniquitous bill. You have impressed their horses and mules and cattle and provisions, and taken from them the means of cultivating their farms. The enemy has overrun large tracts of country in other sections and stolen and carried them off. In many portions of the country the bulk of the male population is in the army and nobody is left at home to make the money with which to pay the taxes now required by law. This hour there are hundreds and thousands of pure and noble wives, mothers and sisters struggling to support helpless families, who are treading the frozen ground barefooted, with insufficient clothing to protect their persons from the chilling blasts of winter. The whole country is filled with aching heads, anguished bosoms, and bleeding hearts—with the weeds of widowhood and the wails of orphanage, and you propose to mitigate their sufferings, conciliate their affections and energize their patriotism by sticking to an irritated public feeling, like the shirt of Nessus, the exhausting provisions of this monstrous measure.

There are burdens necessarily incident to war, and it is a sacred duty that Congress owes to the people to mitigate their weight and severity as far as possible; to let them feel that the government respects their rights, appreciates their sacrifices and sympathizes with their sufferings. When this is done it will revive the hopes of the army and people, re-invigorate and re-inspirit them, and they will continue this struggle, until their patience and valor shall win a glorious independence for their country.

Sir, flings have been made at the fidelity of Georgia. That grand old commonwealth needs no vindication from me. In the language of a great statesman, on a great occasion, "I shall enter on no encomium upon Georgia. There she is, there is her history, the world knows it by heart." There is her Chicamauga, Ringgold, Resaca, Kennesaw, New Hope, Atlanta and Jonesboro, and there they will remain forever. Every foot of her soil from her northern border to the Atlantic coast has trembled under the consecrating seal of a baptism in blood. Her gallant sons have mingled their blood with the soil they died to defend, upon every battlefield from Gettysburg to the Rio Grande. Every altar liberty has erected in this struggle is red with Georgia's sacrificial libation. Her devotion to the imperishable principles of constitutional liberty and inalienable right of self-government has been illustrated by the self-sacrificing spirit and heroic suffering of her soldiers in the field and her people at home. I would institute no invidious comparisons between the contributions of Georgia and the other States to this revolution, but I state a historic fact, and challenge contradiction, when I assert that she has sent more men into the field and paid more money into the treasury than any other State in the sisterhood. You could not remain here in security twenty-four hours if you withdrew the bayonets that gleam around the national capital from her shattered battalions. She has entwined with the laurel that blooms on her brow, the cypress that symbolizes her sorrow. Fifty thousand of her martyred dead have been entered upon her roll of honor and embalmed in historic immortality.

> On fame's eternal camping-ground,
> Their silent tents are spread,
> And glory guards with solemn round
> The bivouacs of her dead.

Atlantic and Great Western Canal.

Speech of Hon. Hiram P. Bell, of Georgia, in the House of Representatives, February 14, 1874.

Mr. Speaker, the question of increased facilities for more and cheaper transportation is the great question to which the attention of Congress is now called by all classes and interests in every section of the Union. This question overshadows all others in its grandeur and magnitude. The public opinion of the country has exhausted all the forms of expression through which it could be heard in favor of the adoption of some means for its accomplishment. The press, public meetings, boards of trade, chambers of commerce, conventions of governors, of members of Congress, of States, and of the nation, and official reports of congressional committees, have all spoken the same language upon this subject without a single note of discord. They have all recognized its necessity and sought its solution. The mineral, mechanical, agricultural, commercial and manufacturing interests are all vitally interested in this great question. The representatives of the people can not, dare not, postpone favorable action upon it.

The rapid increase in the population and productions of the country has created the necessity for cheaper means of putting these productions upon a market that will facilitate the exchange of commodities, enhance the value of labor, and thus reward the toils of industry. Experience has demonstrated the inefficiency of railway transportation to meet the exigencies of the case; hence the public attention has been directed to the feasibility of opening waterways for commercial communication between the great valley of the Mississippi and the Atlantic Ocean. Among the various lines that have interposed their claims to favorable consideration, and pre-eminent among them in the superiority of its advantages, stands the Atlantic and Great Western Canal. Basing its claims upon the superiority of its advantages, it challenges the aid which I invoke from the Government for its construction.

The President, in his annual message to the second session of the Forty-second Congress, indicates his readiness to recommend Government aid to such enterprises as will cheapen transportation and facilitate the exchange of commercial commodities, whenever it is clearly shown that they are of "national interest, and when completed will be of a value commensurate with their cost.

Now, in regard to the Atlantic and Great Western Canal, I undertake to demonstrate the following propositions:

First. That it is feasible.

Secondly. That when completed it will be of a value commensurate with its cost.

Thirdly. That it is a work of national interest.

IT IS FEASIBLE.

If these propositions can be established, it follows that it is the duty, as well as the interest, of the Government, to aid its construction. Is the connection of the Mississippi and its affluents with the Atlantic Ocean feasible? Is it practicable? There are two infallible tests of truth, and but two. One is trial, experiment; this test is based upon the evidence of facts. The other infallible test is mathematical demonstration. Tried by both of these tests this enterprise is feasible beyond all doubt.

If the question were left to the speculations of mere theorists, reasonable doubts of its practicability might be safely entertained. But this is not left to the uncertainty of conjecture. The fact is that these highways of trade and transit have been constructed and successfully operated for centuries, increasing the wealth and ministering to the wants of individuals, cities, and nations. They are to-day great arteries through which commerce flows in China, Russia, the Netherlands, Italy, France, Great Britain, and the United States. The genius of DeLesseps has but recently astonished the world in mingling through the Suez Canal the waters of the classic sea that bore Cæsar and his fortunes with those which overwhelmed Pharaoh and his hosts; and thus revolutionized the commerce of the East, if not of the world. Without descending to particulars or referring to details, it may be stated as a historic fact that the feasibility of constructing canals and the utility of canal navigation stand demonstrated upon the evidence of trial and success.

But it may be said that this does not prove the feasibility of a particular canal—of the Atlantic and Great Western Canal. I reply that it unquestionably proves its feasibility, provided it can be shown that there are no physical, no engineering difficulties that render its construction impracticable. This question involves the other test of truth, mathematical demonstration. The proof has been furnished by the actual survey of the route by an able and accomplished engineer, Major McFarland, who reports that "there are no formidable engineering difficulties along the line." It had been supposed that the Sand Mountain presented a formidable difficulty to the construction of this work, yet an actual survey shows it to be perfectly practicable across that supposed barrier.

This engineer, in his report, says that—

"The engineer's survey shows two practicable routes across it, one passing up the valley of Short Creek, the other up the valley of Town Creek, on either of which an abundant supply of water for the service of the canal can be obtained during eight months of the year, while during the remaining four months, by resorting to the use of storage reservoirs, a sufficient supply may be obtained."

The feasibility of this route has been ascertained by precisely the same means that the practicability of all other canal routes has been ascertained, namely, by the actual survey of skilled engineers. It being established that it can be constructed, that there are no engineering difficulties in the way, let us inquire whether,

WHEN COMPLETED, IT WILL BE OF A VALUE COMMENSURATE WITH ITS COST.

The consideration of this proposition involves an examination into the cost of construction, the revenues it will yield when completed and the contribution it will make to the material wealth of the country. And here we enter upon no unexplored wilderness of speculation, or wild dream of fancy, but we are guided by the safe and steady light of experience. The engineer estimates the cost of opening this line of water communication from Guntersville, on the Tennessee River, to Brunswick, Georgia, on the Atlantic coast, suitable for barges carrying one hunlred and seventy tons during the low-water season and three hundred tons during the ordinary stages of water, upon a liberal basis, at $34,354,291, including river improvements.

The entire cost of the Erie Canal up to the 30th of September, 1862, was $38,977,831.16, which, with interest up to that date, amounted to $52,491,915.74; and after deducting expenses $12,518,860.03, there remained a net profit of $59,264,810.62, not only sufficient up to that time to pay the entire cost of construction with interest but leaving a balance or surplus of nearly $7,000,000 for the State of its gross earnings. Since the 30th of September, 1862, the net earnings were about $20,000,000 more. Since the completion of this great work, less than a half century, its income has paid the entire cost of construction and yielded a net profit of $27,000,000.

These facts furnish a safe basis for the calculation of the revenues which the Atlantic and Great Western Canal will yield when completed in the way of tolls. Indeed, all the advantages of cost of construction, distance of route, climatic obstructions, etc., are in favor of this, and against the Erie Canal.

The distinguished engineer, in his report referred to, says of this line, comparing its merits with the lake and canal, the James River and Kanawha, and the Mississippi routes, that—

"It may be said for it, that it enjoys every advantage possessed by the others; it is superior to them all in this, that it will never be obstructed by ice; will never be rendered impassable by drought; does not descend sufficiently low in the heated regions to have its cargoes injured by heat or moisture; will require no rehandling of cargoes between the points of shipment and discharge; and will cost but little more than the Erie Canal enlarged, while its capacity will be greater, and no doubt it will, like the Erie Canal, pay for the original outlay, interest, expenses of repair and service, with a large balance to its credit, in the course of thirty years."

Taking St. Louis as the great center of trade in the valley of the Mississippi, and the point from which Western products start in search for the Atlantic coast and a foreign market, the advantages of distance in favor of this line are as follows:

	Miles.
From St. Louis by lakes and Erie Canal to New York	1,950
From New York to Liverpool	3,150
Total distance	5,100
From St. Louis to New Orleans	1,270
From New Orleans to Liverpool	4,756
Total distance	6,026
From St. Louis to Savannah by proposed canal	1,508
From Savannah to Liverpool	3,390
Total distance	4,898

The distance in favor of the Atlantic and Great Western Canal against the lake and Erie route is 210 miles, and against the Mississippi, via New Orleans, is 1,136 miles, with a corresponding difference in favor of the Savannah, in the cost of transportation. Superadd the fact that this route is unobstructed by ice, while the Erie is annually obstructed for four or five months; and that no damage results to cargoes from climatic causes, as is the case with the Mississippi route, and the question of advantages between these lines, ceases to be debatable.

It is not my purpose, however, to disparage the claims of any route, but to show the superior advantages of the particular one whose claims to favorable consideration I am now urging. The necessities of the country demand the construction of every line that will develop our domestic commerce and secure an outlet to the ocean for our trade abroad.

If the Erie Canal has shown such results under these comparative disadvantages, what may we not safely expect from the Atlantic and Great Western, with the superior advantages which it possesses. To these may be added the greater necessity now for transportation than when the Erie was constructed. It developed and built up the commerce upon which it has fed. While the subduing of the wilderness and the honest industry of toiling millions have crowded the great valley of the Mississippi with a vast surplus, that wastes and rots while thousands in the East are perishing with famine, whose hunger our bounty could appease if we could but convey it to them. But it is not only in India that bread is needed—the exhausted States of the ruined South likewise want it.

The Committee on Commerce of the House of Representatives, in the second session of the Forty-second Congress, in their able report say that—

"The census of 1870 shows that Georgia, South Carolina, Alabama and Florida produce 57,215,600 bushels of grain. Their average consumption, according to data furnished by the Bureau of Statistics, is 104,521, 470 bushels. This leaves a deficit of 47,305,870 bushels to be supplied by other States. As the larger portion of this grain is needed along the seaboard, in what is known as the cotton belt, we may assume the distance from St. Louis to Savannah as the average distance this grain is moved. This would make the cost of transportation on each ton $14.40, at 1¼ cents per ton per mile. The cost for the same distance by this canal would be $4.88. This is a saving of $9.52 upon each ton, and an aggregate of $13,647,024.72 upon one article in a single year; the development of a latent value of nearly $14,000,000, to be divided between the producer and the consumer."

To state the case in other words, this canal would save to the producers of the West and the planters of the South in the transportation of corn alone for one year nearly $14,000,000; and this amount alone, for three years, would more than pay the cost of the canal. This single fact, undisputed and undisputable, demonstrates the value as well as the necessity of this great work.

IS THIS A WORK OF NATIONAL INTEREST?

Unquestionably it is. The development of the productive resources of the country, the increase of its wealth, and the expansion of its commerce, foreign and domestic, are all matters of national interest; and if these interests of the country are promoted by the construction of this highway of trade, then it is a work of national interest. Will it affect favorably the productive resources of the country?

Let us examine this question a moment.

The States of South Carolina, Georgia, Alabama and Florida are adapted to the production of cotton, while large portions of these States are not well adapted to the production of grain. The average yield of corn is less than ten dollars per acre, while the average yield of cotton is about forty dollars. It is of course to the interest of the farmers to cultivate cotton, because it yields a greater profit; it pays better than grain. But it is cheaper to raise grain than to purchase it even at a nominal price in the West, because of the expense of transporting it.

The Committee on Commerce, heretofore referred to, say that in those States—

"The scarcity of food and the high prices demanded for it force more than five million acres into grain. This takes away from the production of cotton about one-half of the labor and capital of the South. These acres planted in cotton would add two million five hundred thousand bales to our exports, and increase the value of the exports $200,000,000 annually, which would cause the wealth of the world to flow to us instead of away from us, as it has been doing in times past."

Statistics show the values of imports and exports for the eight months ending August 31, 1871, as follows:

Imports $408,503,331

Exports	389,242,497
Leaving against us	19,260,834

For the same period in 1872:

Imports	$479,924,793
Exports	391,920,267
Leaving balance against us	88,004,526

This balance, together with the interest on the foreign debt, must be paid in coin. Yet if this channel of trade were opened so that the planters in these four States of South Carolina, Georgia, Alabama and Florida could obtain their grain supplied from the West cheaper than they can make them on their exhausted lands, they could and would put these five million acres now in grain into cotton, and raise thereon two million five hundred thousand bales, contributing annually to our exports $200,000,000, which alone, in the year 1872, would have turned the tide of foreign trade in our favor to the extent of $112,000,000.

Cotton constitutes our most valuable export. The statistics show a most startling diminution in its production for the last year, which results from the necessity to diversify the crops in the cotton States. A corresponding diminution in our exports and a corresponding increase in the balance of trade against us necessarily ensue. If this state of things continues long, with the competition in the production of cotton, the foreign market will be mainly supplied from the East, and we will make but little, if any, more than will supply our own factories. How can this result be obviated?

It can only be done by reducing the cost of transportation, so that these cotton States can obtain their supplies of bread and meat from the crowded granaries of the West at a less cost than it requires to make them. Then the entire labor and capital of the cotton States will be directed to the production of cotton. The coin will be kept in the country, the West will be supplied with a market that will compensate labor, the currents of commerce will be stimulated, and the productive energies of the country vitalized.

The development of the resources of the country, of any element of wealth or power, in any State or section, assumes the importance and rises to the dignity of a national interest. The constantly multiplying wants of society have increased, and are increasing, the demand for two articles especially at a rate not hitherto known. I allude to iron and coal.

There is on the line of this proposed canal a region in which iron and coal are found, unsurpassed, if equalled, in the extent of its quantity or the superiority of its quality. This belt of iron-ore and coal lies at the eastern base of Lookout Mountain, and extends from near Chattanooga to the Coosa River at Gadsden in Alabama, a distance of about eighty miles. The superior quality of both the ore and coal has been shown by practical tests and scientific analyses. Boundless forests and exhaustless water power are in proximity to these great elements of national wealth, yet they are almost wholly valueless, practically, for the want of transportation.

The development of these interests would not antagonize the coal and iron interests of other sections of the country, because the demand for them is an ever-increasing one. On the contrary, similarity of interests identifies the different sections of the Union, harmonizes conflicting views of constitutional construction and administrative policy, and thus unites the different sections of the Union. It is a great mistake to suppose that because this great country is diversified in climate, soil and productions, therefore the interest of the different sections is antagonistic. This very diversity is the bond of unity. What one section has, another has not, and what one section does another does not, so that the producer, the manufacturer the merchant, and the common carrier are all mutually and relatively dependent on each other.

The country needs a statesmanship whose grasp comprehends the interests of all, and a patriotism whose ardor, ignoring local prejudices, embraces the entire Union.

I present another fact, showing the national importance of this waterway. It will give an outlet to the Atlantic Ocean, to sixteen thousand five hundred miles of inland navigation, embraced in the term "Mississippi and its tributaries," and will connect with it five thousand miles of similar navigation, penetrating every portion of four States, connecting with the Atlantic, thus distributing at home and pouring into the foreign market by the shortest and cheapest route the treasures of the most productive region on the globe, drained by twenty-one thousand, five hundred miles of inland navigation. The simple statement of these facts startles us with the stupendous magnitude and national grandeur of this enterprise.

With every element of wealth, surrounded with profusion and burdened with excess, we are starving at a banquet and famishing at a fountain.

The national debt amounts to $2,293,170,689.43, upon $1,712,749,200 of which we pay interest in coin. The revenues fail to meet current expenses on a peace basis. Commerce decaying; labor disorganized in the South, and unproductive in the West; starving freedmen imploring the Government to feed them upon rations issued from the War Department; finances deranged; factories running on half time, and thousands of operatives turned out of employment in the North; agrarian mobs and communistic associations clamoring for bread or blood in the cities; railroad magnates monopolizing the profits of industry, and money changers defiling the temple with a heartless idolatry at the shrine of mammon—this state of things must be changed. These evils must be corrected. If we would avert from the country the fearful crisis which the deadly conflict between capital and labor, already inaugurated, will precipitate upon us, we must provide channels for the distributions of the productions of the country, the expansion of its commerce, the development of its resources, and the reward of its labor.

How can the means be obtained?

The bill now pending provides them. Its passage, in my judgment, will secure the completion of this work in a short time, and without any liability to the Government except the use of its credit.

The bill provides that upon the completion of each section of ten miles, to be certified by an engineer under the direction of the War Department and approved by the Secretary of War, the Secretary of the Treasury is required to indorse said certificate upon the bonds of the company, not to exceed $80,000 per mile, the bonds to constitute a first mortgage upon the canal and all the property of the company. The bonds may be deposited with the Comptroller of the Currency, who shall thereupon issue to the company currency notes, not to exceed in amount the bonds deposited. As soon as the work is completed the company shall pay into the Treasury annually not less than 6 per cent. of the whole amount of the currency so issued for the redemption of said currency; and as the notes are redeemed the bonds shall be canceled. If the company fail to pay the 6 per cent. annually within thirty days after it becomes due, the Secretary of the Treasury may take possession of it and apply its earnings to the redemption of the currency.

This scheme will secure the means to open this line. It involves no danger to the Government; no taxes are to be imposed; no money to be borrowed, and no risks incurred.

The notes are not to be issued until ten miles of the work or line is completed, and upon that, and each consecutive ten miles, the certified bonds of the company will constitute a mortgage. The Government will be amply secured. It will pay no interest, and the company will pay no interest. The annual payment of the 6 per cent. will redeem the currency in sixteen years;

and if the company fail to pay it within thirty days after it becomes due the Government may take charge of it and apply its income to the redemption of the notes.

These notes would be distributed among the laboring class, men of small means, who greatly need it; and in a section where the circulation does not exceed two dollars *per capita,* and where the people are clamorous for an increase of currency. It would be placed beyond the control of bank and railroad monopolists; and thus open this great national highway of trade, and at the same time supply the people in the South and West, where they most need it, with money.

The necessity for the means of exchanging commercial commodities without absorbing the profits of labor, and a desire for relief from the dominion of extortioners and the monopoly of corporations, have united the honest, toiling masses of the country in the demand for legislative interposition. Nor will they cease until this demand meets with a response from their representatives. If we fail to respond they will fill our places with those who will. Already hundreds of thousands of patriotic men have sundered the ligaments that bind them to party, and united upon this question; and their voice comes up to this Capitol, like the roar of gathering waters, demanding a market unburdened by monopoly and extortion for the products of their labor.

These hardy farmers of the South and the great West demand something more than the repeal of the salary bill. They are for economy; but it is not that sort of economy that keeps up the expenses of thirty custom houses that yield no revenues to the Government; that sort of economy that expends annually millions of the public money in paving the streets and beautifying the grounds of this magnificent city while their homes are covered with mortgages. They want that sort of economy that equalizes the burdens and benefactions of the Government; that distributes its productions, husbands its resources, and develops its wealth.

Argument of Hon. H. P. Bell, of Georgia, Before the Senate Committee on Revolutionary Claims, April 27, 1874, *on the Bill to Refund to the State of Georgia the Sum of Thirty-five Thousand, Five Hundred and Fifty-five Dollars and Forty-two Cents, Expended by said State, for the Common Defense in 1777.*

Mr. Bell said:

Mr. Chairman and Gentlemen of the Committee:

The bill under consideration provides that the Federal Government shall refund to the State of Georgia the sum of thirty-five thousand, five hundred and fifty-five dollars and forty-two cents, which amount the State expended for the common cause of independence in the Revolutionary struggle in 1777. This debt was incurred for supplies purchased by the agents of the State from Robert Farquhar, a merchant of Charleston, South Carolina, for the troops, at Savannah, under the command of General James Jackson. These troops were engaged in the common struggle for independence, and utterly destitute of clothing. The debt was contracted for clothing. After the settlement of the accounts of Georgia with the general government, this account was audited by the auditing officers of the State and certificates of indebtedness issued for the sum of five thousand pounds sterling. Peter Trezvant married the daughter, and only child of Robert Farquhar, and by virtue of his marital rights became the heir-at-law of Robert Farquhar, and the legal owner of these certificates of indebtedness against the State. In 1838, while a resident of Great Britain, he memorialized the Legislature of the State, praying the payment of these certificates. The Legislature adopted the following preamble and resolution upon this subject, to wit:

"Whereas, several claims upon the State have been presented to the present session of the legislature, which claims have been dormant for many years; and whereas the policy of the State, as declared by the acts of past legislatures (which run nearly contemporaneous with their creation), has prevented the authorities thereof from discharging and paying the same; and inasmuch as it is impossible that the legislature can, through any of its committees, investigate the same during its session; and, public justice never requiring the refusal of a just debt nor the payment of one of such antiquated existence, without a due investigation of the same, to the end that justice may be done the claimants and the State—

"*Be it resolved by the Senate and House of Representatives in General Assembly met*, That his Excellency the Governor, appoint three fit and proper persons to investigate fully the claims of Peter Trezvant, R. M.

D. J. Elliott and Milledge Gaulphin, in behalf of himself and others, and that said persons report to the next session of the Legislature the *entire facts connected with the same, the liability of the State to pay them or any part of them, and whether interest is allowable upon the same, together with such facts, if any exist, showing the discharge of the State from such liability, and all other facts connected with each of said claims as shall be useful in determining their validity."* (Acts of 1838, page 276.)

Under this resolution, Joseph H. Lumpkin, William Law and David C. Campbell were appointed to discharge the duties which it imposed—gentlemen distinguished for their talents, their learning, and their virtues. They were charged with the duty of "reporting to the next session of the Legislaure the *entire* facts connected with the same, the liability of the State to pay the claim, or any part of the same, and whether interest was allowable upon the same, together with such facts, if any exist, showing the discharge of the State from liability, and all other facts connected with each of said claims as shall be useful in determining their validity."

It will be perceived that every question of law and fact involving the validity of this claim, and the liability of the State to pay it, was submitted to this commission. After a most searching, thorough and able investigation of the justice of the claim, the consideration upon which it was based, and the question as to whether it was barred by lapse of time, and at a time when the popular judgment and prejudice were opposed to the payment, they unanimously reported in favor of the justice of the claim and the obligation of the State to pay it. In their very elaborate report they say (I quote from the original manuscript report now before me), "we have, as we conceive, fully established that the certificates were rightfully issued—that they are genuine, and that they have never been paid."

Again: "The reasons which have now been assigned have brought us to the conclusion that the State is bound by every principle of honor and justice to redeem the certificates held by Mr. Trezvant."

Notwithstanding the thorough examination of the facts and legal questions involved, and the decided conviction and judgment in favor of the justice of this claim, and the obligation resting on the State to pay it, the Legislature hesitated for years, before making provision for its payment. Finally, pressed with the irresistible conviction of its justice, the Legislature, in 1847, passed an act, which was approved December 25 of that year, providing for the payment of the sum of twenty-two thousand two hundred and twenty-two dollars and twenty-two cents, being the original principal of the debt of five thousand pounds reduced to Federal money. And for this sum, the State issued her bonds bearing date on the first day of January, 1848, at six per cent. interest per annum. Those bonds were paid at maturity on the first of January, 1858, the principal and interest amounting to the sum of thirty-five thousand five hundred and fifty-five dollars and forty-two cents, which amount this bill provides the General Government shall refund to the State of Georgia.

The State presented her memorial to the Thirty-sixth Congress, praying the passage of an act refunding this amount to her. This memorial was referred in the Senate, to the Committee on Revolutionary Claims. After a careful examination of the claim the committee was unanimously of the opinion that the claim was just and ought to be paid, and unanimously reported a bill for that purpose. The bill was not reached on the calendar, and thus failed.

See Senate Report, No. 94, first session Thirty-sixth Congress.

See Senate Bill No. 231, first session Thirty-sixth Congress.

Senate Bills and Resolutions, Part 1 to 258.

The existence and justice of this claim, the consideration upon which it was based, the obligation of the State to pay it, and the payment by the State are all abundantly established by the report of the commissioners appointed by the Legislature to examine it, by the act of the Legislature providing for its payment, and by the report of the committee of the Senate, in 1860, to which reference has already been made.

Unquestionably the State of Georgia expended this sum in prosecuting the common struggle for independence in 1777. She now asks that it be paid back to her, as like indebtedness or expenditures of other States, all for the same purpose and in the common cause, have been repaid to them. This claim was not presented by the State, and, therefore, not allowed in the adjustment of the accounts between the Federal Government and the State, under the assumption act of 1790, because its justness was not admitted by the State at the time of the settlement. But after the settlement, in 1794, this claim was audited by the auditing officers of the State, the amount due ascertained, and certificates of indebtedness issued. It is supposed that the non-residence of Mr. Trezvant accounts for the delay in presenting it for payment. When presented, no means could be found to avoid the payment, except the repudiation of a just debt, which involved a violation of faith and a sacrifice of honor, for which the State was not prepared, and of which her patriotic people were incapable.

Shall the Federal Government reimburse the State?

Congress passed an act, which was approved August 5, 1790, by which the Federal Government assumed, and provided for the payment of all the debts of the several colonies, or States, incurred by them in the prosecution of the common cause, and appointed a commission to adjust the matters of account between the General Government and the several States, growing out of expenditures made in support of the war prosecuted by the colonies against Great Britain for the establishment and maintenance of our independence. Under this law the accounts were settled, the States being charged with the amounts advanced to them by the Colonial Congress, and credited with the amounts severally and respectively expended by them. It is believed that all the claims which the States, or any of them, held against the Government, so far as their existence was known and their validity recognized, were adjusted. The validity of this debt was not admitted, if its existence was known, until after the settlement between the States and the United States. Indeed, the validity of this claim against the State was never fully recognized by the State until the passage of the act providing for its payment, approved December 25, 1847.

Certainly the State would not have been justified in presenting to the Federal Government, for payment a claim, the justice and validity of which she did not admit; and the fact that the claim was either unknown, or disputed was a sufficient reason why it was not or should not have been presented for payment, by the State, in her settlement with the Government of the United States.

The act of Congress of August 5, 1790, established and settled the policy of the Government in the assumption of the debts incurred by the several States on account of the common cause of independence. It has been the policy of Congress to provide for the payment of such debts, where they existed, as were not included in the settlement between the several States and the general Government. I refer to an instance illustrating the truth of this proposition. A short time before the close of the Revolutionary War, the State of Virginia enlisted a number of troops to serve during the war with the express stipulation that if they served out the term of their enlistment they were to receive full pay, and if they were not called into service, they should receive half pay. The surrender at Yorktown closed the war before these troops were called into the service. The officers and privates claimed, under the stipulation, their half pay. Virginia declined to pay, on the ground that no service had been rendered. This claim was in existence at the time the accounts of Virginia with the General Government were settled. They were not included in the settlement. Afterwards Virginia opened her courts and allowed the claimants to test the validity of their demand. Suits were instituted and judgments were rendered in favor of the claimants against the State.

Congress passed an act in 1848, which provided for the repayment to Virginia of the sums thus recovered. This provision is contained in an appropriation act, and is in the following words: "For repayment to Virginia of money paid by that State, under judgment of her courts against her, to Revolutionary officers and soldiers and their representatives, for half pay and commutation of half pay, a sum not exceeding eighty-one thousand, one hundred and seventy-three dollars and seventeen cents, provided, however, that the agent of said State shall deposit authenticated copies of the acts or judgments under which the money was paid by the State of Virginia."

Georgia, like Virginia, denied her liability to pay this claim. Virginia opened her courts to the claimants against her, who instituted suits, and recovered judgments. Georgia referred the claim against her to commissioners, whose investigation and report established the justice of this claim, and her Legislature passed an act providing for its payment. Virginia paid the claim against her, and Congress pased an act to repay the amount to Virginia. Georgia paid the claim against her, and asks Congress to repay—to do that justice to her which was done to Virginia. If it was the duty of the General Government to pay Virginia, why is not also the duty of the Government to pay Georgia? The debts were contracted by the States in both cases for the same purpose—the public defense. In the case of Virginia the debt was paid for service which was never rendered. In the case of Georgia the debt was contracted and paid by the State for clothing, for her troops while actually engaged in the service. There can, therefore, be no question of the justice of this claim or the liability of the Federal Government to pay it.

Louisiana.

Speech of Hon. Hiram P. Bell, of Georgia, in the House of Representatives, February 10, 1875.

The House being in Committee of the Whole on the President's annual message.

Mr. Bell said:

Mr. Speaker, the people of this country were startled at the announcement of the events that transpired on the 4th day of January, 1875, at the capital of the State of Louisiana. On that day, at that place, in a time of peace, the soldiers of the United States Army, with fixed bayonets, entered the capitol of the sovereign State of Louisiana and broke up and dispersed by armed force the representative branch of her General Assembly. This outrageous act of tyranny and military despotism was committed upon the order of the person who claimed to be the governor of the State, and was approved by the President of the United States and his Cabinet ministers.

The sole pretext for this high-handed usurpation was that in the opinion of William Pitt Kellogg, the House of Representatives was an illegal assembly. The members were chosen by the electors of Louisiana at the time and place and in the manner prescribed by law. The House of Representatives had assembled at the time and place fixed by law for the meeting of the Legislature under a written constitution, which provides, among other things, that—each House of the General Assembly shall judge of the qualification, election, and return of its members.

The returning board failed to pass upon the election of five persons claiming to have been chosen, and expressly referred the question of their election to the House of Representatives. The House, in the exercise of a plain, constitutional right, adjudged that they were entitled to seats, and adopted a resolution seating them as members, subject of course to any contest that might be filed. And this is the ground of alleged illegality upon which Kellogg based his order or request to the military to dispose of the House. What law made Kellogg the judge of the qualification, election, and return of the members of the House of Representatives? The constitution of Louisiana made the House itself the judge of that question; and the assumption on the part of Kellogg to determine the question of who were or who were not qualified, elected, and returned as members was a plain and palpable violation of the Constitution which he had sworn to support. Claiming to be the chief magistrate of a great State, the guardian of her rights and the defender of her Constitution, he tramples that Constitution into the dust at the expense of his official oath, and sacrifices the rights and liberties of the people to personal aggrandizement and party supremacy, and thus embalms himself in historic infamy as a usurper and a tyrant. There are none so stupid as not to know that Kellogg invoked the arm of military power to disperse the House of Representatives, not because it was illegal, not because the five members were improperly admitted, but because a majority of the members were not in political sympathy with him and the party with which he is allied, and of which he is the fit representative and exponent in the South. The incipient step, therefore, in all this trouble on the 4th of January was a usurpation. The whole difficulty arose from the claim of that burlesque, upon the idea of a governor to judge of the qualification, election, and return of the members of the House of Representatives, a right which the Constitution secured to the House itself, and a right about which there could not possibly be any doubt.

The American people begin to understand, and history will faithfully record, the extent to which the irrepressible carpet-bagger has exhausted Southern patience and fatigued Southern indignation. And by whom was this judgment of illegality pronounced? By a man who held the office of governor by virtue of an order issued ex parte at the dark hour of midnight by a judge who resigned to avoid impeachment by his own party, for granting that order, upon the ground that he had no jurisdiction in the matter. If Durell had no right to grant the order, for the want of jurisdiction, that practically kept Kellogg in office, then the judgment was a nullity and Kellogg took nothing by it. If Kellogg held the office by virtue of a popular election, and in accordance with the popular will, why was it necessary for a corrupt judge to draggle the judicial ermine in the mire of party politics to sustain him?

The next step in this drama of usurpation and outrage was the invasion and dispersion of the House of Representatives by armed Federal soldiers, supplied by the Federal Government upon the application of Kellogg. The ground upon which this interference is based is not that there was an invasion of Louisiana, not that domestic violence existed, but that in his opinion the House of Representatives was an illegal assembly. And the Federal authorities coincided in judgment with Kellogg and granted his request, dispersed the representatives chosen by the people according to the Constitution and laws of Louisiana, and installed in power those whom the people had rejected but whom the returning board, by the most stupendous fraud, declared to have been elected. But concede that it was an illegal assembly; concede that the five men sworn in as members under the resolution of the House were improperly, were illegally admitted; what law constituted either Kellogg or the armed military the judge of the qualification, election, and return of these members? What constitution authorized them, or what law, State or Federal, authorized them to break up and destroy one branch of the General Assembly of a State of the

American Union? Whether the House of Representatives was an illegal assembly or not is not the question. But the question is, by virtue of what authority the Federal Government took it upon itself to judge of the legality of the assembly, and by virtue of what authority of law the Federal Government enforced with the relentless arm of military power the judgment which it pronounced adverse to its legality. These are the questions which the law-abiding and liberty-loving people of the United States, in a thousand forms and through a thousand instrumentalities, are pressing with the earnestness of alarm upon the Chief Magistrate and his constitutional advisers. Failing to show the authority demanded, the act stands a naked usurpation.

Is there no cause for alarm when the Chief Magistrate of the Republic, clothed by law with vast power and patronage, the chief of a powerful party, distinguished for military prowess and achievements, destroys by the fiat of power the Legislature of a State and strikes down at one blow the constitutional liberty of the people?

The question still recurs, by what authority of law can this interference be justified? Section 4 of article 4 of the Constitution is invoked in vain for this purpose. It provides: That the United States shall guarantee to every State in this Union a Republican form of government, and shall protect each of them against invasion, and on application of the Legislature, or of the executive,when the Legislature can not be convened against domestic violence.

This section neither binds nor authorizes the President of the United States to guarantee to each State a Republican form of government. The usurpation of this power by a Republican President was one of the grounds of impeachment alleged against him by a Republican House of Representatives.

In the case of Luther *vs.* Bonlen Chief Justice Taney said: It rests with Congress to decide what government is the established one in a State; for as the United States guarantees to each State a Republican form of government, Congress must necessarily decide what government is established in the State before it can determine whether it is Republican or not, and when the Senators and Representatives are admitted into the councils of the Union, the authority of the government under which they are appointed, as well as its Republican character, is recognized by the proper constitutional authority, and its decision is binding on every other department of the government, and could not be questioned in a judicial tribunal.

But no question is made upon the form of the government of Louisiana. All concede that her government was Republican in form. If the question were involved, Congress and not the President would be the judge. Does the provision of the section under consideration, which guarantees to each State protection against invasion and domestic violence, justify the dispersion of the House of Representatives by the armed military? Unquestionably not, because there was no invasion and no domestic violence, and for the additional reason that the Legislature must make the call, if it can be convened. The Legislature was convened, and did not make the application for the interposition of the military. The state of facts upon which alone the governor was authorized to call for Federal assistance did not exist. This call for Federal troops was made by Kellogg when the Legislature could have been convened, when it was actually convened, and for that reason Kellogg had no constitutional right to make it, nor any other power except the Legislature. The application of Kellogg was itself a violation of the Constitution. It was the exercise of a power which depended upon the happening of a contingency, when the contingency upon which the right attacked had not happened.

Again, domestic violence did not exist in New Orleans at the time. If it is said that white men were armed, or that white-leaguers were armed, the reply is that the Constitution protects white men and white-leaguers in the right to keep and bear arms. And the truth is that they were compelled to bear them in New Orleans to prevent the armed police from stealing them.

The exercise of a constitutional right by the people of Louisiana, or any other State, can not justify the dispersion and destruction of the House of Representatives by armed power.

The American people thoroughly understand the reason why Kellogg appealed to force, and the alacrity with which the force was supplied, and the vigor and promptness with which it was used. It was not to protect the State against domestic violence, because domestic violence did not exist, in the sense in which that term is used in the Constitution. The expulsion of a legal, and the induction of a fraudulent House of Representatives was not protection against domestic violence. The plea of domestic violence is a pretext, a sham. The aid of the Federal arm was invoked to dissolve the House of Representatives because that house was adverse to Kellogg in political sentiments and party affiliation. It was invoked to maintain a government that did not derive its powers from the consent of the governed. It was invoked to maintain a usurpation, in defiance of the popular will, originating in fraud and upheld by the midnight order in chancery of a judge driven to resign by an impending impeachment, and a government that is still maintained by the unconstitutional interference of armed Federal power.

I have characterized Kellog as a pretended governor, and I have the very highest official authority for insisting that he is not and never was the rightful governor of Louisiana. The President of the United States, in his special message to the Senate upon the question of Kellogg's election, says:

"It has been bitterly and persistently alleged that Kellogg was not elected. Whether he was or not is not altogether certain, nor is it any more certain that his competitor, McEnery, was chosen. The election was a gigantic fraud, and there are no reliable returns of the result."

The President's recognition of Kellogg as the governor is not based upon the fact of his election, for the election under which he claims to have been chosen is pronounced to be a gigantic fraud. And it is expressly declared that there are no reliable returns of the result of that election.

From these two facts it would seem to be impossible that Kellogg should be the governor. If the election was a gigantic fraud, then nobody was elected. Fraud vitiates elections as well as contracts. No person ever did or ever can rightfully exercise the functions of an elective office when the election itself is a gigantic fraud. The President says that "there were no reliable returns of the result." Then there is no evidence of his election; because the only legal evidence of his election is reliable returns of the result, and that evidence the President declares does not exist. The presidential recognition is based upon the ground that "Kellog obtains possession of the office, and in his opinion had more right to it than McEnery." But how did Kellogg obtain possession of the office? By reliable returns of the result of the election, the only way in which he could rightfully obtain it? Not at all; but virtually and practically by the midnight *ex parte* order of a Federal judge, who was compelled to resign to avoid impeachment by a Republican House because he granted that illegal order in the exercise of a usurped jurisdiction. And this is the governor who appealed to bayonets to determine a question that the Constitution of Louisiana declares the House of Representatives shall decide!

The Constitution of a sovereign State of this Union has been trampled into the dust in the capital of that State beneath the ruthless tread of an armed soldiery, and the patriotic citizens of the Republic, East, West,

North and South, in alarm demand to know by what authority of law the deed was done, and with united voice and earnest hearts they press the question. The leaders of the Republican party have shrewdly attempted to divert the public attention from this thrilling inquiry by the oft-repeated and threadbare cry of outrages, proscription, murder, and insecurity of life and property in the South. Is this a manly meeting of the issue? Do they suppose that the American people will accept this old story, repeated a thousand times and as often refuted, as a justification of this wrong done to Louisiana? Crimes always have been and always will be perpetrated by all classes in every form of government and in every type of civilization. Lawlessness, crime, and bloodshed exist to a greater or less extent in every State in the Union. This is to be deplored; it can not be prevented; it can only be punished. If crimes are not punished in the States of Louisiana and Mississippi, who are to blame for it? The Republican party has had control of these State governments in all their departments, executive, legislative and judicial, ever since they were reconstructed; whether rightfully or by usurpation, they have had control. Why has crime not been punished? Why is the judicial arm of those States under the domination of the colored Republican officials? Why does it not afford protection? The admission that crime can not be punished is a confession that the Republican party is incapable of governing in those States at least. In every State under Democratic rule and government in the South, crime is punished, rights are protected, law enforced, and peace and order assured. This difference does not arise from a difference in the people to be governed, but from the difference in the capabilities and methods of those who govern.

Everybody knows that the lamentable state of affairs in Louisiana has resulted from the efforts made to secure power and plunder by the miserable rival factions of the Republican party, headed respectively by Warmoth and Kellogg. Yet this wretched abortion of a State government, brought into being at the dark hour of midnight by the order in chancery of a judge then drunk and since abhorred, confessedly unable to protect life or punish crime, is the government which Federal soldiers overthrew the Constitution of Louisiana to perpetuate over a people that have the right to be free. What agency General Sheridan had in this affair does not appear. The President informs us that he—

"Requested him to go to Louisiana to observe and report the situation there, and if in his opinion necessary, to assume the command; which he did on the 4th instant, after the legislative disturbance had occurred, at nine o'clock p. m., a number of hours after the disturbance."

Whether he was sent down with the view of hurting somebody we are left to conjecture. It is clear he was on the ground at the time, and deemed it necessary to assume command and "report." He reports as follows:

"W. W. Belknap,

"Secretary of War, Washington, D. C.

"I think that the terrorism now existing in Louisiana, Mississippi and Arkansas could be entirely removed and confidence and fair dealing established by the arrest and trial of the ringleaders of the armed White League. If Congress would pass a bill declaring them banditti, they could be tried by a military commission. The ringleaders of this banditti, who murdered men here on the 14th of last September, and also more recently at Vicksburg, Mississippi, should, in justice to law and order and the peace and prosperity of this Southern part of the country, be punished. It is possible that if the President would issue a proclamation declaring them banditti no further action need be taken except that which would devolve upon me.

"P. H. SHERIDAN,

"Lieutenant-General United States Army."

To which report the Secretary of War replied:

"Your telegrams all received. The President and all of us have full confidence and thoroughly approve your course."

The simple proposition in this suggestion is that Congress suspend the writ of habeas corpus in Louisiana, Mississippi and Arkansas, and turn the destinies, rights, liberties and life of the citizens of these States, in a time of peace, over to the tender mercies of a military commission appointed by General Sheridan. But reflecting that Congress might not see it in that light, and might still have some little regard for the Constitution and the liberties of the people, he recommends a shorter and more summary method of disposing of the white citizens of three States:

"Let the President issue a proclamation declaring

them banditti, and no further action need be taken except that which would devolve upon me."

That would settle the question truly. That would put a quietus to strife; that would protect law and suppress terrorism; that would give peace to these States; the peace that Hastings gave to Hindostan; the peace that Austria gave to Hungary; the peace that Russia gave to Poland—*the peace of death.* Yet this advice is given by the second officer in rank in the United States Army, coolly, deliberately, in a time of peace, to the Republican President of the United States, and the lightning flashes back the presidential expression of confidence and approval. And all this under a Government whose written Constitution declares that the privilege of the writ of habeas corpus shall not be suspended unless when in cases of rebellion or invasion the public safety may require.

Mr. Speaker, it is singular that so much horror is manifested at the White Leagues of the South and none against the black leagues. It is notorious that almost the entire body of colored voters in the South are members of oath-bound leagues, meetings in darkness, and many of them armed and incited to the most deadly hostility to white men by bad men of the Republican party for selfish partisan ends. But no words of complaint or rebuke escapes Republican lips, no Republican press teems with denunciation of them, and no arm of Federal power is bared for their suppression.

The midnight heavens blush in redness with the flamess of burning dwellings and gin-houses in South Carolina, and the lieutenant-general of the army advises no suspension of the writ of habeas corpus that he may summarily try the incendiary and punish the arson. Why is this? Is it because the turpitude of crime consists in the color of the perpetrator; or is it because it is done by those who maintain a negro despotism over the people of that suffering State? Why is there no condemnation of the black leaguers in the South? Is it because they were organized by adventurers in the interest of the Republican party that they are not condemned?

Why are not the armed organizations and hostile demonstrations of the negroes in the South denounced? It was this state of affairs that created the necessity for White League organizations. It is because the negroes have been armed and incited to hostility to the whites by Republicans to secure power and plunder in defiance of the popular will. This denunciation of the White Leagues, this cry of lawlessness and insecurity of life and property is raised to evade the issue and divert the public attention from the true, the vital question involved. That question is by virtue of what authority of law the armed soldiers of the United States dispersed the House of Representatives of the State of Louisiana. It is no answer to this question to say that lawlessness, violence and intimidation exist in Louisiana. This is the answer of the lieutenant-general of the army. Three bishops of different branches of the Christian church, and the pastor of the synagogue caveat the truth of the allegation in these words:

"We, the undersigned, believe it our duty to proclaim to the whole American people that these charges are unmerited, unfounded and erroneous, and can have no other effect than that of serving the interest of corrupt politicians who are at this moment using the most extreme efforts to perpetuate their power over the State of Louisiana."

I do not care to discuss the issue of fact thus joined. But I will be allowed to state that the very able report of the committee of this House, a majority of whom are distinguished Republicans, explicitly and unequivocally sustains the bishops and contradicts the general. But admit that disorders exist in Louisiana; who is responsible for them? If crime is unpunished; if life and property are insecure; if business is deranged and ruined; if property is depreciated in value; if taxation amounts to confiscation, in the language of your committee, and if the people are discontented, who is responsible for it all? This deplorable state of affairs is the legitimate result of the misrule of rival Republican factions utterly unworthy of public confidence and wholly incapable of securing the objects for which government was instituted. And it was to sustain those in power, thus unworthy, thus incapable, and of whose election there were no reliable returns, that the Federal soldiers broke up the House of Representatives.

It is the duty of the State government to punish crime, to enforce law, and to protect right. And that government that fails in these objects, fails to execute the high trusts with which government is invested for the public good. In the State of Georgia, under Republican rule, crime was not punished; but it is due to the courts of that State to say that it was no fault of theirs.

A Republican governor, himself a fugitive from justice, pardoned the most outrageous cases of murder, both before and after conviction, and in many cases after convictions had been affirmed by the Supreme Court. The corruption of the executive palsied the arm of the judiciary, and the criminal went free.

It is true, and the people of this country know that it is true, that crime is punished, right protected, and order maintained in every Southern State in which the Democracy is in authority. Why? Because Democrats have been placed in power by the popular will. The people govern themselves. If disorder exists in Louisiana, Mississippi, and Arkansas, they were produced by the struggle for power by rival Republican factions in Louisiana and Arkansas, and by a carpet-bag, negro government in Mississippi that was incapable of discharging the functions of government.

I can not relieve my mind from the conviction that there is "method in all this madness." I think that Kellog disclosed the secret, when, in his communication to the President at Long Branch of August the 19th he despondingly says that Louisiana is now the last State in the southwest, except Mississippi, that remains true to the Republican party. It would seem, then, that the supremacy of the Republican party after all was the great question. If Louisiana remains true to the Republican party, why is not the Republican party able to govern Louisiana?

A distinguished leader in that party in high official power says, speaking of the Southern people:

"What they want is to be let alone, and then they will take possession of Louisiana, and they will take possession of Mississippi in the same way, and they will take possession of Florida in the same way, and they will take possession of South Carolina in the same way, and thus they intend to secure a solid Democratic South."

Can it be possible! Is it credible that peace, quiet, law, and order in these States are to be sacrificed to party supremacy; and still who doubts it?

It is boldly proclaimed by one of the first men in ability and position in the Republican party that if the white people of the South are let alone it will secure a solid Democratic South. And that is literally true. If let alone by the Federal Government, if left to exercise the constitutional right of local self-government, there would soon be a solid Democratic South. This is the reason why the Federal soldiers did not let Louisiana alone. When let alone, the people are opposed to usurpation; when let alone, they are in favor of the subordination of the military to the civil authority; when let alone, they are capable of punishing crime, of preserving peace, and of enforcing law.

The trouble with Louisiana has been that she was not let alone.

Massachusetts, New York, Pennsylvania, Ohio, Indiana, and other States were let alone, and they recently went solidly Democratic. And leave the South alone, and every State will soon be solidly Democratic. This is the reason why the armed soldiery of the United States did not let the House of Representatives of Louisiana alone. It was, if let alone, Democratic. It may soon become necessary to apply the method adopted in Louisiana to Massachusetts and New York. It is a very effective way to convert Democratic States into military despotisms. But just now a universal demand comes up from the people to be let alone. They are honest, they are capable, they are patriotic, and when let alone they will maintain public liberty, they will preserve free institutions, and will transmit unimpaired to posterity the blood-bought heritage of constitutional government. The complaint they make is that they are not let alone; that the armed soldiers of the United States determined a question by force which under the Constitution the House of Representatives alone had the right to determine. Our fathers intended that they should be let alone in the exercise of those rights which were not expressly delegated to the Federal Government; hence they said in article 9 of amendments to the Constitution that—

The enumeration in the Constitution, of certain rights shall not be construed to deny or disparage others retained by the people.

And in article 10 of the same amendment that—

The powers not delegated to the United States by the Constitution, nor prohibited by it to the States, are reserved to the States respectively, or to the people.

The people of this country have the right to be let alone in the exercise of all the rights and powers which were not surrendered by them in the Constitution to the Federal Government, and this is the difference between the creeds of the Democratic and Republican parties. The Democratic doctrine is the freedom of the people to exercise those rights of local self-government not surrendered in the Constitution to the Federal Government; while the Republican party maintains the supremacy of the Federal authority over the local affairs of the States, even to the installation and maintenance in power of a governor never elected and the dispersion of a House of Representatives duly elected, and that this power may be rightfully exercised by the executive through the arm of the military. This issue is fairly and squarely made. Louisiana is the illustration. It can not be evaded. This usurpation must be sustained or repudiated. If sustained, constitutional liberty in this country is dead; if repudiated, the supremacy of the Republican party is ended. It remains for the American people to decide it. No graver question ever engaged the attention of any people or the deliberations of any assembly, the number of public meetings throughout the country shows with what intense anxiety the great heart of the American people throbs at its contemplation.

This question of usurpation can not be answered by charges of treason and rebellion in the late deplorable war. That national calamity is past. The issue it involved was submitted to the arbitrament of the sword, and the award was against the South. The people of that section accept the situation and abide the result. They pressed their bleeding lips to the oath of allegiance which you presented, and repledged their fidelity to the

Constitution and the Union. By that pledge they stand, and in its maintenance they would perish. The brave men of the South will defend the flag of the Union with the same heroism that they bore it on the bloody hillsides of Buena Vista and Cerro Gordo. But they want liberty with the Union. They re-echo the immortal sentiment of New England's greatest statesman, "Liberty and Union, now and forever, one and inseparable."

When the people of this great Republic meet at the approaching centennial, they want no State crushed beneath the iron heel of military despotism, bound by the cruel chains of slavery, bleeding in the dust from wounds inflicted by Federal bayonets. They wish to meet the people of this country on that occasion from the East, North, and West as brethren, identified in interest, sharing the same hopes, animated by the same patriotism, and involved in a common destiny, and in the spirit of magnanimity and fraternity forget and forgive the bitter and unfortunate past; and drawing inspiration from the spirit of our fathers, on that hallowed ground, rekindle on the altar of a common country the flame of freedom. The institutions of this country can not be perpetuated by force. They rest for support upon the hearts and affections of the American people. Then let justice be done to suffering, down-trodden Louisiana. Let the Federal soldiers be withdrawn from her soil; leave her ruined yet patient people to govern themselves. And let us inaugurate an era of equality among the States and of devotion to the Constitution;

an era of peace, of justice, of friendship. And let us maintain and transmit to posterity unimpaired the sacred trust of free institutions and constitutional liberty secured to us by the heroism and blood of our fathers.

SPEECH.

Delivered in the House of Representatives, November 14, 1877.

Speech of Hon. H. P. Bell, of Georgia, in Support of the Bill Reported by Mr. Ewing from the Committee on Banking and Currency to Repeal an Act Entitled an Act to Resume Specie Payment.

The bill for the repeal of the resumption clause being under consideration—

Mr. Bell said:

Mr. Speaker, on the 14th day of January, 1875, the act known as the resumption act was approved. *It* originated in the Senate and was passed in the House of Representatives under the operation of the previous question. No debate was had upon the bill in the House and no opportunity for debate allowed by those who had the matter in charge. After testing the wisdom of this law by its practical operation, a large portion of the American people have arrived at the conclusion that at least that provision of the third section which relates to the redemption in coin of the United States legal-tender notes should be repealed. A majority of the Committee on Banking and Currency, acting in obedience to what was supposed to be popular will, as well as in conformity with the convictions of their own judgment, reported, at the first opportunity, the bill under consideration for that purpose. The question thus raised, though simple in its statement, involves, in anything like an extended discussion of it, the consideration of every material interest in this great country. If I were capable of so doing, I should not attempt an elaborate discussion of all the questions of interest that legitimately belong to it. I shall, therefore content myself with a brief statement of the reasons which induce those whose interest and opinions I represent to desire the passage of the bill as well as those which control my own judgment in supporting it.

I submit and undertake to maintain the following propositions:

First. That it is impracticable, if not impossible, for the Government on the 1st day of January, 1879, to redeem in coin the United States legal-tender notes outstanding.

Second. That, if it were possible or practical it would be unwise in policy and ruinous in results to do so. Can the Government, in view of all its obligations and its available resources, present and prospective, redeem in coin its outstanding legal-tender notes on the 1st day of January, 1879? In view of the distressed condition of the country, can we afford to risk the experiment? How will resumption affect the volume of the currency, the amount in circulation, the price of property, the value of labor, and the prosperity of all the great industries of the country? These are grave, practical questions which the tax-burdened and poverty-stricken millions of this land are pressing with more than an ordinary interest and earnestness. It seems to me that the amount to be redeemed and the means of redemption are important factors in the solution of the problem.

The amount of United States legal-tender notes outstanding now is $354,490,892. How much this amount may be varied before the first day of January, 1879, it is impossible to tell. I assume that it will not be greatly changed. What the means of the Government for the redemption of these notes will amount to on the 1st of January, 1879, is left to conjecture. But if the Government owned and controlled all the coin and bullion now in the country, and could use every dollar of it in the redemption of the notes, it would pay but little over 50 per cent. We do know from authentic official resources that the amount of United States legal-tender notes now outstanding is $354,490,892. And we know from the same source (the report of the Comptroller of the Currency) that the whole amount of gold and silver coin and bullion in the entire country is estimated at only $186,678,000, which, deducted from the amount of the notes leaves an excess of $167,812,892 of the notes over the entire amount of coin and bullion in the whole country. So that if the Government now owned and controlled all the specie in the country and was in a condition to use every dollar in redemption, it could redeem but little over one half of the notes. But it is not true that the Government owns all the gold and silver coin and bullion in this country, or that it can control it all.

The precise amount of coin in the Treasury belonging to the Government on the 1st day of November, 1877, is $97,479,643.94. The difference between this sum and $354,490,892, the amount of legal-tender notes, outstanding at same date, is $257,021,248,06. To show the ability of the Government to redeem these notes, the opponents of this bill encounter the difficult task of proving that $97,479,892.94 in coin will redeem at par, $354,479,892 in legal-tender notes. To do which they will have to invent a new system of mathematics, for it certainly can not be by any mode of calculation with which the world is now acquainted; or they will have to do what is equally difficult; show that with decreasing revenues and a public debt of $2,047,350,700.75, less cash in the Treasury, the Government, on the first day of January, 1879, after discharging all its indispensable obligations, will be able to redeem, at par, in coin, its outstanding legal-tender notes. He is a bold man who will undertake it, and will succeed in convincing the world that he has a larger endowment of courage than judgment.

It is unquestionably clear that resumption now would be an impossibility. It is not within the reach of any human power to show that it will be possible or practicable on the first day of January, 1879, to show that the amount to be redeemed and the means of redemption will be so varied by that time from what they are now as to attain an equality.

Resumption is not to be gradual. The obligation imposed upon the Government by the law which it is proposed to repeal is to redeem in coin the outstanding

United States legal-tender notes on the first day of January, 1879. The only qualification is that the notes shall be presented in sums of more than $50. That one gold dollar will pay, at par, five paper dollars, is a logical as well as a mathematical absurdity. There can be no great change in the amount of coin required to pay the interest on the national debt between the present time and the time fixed by law for redemption.

There is no reasonable probability that the production of gold in this country will increase, or that there will be an influx of it from abroad, since Germany and Great Britain, as well as some other European Governments, have adopted it as the sole standard of value. The public revenues are falling off and taxation has reached the utmost limit that can be borne by the people. How can the Government be able to resume specie payments at the time prescribed by the resumption act? Where is the coin to come from? How is it to be obtained? Will the bankers of the House and the opponents of this bill enlighten the country upon these questions? Star-spangled banner and spread-eagle speeches do not answer the question nor satisfy a suffering people. To say that the effect of resumption will be to appreciate the legal-tender notes to an equality in value with gold, and that therefore the holders of the notes will not want the gold and will not present them for redemption, is to trifle with the question. With the experience of the last ten years in the fluctuations in values of money and property, does any one suppose that the holders of these non-interest-bearing notes would keep them a day after they could be exchanged for gold. To suppose that they would is to suppose that human nature will be changed and men will cease to love gold, or that human reason will be lost and men will cease to understand values.

Some of the most ardent oppnents of this bill, as I understand, admit that it is impossible, as a matter of fact, for the Government to redeem these notes in coin at the time provided in the resumption act. They would insist, I suppose, that the Government can begin to redeem them, and as soon as redemption is commenced the holders of the notes will take the will for the deed; by a sort of etherealized imagination take it for granted that resumption is an accomplished fact. This logic may convince resumptionists, capitalists, and gold gamblers, but the honest and unfortunate debtor, whose property is sacrificed at sheriff's sale, and the unemployed laborer, whose starving family stretch out their skeleton hands for bread, will not understand a piece of financial jugglery that fattens wealth and famishes want. It may be insisted that the Government can borrow the coin from abroad that may be necessary to redeem its notes. I prefer to let high Republican authority answer that suggestion. A former Secretary of the Treasury, Mr. Boutwell, upon this subject, says:

"The Bank of England, foreseeing that there would be an accumulation of coin to the credit of the United States which might be taken away bodily in specie, gave notice to the officers of the Treasury Department of the United States that the power of that institution would be arrayed against the whole proceeding unless we gave a pledge that the coin should not be removed, and that we would re-invest it in the bonds of the United States as they were offered in the markets of London. We were compelled to comply. It was in the interest of the Government that we should do so, because we did not want the coin and we did want the bonds. But it shows the feeling that animates the central financial power of Great Britain. And it shows a policy on the part of that institution, and of every kindred institution on the continent of Europe, sustained by all the banking and commercial classes, by which, if it were necessary and this proposition should become a law, the bonds of the United States would be excluded from the stock market of every financial city. There are in the nine great banks of Europe only $600,000,000 in specie. That specie is held as a reserve with reference to their local business and with reference to the great transactions that take place between the countries of continental Europe and Great Britain.

I may say, without disparaging the author of these propositions, that it is useless for Congress to waste time looking in that direction. There is another fact, known to all. We recovered at Geneva an award against Great Britain of $15,500,000. When this claim was maturing, the banking and commercial classes of Great Britain induced the government to interpose, and by diplomatic arrangement through the State Department here, operating upon the Treasury Department, secured the transfer of securities, and thus avoided the transfer of coin.

In the presence of these facts, is it to be assumed for a moment that we can go into the markets of the world and purchase coin with which we can redeem four, three, two or even one hundred millions of outstanding legal-tender notes?

This is the judgment of a gentleman whose position and relation with the financial world enabled him to thoroughly understand the question whether the Government could borrow coin to redeem the legal-tender notes. It has been shown that the Government can not redeem these notes because it does not possess and can not control the means to do so.

I consider the second proposition: That, if it were possible or practicable, it would be unwise in policy and ruinous in results to do so at the time specified. Suppose the Government were to redeem every dollar of outstanding legal-tender notes on the first day of January, 1879. This redemption would necessarily withdraw them from circulation and leave in circulation only $351,861,450 in national bank notes. Assuming that there would be no change in the amount from the present time until the time fixed for resumption, what would be the inevitable result of such diminution in the amount of the currency? It could not be otherwise than disastrous in the extreme. Of course, the gold would not enter into circulation, it would be hoarded. A circulation so inadequate to pay the debts and carry on the business of the country, the shrinkage in values, the paralysis of all the industries, and the starvation of the laboring classes would involve us in such ruin as the world has seldom witnessed.

Resumption does not mean the appreciation of the legal-tender notes to an equality with the present value of gold, but it means an immeasurable increase in the price of gold and its banishment into the vaults of banks and the coffers of misers, with a corresponding decrease in the value of all kinds of property, and a reduction in the wages of labor, for which the country is not prepared, and to which it would not and ought not to submit. If you ask how the people will help themselves, I answer, at the ballot-box. Capital is not the only power in this country. The popular intuition, even before the demonstration of experience, discovered the mischief of the resumption act, and it will find the remedy. The remedy for political evils and unwise legislation may come slowly, but it will come surely.

I but state a truism when I say that when money is high, and the price or value of property falling, money is the most valuable, and therefore the most desirable form of wealth, and "like the leaves of sibyl," it increases in value as it diminishes in quantity.

If redemption on the first day of January, 1879, were practicable, and gold with which the notes were redeemed and withdrawn from circulation would be hoarded until the falling prices of property and labor resulting from the contraction in the volume of currency, produced thereby, had reached the bottom, and then it would appear to possess the one and control the other. The country is overwhelmed with a burden of debt—national, State, county, municipal, and individual—estimated at seven and a half billions, an amount that almost defies the computation of figures. In the opinion of many the amount of money now in circulation is not sufficient to meet the wants of forty-five millions of people in the highest state of civilization, with wants constantly multiplying and demands for money daily increasing, crushed with debt and burdened with an exhaustive and unjust system of taxation.

Upon the assumption that resumption succeed and the legal-tender notes should be redeemed, the national-bank notes, which, as we have seen, now amount to only $316,775,111, will constitute the only circulation with which the people can pay their debts and carry on the business of life. This is to take place suddenly, at a time arbitrarily fixed by law, when the public revenues are diminishing, labor unemployed and unfed, clamoring for work and suffering for bread, property of every description rapidly depreciating, and the gold-bearing securities of the Government as rapidly appreciating in the hands of purchasers who obtain them at prices under the nominal value, and universal bankruptcy impending over millions of people, who at the same time possess a country without a parallel in history in the extent, variety, and richness of its resources. Is it not singular that the people should challenge the wisdom of a policy under which all these evils are found to exist and seek to change legislation in which they are believed to have their origin? And it is not strange that Representatives fresh from them should be in haste to present and press bills to remonetize silver and repeal Procustean resumption acts.

Does any one insist that the amount of the currency is larger than the necessities of the people require?

Does any one deny that activity, enterprise, and improvement are co-incidents of a large circulation? Does not every one at all familiar with the subject know that, when money is abundant and cheap, forests are felled, factories are built, railroads are constructed, and that town and cities spring up where savages roamed and solitude reigned.

These facts are known by the testimony of all financial experts and political economists, and by the more reliable evidence of experience in all nations and ages. Upon this subject one of the greatest men this country ever produced, and at one time Secretary of the Treasury, William H. Crawford, said, "that all intelligent writers on currency agree that, where it is decreasing in amount, poverty and misery must prevail."

The American Review for 1876, upon the same subject, says:

"Diminishing money and falling prices are not only oppressive upon debtors, of whom in modern times States are the greatest, but they cause stagnation in business, reduced production, and enforced idleness. Falling markets annihilate profits, and it is only the expectation of gain which stimulates the investment of capital, inadequate employment is found for labor, and those who are employed can only be so upon the condition of diminished wages. An increasing amount of money and consequently augmented prices are attended by results precisely the contrary. Production is stimulated by profits resulting from advancing prices. Labor is consequently in demand and better paid, and the general activity and bouyancy insure capital a wider range and higher remuneration.

This is but a history of a small and large circulation always and everywhere.

The following statement compiled by an intelligent gentleman formerly in the United States Treasury (Mr. Alexander Delmar), shows the effects of expansion and contraction in this country from 1832 to the present time to be as follows:

YEARS.	PER CAPITA.	EFFECT.
From 1832 to 1837	Expansion from $7.50 to $14.00...	Activity.
From 1837 to 1843	Contraction from $14,00 to $6.90..	Deprossion.
From 1843 to 1857	Expansion from $6.90 to $16.70...	Activity.
From 1857 to 1861	Contraction from $16.70 to $18.70	Depression.
From 1861 to 1865	Expansion from $13 70 to $28 50..	Activity.
From 1865 to 1870	Contraction from $28.50 to $20.80	Depression.
From 1870 to 1873	Contraction from $20.80 to $14.00	Bankruptcy.
From 1873 to 1877	Contraction from $14.00 to $10.00	Beggary'crime, strikes and suicide.

Much has been said in this discussion of the amount of currency and coin in France, and the prosperity which prevails in that country. Upon this subject Mr. Delmar says:

France has a population of thirty-three millions and a national currency of $2,000,000,000, or more than $60 per capita. We have not half that amount, with a population of forty millions (I may add nearly forty-five millions,) with a per capita currency of less than $10. France is prosperous and we are pressed beyond endurance.

If we have had a terrible war, so has France. If our national resources were exhausted so were those of France. What makes the difference?

The debate in this House has developed the fact that precisely the same results followed contraction and expansion in Great Britain from 1818 to 1826. The gentleman from Pennsylvania (Mr. Kelly) showed from Tallis's Illustrated Atlas of Modern History of the World the following:

YEARS.	CIRCULATION.	EFFECTS.
1818	£47,727,000	Prosperity.
1819	41.358,948	Distress.
1820	35,129,405	Distress.
1821	23,699,500	Great distress, county meetings for relief.
1822	26,743,260	
1823	29,502,422	
1824	33,124,658	Great prosperity and speculation.
1825	34,220·738	
1826	30,911,323	

Here stand the facts. What do they teach? What do they mean if they do not mean that distress follows contraction and that activity and prosperity follow expansion? Will the opponents of this bill interpret these facts if they do not teach that bankruptcy and ruin will follow the withdrawal of $354,490,892 United States legal-tender notes from the circulation with no provision to supply them with something in their stead? It is worse than idle to insist that gold will take their place in the circulation. Resumption of specie payment in Great Britain, in 1821, brought ruin upon a generation in the reduction of the value of property and the wages of labor. It will do precisely the same thing in the United States, in 1879, unless the bill under consideration becomes the law of the land.

It will be conceded that the great bulk of the indebtedness of the country was contracted upon the basis of an inflated currency and exorbitantly high prices, either during the war or since its close. Payment is demanded when the currency is contracted and when prices of property are ruinously low. But one result has followed, but one result can follow, inability to pay.

The third section of the resumption act has done much toward reaching this result. The country was assured and understood that while that section provided for resumption, it provided for it in a way that would not affect the volume of the circulation. But this turns out to be a delusion. Whether it was pressed through the House of Representatives under the previous question to prevent the discovery of this delusion, I will not undertake to say. But one thing is clear from the official statement of the Comptroller of the Currency, and that is that under the construction of the Treasury Department it is a most vigorous measure of contraction. Under its operation there have been withdrawn directly of national bank notes in less than two years, $35,086,339; of United States legal-tender notes, $27,595,447; making in the aggregate, $62,681,786. The gentleman from Kansas (Mr. Phillips) showed that about $44,000,000 more had been retired in various ways under the operation of the act.

We have had abundant crops, a large excess of imports over exports in our foreign commerce. We have cut down the expenses of the Government; still debts are unpaid and interest accumulating; values are shrinking and labor is almost starving.

I will not stop to speculate upon the amount the

country is daily losing in the stagnation of its business and the idleness of its labor. If these damaging effects have resulted from a contraction that is gradual and continual, covering a period of two years, how can ruin be obviated from the revulsion ensuing from contraction by the withdrawal suddenly and certainly of more than one-half of the currency now in circulation without an equivalent to take its place? It will as certainly follow as effect follows cause. We can not imperil the fortunes of this country upon an experiment so hazardous to every interest, public and private. The recent "strike," that startled the country from its center to its circumference with the magnitude of its proportions, the celerity of its movements, and the destructiveness of its operations, involving the loss of many lives and millions of property, contains a lesson from which capital may take warning and the Government derive wisdom.

The charge that the repeal of the resumption act means the repudiation of the obligation of the Government to redeem the United States legal-tender notes, scarcely rises to a dignity that entitles it to contempt. The question of repudiation is not involved in this question of repeal, either directly or indirectly, immediately or remotely. No time is specified in the obligation, when redemption shall take place. The law passed long after the obligation was incurred, fixing the time when it should be discharged, is no part of the obligation. The law can be repealed and no time fixed, leaving the question of time undetermined, as it was before the resumption act was passed, without affecting the obligation and without violating the public faith in the slightest degree whatever. There is not the least danger that the Government will ever repudiate its obligation to pay the legal-tender notes, for two reasons: first, nobody in the United States favors it, and in the second place, the Constitution declares that the validity of the public debt shall never be questioned.

The question is not whether the Government shall ever redeem them, but whether a law that fixes without reason a time for redemption, shall be repealed. I apprehend that every friend of repeal on this floor and in this country wishes to see the Government pay every debt it owes. But they do not wish to see the property and prosperity of the country destroyed in an effort to do a thing which the Government is unable to do and under no obligation to do, to wit, redeem $354,490,892 in legal-tender notes on the 1st day of January, 1879, when it never promised to redeem them on that nor any other specified day. I look for a time in the near future when the Government will be able to redeem every dollar of these notes. This house, in my judgment, has taken an important step in that direction in passing the bill to remonetize silver. If this should be done, it will convert the large amount of silver in the country from a commodity to a currency, and to the extent of its production swell the volume of the currency. It will depreciate the value of gold, because equally with gold it will be a legal-tender in the payment of customs duties and all debts except those required by the terms of the contract to be paid in a different currency.

If the country can be saved from the ruin which the

resumption act is precipitating upon it by its early repeal and the statesmanship of the country rises to an equality with the emergencies upon it, there will be but little difficulty in returning within a few years to specie payments. It can not be done, however, while the bane of all prosperity, fluctuation in the value of money and property, shall continue. It can only be done when the volume of the currency becomes steady, the values of money and property become settled, the laws of supply and demand are restored to their normal relations, labor and capital re-adjust their relations upon the basis of reasonable profits for the one and just compensation for the other.

The question has been raised in this debate why labor was cheaper in Europe than in the United States. The reason is obvious. Capital has accomplished there what it seeks to do here. It has dictated the price of labor, and the large standing armies of the European despotisms suppressed complaint. The people of these United States do not intend to allow capital to control labor, nor do they intend to support a large standing army in times of peace to suppress the expression of opinion or hush the cry of want.

I have endeavored to show that the resumption act should be repealed, because it is impossible for the Government to discharge the obligation which it imposes upon it, for the reason that it does not possess and can not obtain the coin necessary for that purpose. And that if it were possible to do so, it would necessarily withdraw from the circulation, already small as compared with that of other countries, an amount that would leave the people without the means of paying debts and carrying on the affairs of life; that it would depreciate gold and drive it into the vaults of banks and coffers of misers, and so reduce the value of property and labor as to destroy the one and starve the other, and thus overwhelm the country in bankruptcy and ruin. That these results must inevitably follow, a very large portion of the people of this country have not the slightest doubt.

With discreet legislation, the future of this country is full of hope. We are returning to constitutional methods of administration. The ballot dominates the bayonet. Military despotism has ceased in the South. The virtue, intelligence, and honor of her people find expression in the character and patriotism of her representatives upon this floor and in the Senate. Sectional animosity has been displaced by national concord and fraternity. The reign of the carpet-bagger has closed; universal contempt has embalmed him in infamy and sent him to history. It is but just to the colored people of the South to say that since let alone, they conduct themselves with propriety. High responsibilities devolve upon us. The inauguration of a system of legislative and administrative policy that will develop all the material resources of the country, extend its commerce, correct the disorders of its finance, reward its labor, protect its capital, maintain its faith, reform its revenue system, and mitigate the burdens of the people are the high obligations we have assumed upon entering these halls, and, for the fidelity with which we discharge them, we must answer at the bar of an enlightened public judgment.

I now yield the balance of my time to my colleague.

Pensions to the Soldiers of the Mexican and Indian Wars.

Speech of the Hon. H. P. Bell, of Georgia. Delivered in the House of Representatives, February 9, 1878.

The House being as in Committee of the Whole on the state of the Union upon the subject of the bill (H. R. No. 257, reported by Mr. Hewitt, of Alabama, from the Committee on Invalid Pensions, at the first session of the Forty-Fifth Congress), granting pensions to the soldiers of the Mexican, Seminole, Creek, and Black Hawk Indian wars—

Mr. Bell said:

Mr. Speaker: Governments, under all forms, in all ages and every type of civilization, have manifested in some way their appreciation of the public service of their citizens or subjects. The achievements of statesmen and the triumphs of warriors are carved in bronze, chiseled in marble, or colored on canvas, and thus distinguished virtues and great deeds are preserved to history and transmitted to posterity. This tribute of admiration to greatness is creditable to human nature, although its expression is often long delayed and frequently partial when bestowed.

The highest evidence of right to public gratitude

which the citizen of this or any country can give is the offering of his blood and his life to the Government in the defense of its liberty, the vindication of its rights, and the honor of its flag.

The Government of the United States has evinced its appreciation of the service of its citizen soldiery in providing by law, in the form of pensions, a support for them when disease contracted in camp or wounds received in battle or advanced age or physical infirmity rendered them unable to secure it for themselves. This may be regarded as the settled policy of the Government, the only exception to it being the in the case of the soldiers of the Mexican war and the Seminole, Creek and Black Hawk Indian wars. Whether the support is always commensurate with the merits or necessities of each particular case, or whether the pension in some particular instances may not be fraudulently obtained, are questions that I do not now propose to consider. There is no American citizen who does not now feel that the pittance granted to the heroes of the Revolution of 1776 was a poor return for the heritage of freedom won by their valor on the field and embodied by their wisdom in the Constitution. And there is no American citizen, I apprehend, who does not regret, since the death of the last of that band of heroes, that more liberal and just provision was not made by the Government for their comfort and support while living. But the opportunity to cancel that high obligation is now gone, and those who had it in their power to discharge it and failed to do so are left to the reflections which remorse alone can suggest, the never-failing penalty of neglected duty.

The soldiers of the Mexican war, and of the Seminole, Creek and Black Hawk Indian wars, after waiting thirty years for the Government to do them the same measure of justice it has its soldiers in other wars, in conformity with its established policy, and waited in vain, have at length appealed to that Government which they so faithfully served for that right which has been so long deferred and so persistently refused. These veterans pay without complaint their proportion of twenty-eight millions annually in pensions to the soldiers of the Union Army in the late war between the States. They likewise pay their part of thirty-eight millions annually to support a skeleton army of commissioned officers to guard the Texas border from incursions from the banditti whose country the Mexican soldiers conquered. They pay taxes also to support the establishment at West Point for the education, at public expense, of future officers of the army of the United States, to be maintained, at the public expense, in peace as well as in war.

They do not understand how the Government can deny their claim and at the same time exhibit such princely liberality in granting, in subsidies, $4,500,000 to the Pacific Mail Steamship Company to transport Chinese into California to be sold into slavery, and $1,387,500 to the United States and Brazil Steamship Company, and $64,623,512 in bonds and thirty-one millions of acres of the public lands to the Pacific Railroad, and yet be unable to pay a pension of $8 per month to a few hundred old men whose valor won an empire from a foreign foe, and cast it, glittering with gold, at our feet.

There is no difficulty in understanding how the Government became able to give so much land and money away; the soldiers recovered it for the Government from Mexico. But the difficulty consists in reconciling the conduct of the Government, according to the standard of any nation, civilized or savage, with right of justice, in *giving* the domain and treasure bought with the blood of the brave, to soulless corporations, and refusing to pay to the soldier that which in all other instances the Government itself has recognized to be the highest obligation. If the wish of the people of this country could have found expression through the forms of law, justice to these men would not have been denied in the past; and if it is now permitted to have utterance, it will not be delayed for a day in the future.

To subject them to the humiliation of asking for a right so manifestly clear, is itself an act of gross injustice. A government inspired with gratitude for distinguished public service would have magnanimously shown it when the first occasion was presented. I do not propose to discuss the details of the bill reported to the House by the committee. I shall certainly give it a most cheerful support, and would prefer it if it were even more liberal in its provisions for the widows and orphans of the dead soldiers. What I propose is to examine the ground upon which the claim for pensions is based, and to insist, with all possible earnestness, upon its earliest recognition. Who are these men? What service have they rendered to the Republic? Engaged in the peaceful pursuits of civil life, surrounded with domestic joys in the charmed circle of home, unused to the discipline of the camp, and untrained in the art of war, when their country became involved in the war with Mexico, without a regular army, upon its call for volunteers they came from the field, the counter, the office, and the shop, unallured by the phantom of glory and uninspired by the god of ambition to respond to that call. The ardor of their patriotism superseded the training of discipline, and their first field developed volunteers into veterans—a community of citizens at home into an army of conquerors in Mexico.

Their example taught the world that large standing armies, the instruments with which tyrants destroy liberty, are not necessary to the security of free States; that while the genius of our system vests or acknowledges power in the people, it rests for its support upon their affection. It demonstrated that the United States could improvise an army of citizen soldiers equal to any emergency of defense or conquest, of which truth the war with Mexico was at once the illustration and the evidence, and that while with the mercenary war is a trade, with the volunteer citizen right is the object and patriotism the inspiration. Upon the close of the war, reversing the order of transformation of citizen to soldier, from soldier back to citizen, and equally a patriot as citizen or soldier, they resumed their places in civil life without a ripple upon the surface of society, the pride of the country and the admiration of the world. In all the world none could be found who failed to appreciate their patriotism and the trophies of their valor, save the Government they so faithfully served, whose honor they so signally vindicated, whose prowess they so gloriously illustrated, and to whose domain their heroism added an empire richer than all the Orient.

If these men have accomplished nothing more than the demonstration of a military prowess that placed the United States in the van of the greatest powers of the earth, they would have been entitled to the gratitude of their country and their kind. The war with Mexico showed the possession by the Government of military resources that straightened the labyrinthean mazes and smoothed the rugged pathways of diplomacy, discovering to the great powers of Europe other modes of settling national controversies with us than the last resort of kings—the sword. In considering this claim of the Mexican soldiers upon their Government, their hardships and sufferings are not to be ignored. They were such as are incident to all wars, intensified by an unhealthy climate. Subjection to the restraints of a rigorous discipline, the weary march, the fearful contagion, the dreaded hospital, the anxious uncertainties of life in the hour of battle, the absence of all comfort in the bivouac, and unremitting toil, taxing every resource of physical endurance, and an absence that any hour might make final from loved ones at home—these were all borne with a resignation that never murmured and a courage that never faltered.

The uniform that distinguishes the soldier is the garland that festoons him for the altar. Heroism is exhibited in suffering as well as in doing; as well in the disease of the hospital as in the struggle of the field. Nor should we forget the claims of those stricken ones, whose husbands and fathers fell either by disease or in battle, who were denied the sad solace of dropping on unmarked graves in a foreign land affection's last offering—the tribute of a tear. Their claim is sealed in blood and sanctified by the sorrows of widowhood and orphanage. Can any appeal to the justice or gratitude of their Government be stronger than that which they urge? But let us put this claim on another ground—on what the lawyers would call a *quantum valebant* count—and see how the questions stand in that light. What has the service of these soldiers availed the Government in the increase of its wealth, the expansion of its domain, and the augmentation of its power? What are the results of their triumph? California, Colorado, Nevada, Arizona, Utah, New Mexico, and Wyoming were conquered from Mexico.

Look at California alone! That State now has a population of 800,000, with an area of 188,981 square miles, or 120,947,840 acres more than the combined area of New England, New York and Pennsylvania. In 1872, 3,670 vessels bore to the great commercial emporium of San Francisco 1,237,227 tons of commerce. The State paid into the Federal treasury in customs duties alone, $8,184,481. The same year she shipped in coin, bullion, gold dust, and the precious metals $19,049,048, and paid in taxes $9,500,000. The production of gold in that single State for a period of twenty-five years ending in 1872, amounted to the enormous sum of $990,600,000. With commercial advantages unsurpassed, agricultural resources sufficient when fully developed to supply her own people and feed the famine-stricken countries of the East, unrivaled in the salubrity of her climate, the fertility of her soil, the richness of mines, the magnificence of her scenery, and the activity and enterprise of her people, she stands, if not the envy, the admiration of her older sisters in the Union.

But the wealth and greatness of this State does not exclusively consist in the richness of her mines, the extent of her commerce, or the value of her agricultural products. Twenty colleges and universities adorn her hills and valleys, affording superior advantages for the higher cultivation of the arts and sciences. Two hundred and one newspapers and periodicals, with a circulation of 94,100, enlighten the public mind upon all questions affecting their political, social, and material interests. Sixteen hundred and twelve schools invite her children to the fountain of knowledge, and nearly one hundred libraries, numbering over two hundred thousand volumes, supply the means of continuing an intellectual cultivation begun in the schools. Religious instruction is received at five hundred and thirty-two churches, accommodating 195,585 persons, and how much these elements and instruments of progress and greatness have been increased since 1872 I have no means of ascertaining.

If we add to California the area, population, and wealth of Colorado, Nevada, Arizona, Utah, New Mexico, and Wyoming, we have an area of over 937,875 square miles—an empire in extent, wealth, and population in a high state of Christian civilization, added to the Republic. These are the material results of the war with Mexico, wrung by the valor of the men whose claim I urge, from a foreign foe, on foreign soil, and cast at the feet of a hitherto ungrateful Government. Statesmanship had but little agency in this grand acquisition. Diplomacy only formulated at Guadaloupe Hidalgo what blood had purchased at Buena Vista and Cerro Gordo. What the future of this empire will be, time alone will reveal. Three States are already admitted, and Arizona, Utah, New Mexico and Wyoming will soon add four more to the circle of the sisterhood, with undefined resources of wealth and elements of development, supplying a home for unnumbered millions of free, active, enterprising, and happy people.

These treasures eclipse the trophies of the famous legions of Caesar. The Mexican veterans secured them from the public enemy and presented them to their Government, and ask in return a compensation in the form of a pension which one-sixth of the customs duties paid by California alone into the Federal treasury would annually discharge. And they present as an indorsement of this claim the action of the legislatures of fourteen States of the Union instructing their senators and representatives to support it. That patriotism is intense, indeed, that is not chilled by ingratitude so flagrant. If their claim rested on no other ground than the value of their acquisitions it would be indisputable upon that alone; and posterity will be astonished that a right so clear and a claim so just was not conceded without dispute and paid without delay. But the service rendered by the Mexican soldiers does not consist exclusively nor even mainly in the extent and value of material acquisitions. National greatness does not depend entirely upon area of territory nor richness of resources. The type of civilization, the character of the people, their respect for the rights of others and the courage with which they maintain their own, the institutions which reconcile the largest liberty of the citizen with the most absolute obedience to law, the affection of the people for the Government while it exacts their money for its support and their blood for its defense are far greater elements of power than mere extent of dominion or numbers of population. Greece achieved more glory in the defense of Thermopylæ than Rome won in the conquest of Gaul. The most important service those veterans rendered to their government is found in the position their valor achieved for it among the great powers of the world. It is true that American patriotism and prowess were tested and vindicated in the war for independence and in the war of 1812. But these were defensive wars, where heroism caught inspiration from the spirit of liberty in the defense of homes, firesides, and altars. The great captains of Europe, affecting contempt for free institutions maintained by the affections of the people and defended by a citizen soldiery, predicted disaster to our arms in the invasion of Mexico. The strength of our Republican system was on trial. The interested monarchies of Europe and the East were the anxious spectators. The men who now appeal to you for justice, led by Scott and Taylor, were the arbiters of this great question. How gloriously they decided it history has recorded. Victory mingled its light with the stars that deck the flag on every field, from the firing of the first gun at

Palo Alo until it floated in triumph from the capital of the Aztecs. Invading a foreign country more than a thousand miles from the capital of their own, they were met upon its border by a force four times their strength in numbers, under the leadership of a chieftain already famous in history, aroused by the incentive which the consciousness of defending home and country can alone inspire. With natural advantages for defense seldom found, and obstructions to aggressive advancement rarely met, these heroic men with knightly crests vindicated their country's chivalry, avenged its wrongs and bore its flag in triumph in every fight and on every field from Vera Cruz to the City of Mexico.

Invincible alike in the skirmish of the *chaparrel,* the charge of the plain, and the assault upon the fort, the graves of more than ten thousand who fell by disease consecrate the line of march with monumental patriotism. In a glorious army like this, where every officer and every soldier was equally a hero, comparison is inadmissible. But even at this distant day the names of Clay, Harden, McKee Yell, Ringgold, and Butler, excite a pride, kindle an enthusiasm, and challenge an admiration constituting a heritage of national fame far more valuable than the pension sought by their survivors or the empire won by their blood. Of each one of these it may be truly said—

His was the hero's soul of fire,
And his the martyr's deathless name,
And his was love exalted higher
By all the glow of chivalry.

So profoundly impressed were the people of Mexico with the prowess of our army, that they proposed to invest its commander with the chief magistracy of their republic. These men were as much distinguished for their moderation in victory as their courage in battle. They were at once the finest type and truest exponents of American citizens and American soldiers. Since the war with Mexico the military capacity of the United States for any emergency arising from foreign or domestic complications has ceased to be a question. If this war had been fruitless in other results, the imperishable luster it shed upon our arms would compensate its cost of blood and treasure, and entitle its soldiers to the justice they seek. Much that has been said in favor of the claims of the Mexican veterans applies with equal force to the brave men who served in the various Indian wars mentioned in the bill of the committee. Their military service may not have been distinguished by as many battles nor as brilliant victories, with as large numbers, as that of the army in Mexico. The results in wealth and domain may have been far less, yet their patriotism was identical, their sacrifices and sufferings were equal, and their title to a pension rests upon precisely the same foundation of faithful military service rendered to their country in the hour of its necessity. Millitary merit, in the subaltern or the superior, is not always to be measured by the standard of success. The mode of Indian warfare is not governed by the code which controls the warfare of civilized nations. Its very nature imposes all the burdens, inconveniences, dangers and sufferings incident to all wars, without its "pride, pomp, and circumstances." There is something thrilling in the grand array of opposing forces upon the same plane of civilization, where the destinies of empires are to be determined upon a single field and the current of history changed from the event. The very fact of opposing a foe of equal skill and upon equal terms appeals to soldierly pride for the utmost display of skill and courage, and stimulates the ardor of patriotism by adding the incentive of ambition.

Indian warfare includes all the hideous horrors of war without any of its compensating mitigations. The stealthy approach with uplifted tomahawk to the bivouac, the deadly shot from the secret covert upon the unsuspecting victim upon the march, the blazing house consuming the remains of slaughtered women and children, degenerate Indian warfare into horrible massacre or bloody assassination. It was this kind of warfare in which the courage and patriotism of the soldiers were tested in the Seminole, Creek and Black Hawk wars. They accomplished all that was attainable. They conquered peace; they secured protection to the people; and they vindicated the authority of the Government. They did more: they discharged with fidelity the highest duty they owed to their Government; they have waited forty years for the Government to discharge its duty to them. How much longer shall they wait? How many more in advanced age and extreme poverty will we allow to go down to their graves stung with ingratitude, disappointed in their hopes, and suffering for bread? In the name of the American people, whose sense of justice is outraged at the delay, let us gladden the hearts of these gallant old soldiers as they stand on the confines of the grave by according to them now that which they should have had a quarter of a century before.

It seems to me that the Interior Department has put itself to much trouble to show, upon a basis of calculation utterly fallacious, that there was a great number of these soldiers, and that therefore it would require a large amount to pay the pensions. This logic that a debt should not be discharged because it is large, the country is too dull to appreciate, even if the fact assumed were really true. But it is not true that the number is as large as it is supposed to be. After the most thorough investigation of the question by the Mexican Veterans' Association, covering a period of several years and every State in the Union, the actual number of the survivors of the Mexican, Seminole, Creek and Black Hawk wars amounts to about thirteen thousand and four hundred, including all that would be entitled to pensions under the provisions of this bill.

The committee in its very able report submits this number as the nearest possible approximation to the truth. The committee shows that $1,286,400 per annum would pay the pensions, and that this amount would constantly decrease as the average age of the beneficiaries is about sixty years. Compared with the resources of the Government and the merit of the claim, the amount dwarfs into a trifle. If it were impossible to pay this amount, could we not retrench some extravagant and useless expenditure—some subsidy—and save enough from prodigal waste to discharge an honest obligation? But no such retrenchment, even where retrenchment ought to be had, is necessary for this purpose. These aged soldiers of the Republic have presented their claim. They put it upon the ground—

First. That it is the established policy of the Government to reward in this way the service which they rendered.

Second. They put it upon the ground of value of these services in the expansion of domain and the acquisition of material wealth.

Third. They put it upon the ground of the sacrifices they made and the sufferings they endured for the public welfare.

And, last, they put it upon the ground of the imperishable luster shed upon our arms by their valor. And standing upon this foundation of truth and justice they appeal to the American people, through their representatives in Congress assembled, for justice long delayed but never controverted. Shall they appeal in vain? Will no remorse linger in the consciences of men who who refuse this claim because complaint can not come from the silence of the grave? Can some future Congress relieve the present one from responsibility by granting the pensions when the beneficiaries are dead? Can the Government hope to do justice by granting the pension and at the same time save the money by waiting until nobody is left alive to accept it? Let us save the Government from injustice so monstrous and reproach so shameful.

Refunding the National Debt—Postal Savings Banks.

Speech of Hon. Hiram P. Bell, of Georgia, in the House of Representatives, April 24, 1878.

The House having met for debate, Mr. Vance in the chair as speaker *pro tempore*—

Mr. Bell said:

Mr. Speaker: The financial question is the great economic problem of this country and of this age. Its satisfactory solution is the supreme desire of the American people. With a country the greatest in extent and richest in resources of ancient or modern times, under a system of government the most beneficent that human wisdom ever formed, we present to-day a sad spectacle of poverty, suffering, and distress. The stagnation of business, the paralysis of industry, the idleness of labor, the destruction of property in the shrinkage of values and existing and impending bankruptcy, are expressions with which we have become familiar by daily repetition in these halls since we met in October. Different causes have been assigned and various explanations given for this unfortunate condition of the country. There are those who suppose that they have found the cause in extravagant living, in overtrading, and in wild and reckless speculation. They suggest, of course, economy in personal and family expenditures as a panacea for all our ills. Others have ascertained that the "Iliad of our woes" comes from an inflated, irredeemable paper currency, and recommend as a sovereign specific the resumption of specie payment. This school of political philosophers teaches the paradoxical doctrine that you can relieve the poverty of the people by destroying their property and increasing their debts. This solution finds its equal in absurdity only in that other theory that attributes our troubles to what is called overproduction. The advocates of this theory would insist that the distress which the country now suffers results from the abundance of the products of our mines, fields, and factories.

If this grand discovery that so unceremoniously explodes the doctrines of Adam Smith be true, then the remedy, simple and complete, is at hand. We have only to destroy what we have and cease to produce any more. All this nonsense is worse than trifling with the gravest questions of public interest. The people of this country thoroughly understand the cause of their distress. They find it in the overwhelming indebtedness of the country—the Government and the people—and in the financial policy of the Government manipulated by syndicates in the interest of non-taxed capital, and against the property and labor, upon which class legislation has imposed enormous burdens of iniquitous taxation. That financial policy they have arraigned and denounced, and that financial policy it is the object of this bill to change and improve. A simple statement of what the legislation upon this subject has been is the clearest demonstration of its folly and of its injustice. The national-bank act secures a monopoly of the banking business to the bondholders. This monopoly is protected by a prohibitory tax of 10 per cent.

upon the issues of State banks. The Government pays to the bondholding bankers 6 per cent. in gold semi-annually, and gives them the use of $90,000 on every $100,000 in bonds deposited in the treasury; and all this is done at an annual expense to the people of at least $15,000,000.

Between the years 1862 and 1868 the Government of the United States issued and sold bonds amounting to the sum of $2,059,975,700, for which it realized in gold or gold value $1,371,424,238, a loss to the Government and a gain to the purchasers of the sum of $678,551,-460. The interest on this sum for ten years, at 6 per cent., amounts to the sum of $407,130,876. There is therefore now a debt upon the American people, principal and interest, amounting to the gigantic sum of $1,085,682,336—one-half of the public debt, for which, in fact, the Government never received one cent, and for which the creditors never paid one cent. And this is the fountain from which the bitter waters of distress now deluging the entire country have flowed; and this is the debt around which constitutional guarantees have been thrown. The fourteenth article of amendment to the Constitution declares, among other things, "That the validity of the public debt shall never be questioned." This debt was originally payable in paper money or lawful money. It was not originally payable in coin. The act of 13th of March, 1869, pledged the faith of the Government to its payment in coin; the act of 12th of February, 1873, demonetizing silver, left gold the only legal-tender coin in which it could be paid.

The financial policy which I arraign has fastened

upon the people of this country this vast gold-bearing debt under which they are staggering and with which they are crushed, when the Government received nothing for it, and which in fact constitutes the spoils which war speculators coined out of blood. Since this debt was created and converted into a gold debt, the policy has been to constantly contract the volume of the currency, while the population of the country was rapidly increasing, and the wants and necessities of the people steadily multiplying. The amount of the currency outstanding in 1866, was $1,696,987,643. In 1876 it was only $748,912,072, a reduction in the volume of the currency in ten years of $948,074,570, an annual average diminution for ten years of $94,807,457.

The financial system or policy of the Government, manipulated by syndicates, gold rings, bondholders, and bullion brokers in the interest of capital at the sacrifice of every other interest, culminated in the passage of the act of June 14, 1875. This act required the Government to redeem in gold the outstanding legal-tender notes on the 1st day of January, 1879. To carry out the provisions of this act the Secretary of the Treasury informs us that he has purchased $15,000,000 of coin by the sale of 4 1-2 per cent. bonds, and $25,000,000 with 4 per cent. bonds. The bonded debt of the United States is thus increased the sum of $40,000,000, carrying an annual interest of $1,670,000, to redeem and withdraw from circulation an equal amount of legal-tender notes which bear no interest. And the Secretary informs us that he must have fifty millions more of coin to make resumption practicable, which he proposes to purchase with 4 1-2 per cent. gold bonds, thus increasing the public debt ninety millions, with an annual interest of $3,650,000. And this is what it costs the people to enable the Government to deprive them of the means of paying their debts and prosecuting their business.

With the bonded debt of the United States converted by legislation, not by contract, into a coin debt at a high rate of interest and constantly increased; silver demonetized, leaving gold the only currency in which the debt could be paid; the legal-tender notes redeemed and destroyed or hoarded in the treasury; State banks strangled, taxed out of existence, the people of this country, numbering nearly fifty millions, would have left to them $320,000,000, to pay their debts and conduct their business, of national-bank notes, issued by the Government to the banks, to be let out or drawn in as their interest or caprice might dictate.

This legislation is very rapidly making the stock-jobbers, gold gamblers, and money rings the owners of the property and the masters of the people of this country. Thus the financial legislation stood at the meeting of the extra session of the Forty-fifth Congress, the result of which is seen in the fact that the Government securities were at a premium, the property of the country ruinously depreciated and its business destroyed. After this wicked scheme of class legislation, running through a period of ten years and indorsed by an administration distinguished for its appreciation of gifts, if for nothing else, had been accomplished, and while the saints who worship only at mammon's shrine, jubilant with triumph, were reveling in high carnival, in fancied security, Congress met and the "handwriting appeared on the wall." The people had cast the ballot into the scale like the sword of Brennus, and it outweighed their gold. And all at once there rings through the land, from these Halls and from a subsidized and prostituted press, the cry about plighted faith, public credit, and national honor.

And while the men of this generation and their children are writhing under the burdens this monstrous crime against humanity has imposed upon them, like Laocoon and his sons in the crushing coils of the serpent, it is just discovered that it is extremely unwise for Congress to legislate upon the subject of finance. Political economists and *doctrinaires* tell us that these questions are above legislative control; that they are matters to be regulated and adjusted by commercial values and the laws of trade. The Government contractors, speculators, and bounty-jumpers of the war period now serenely draw semi-annually in gold the interest on their bonds purchased at 50 per cent. of their nominal value and exempt from taxation, while the Government taxes even the match with which poor war widows, North and South, kindle the fire with which they cook their scanty meal. I repeat that the cause of the distress upon the country is to be found mainly in this stupendous national debt, largely contracted without an equivalent, and in that system of legislation which has constantly increased its amount by enhancing its value and diminishing the means of its payment.

Having intrenched themselves behind this legislation,

conscious of the power with which these spoliations have invested them, the extent of their demands is only equaled by the offensiveness of their insolence. One of their organs has made the announcement that—

The American laborer must make up his mind henceforth not to be so much better off than the European laborer. Men must be content to work for low wages. In this way the workingman will be nearer to that station in life to which it has pleased God to call him.

This is an oracular *pronunciamiento* from the money power that the condition of the American laborer is a state of serfdom, and that God has been pleased to appoint him to a station of inferiority in all the relations of life. This is the legitimate result of that class legislation in the interest of money and against all other interests in the country which I condemn and denounce. Yet the laborer pays the taxes and fights the battles of the country. And when we warn the people that this legislation is establishing a rich class and a poor class, and making a line of distinction in men in this Government of freedom and equality, and thus silently but certainly subverting our free institutions and destroying equality and ultimately liberty, arrogant capital, "invisible in war and invincible in peace," concealing its cormorant rapacity by a false pretense to the mild virtue of timidity, raises the cry of agrarianism and communism, and insists upon increasing the army to preserve order and suppress strikes.

This Congress when it assembled addressed itself with commendable dispatch and earnestness to the relief of the anxiety and distress of the country, and commenced to change the mischievous legislation from which our troubles have sprung.

The passage of the silver bill and the bill to repeal the specie-resumption act, if it succeed, will break up the conspiracy between foreign and domestic bondholders to destroy the country. Stop the contraction of the currency and the shrinkage in the value of property. Utilize one of the great resources of the country, diminish the amount of the public debt by making it payable in a cheaper currency and make its ultimate extinction a possibility. The country can never have financial prosperity so long as foreign creditors backed by foreign governments control its financial policy in their own interest. We want the public securities held by our own people and at a lower rate of interest. When this shall have been accomplished and capital is made to bear its just share of taxation, then we can reform our revenue system, reduce taxation, and sooner or later discharge the entire public debt.

In my judgment the bill under consideration will contribute more to this most desirable result than any measure that has been presented or that can be suggested. That if it become a law it will afford practical and speedy relief to both the Government and people I do not entertain the slightest doubt.

In brief, it provides that any holder of money may deposit the same to the amount of $10 in any postal money-order office in the United States, to whom the postmaster shall issue a postal order on the treasury, which, when presented in sums of $10 or any multiple thereof, shall be receivable in exchange for postal savings-bonds of the United States, to be issued by the Secretary of the Treasury in denominations of ten, twenty, fifty, and one hundred dollars, bearing interest at the rate of 3.65 per cent. per annum, the interest payable every three months. These savings-bonds are exchangeable for notes of the United States, and also for 4 per cent. bonds authorized to be issued under and by virtue of the act of 14th of July, 1870. This bill makes every postal money-order office in the United States, for all practical purposes, a savings-bank in which the holder of money may deposit the same in a place of absolute security to him. It involves no additional expense. It requires no legal machinery except what may readily be provided by departmental regulation, adjustable to the test of trial and the suggestions of experience.

The liability of the Government to the depositor is the guarantee of his safety; and such bond as the Government may require under such regulations as the department may adopt secures the Government against loss. It is a safe and convenient place of deposit, in which the earnings of labor and the acquisitions of industry can be preserved in sums of twenty-five cents and upward to as much as $20 in a day. It will furnish an incentive to industry, encourage frugality, foster economy, and soon develop its beneficent results in sheltering the homeless, clothing the naked, and feeding the hungry. If it be true that recklessness and extravagance have been productive of all the mischief claimed, then the wisdom of that measure or policy that educates the people in the direction of economy and supplies them with a safe, convenient, and inexpensive means of preserving and increasing the rewards of their toil can not be questioned.

In those sections of the Union where savings institutions exist it has been found to be true that by this means the daily wages of laborers among the poor have been carefully husbanded. Daily and weekly deposits of small amounts have been made until after a while the aggregate would surround them with comfort. And this has been the case while there was a painful apprehension of loss from the failure of the banks, which, unfortunately, in too many instances turned out to be well founded. And while losses in these institutions have been numbered by millions, and in the midst of wreck and ruin, there is now on deposit in the savings-banks of the Union, as shown by the report of the Secretary of the Treasury, the sum of $843,154,804, deposited by 2,300,000. The American Almanac for 1878 shows the number of depositors in 1875 and 1876, in twelve States, comprising the New England States, New York, New Jersey, Pennsylvania, Maryland, Minnesota, and California, to be 2,414,952, and the amount deposited to be $892,785,553. This is an average of $369.69 to each depositor. The learned editor of this valuable book, after showing that but partial and incomplete returns have been made, says:—

It may be safely stated, however, from the returns which do exist, that the amount of deposits in savings-banks throughout the United States reaches, if it does not exceed $1,000,000,000 held by about 2,800,000 persons.

These facts show the popularity of these institutions.

They also show that the depositors are the poor whom we always have with us, and they further show what a vast sum may be saved by a wise system of economy and frugality. Can any one doubt, in the face of these facts, that an immense amount would soon be saved by the poor people of the United States if they had the facilities for sécure deposit which this bill provides?

The savings-bank is an institution of recent origin. It had its birth in the present century. Its career has been marked by signal success and beneficence. The British government has in successful operation a postal savings-bank system similar in many respects to the one sought to be established by this bill. There were in 1876 in her savings-banks, on deposit, about $350,-000,000. The postal savings-bank, which this bill will establish, possesses the very decided advantage over ordinary savings-institutions of absolute security to the depositor. Money-orders are to be issued to depositors without interest, it is true, but negotiable by indorsement, and therefore valuable and convenient as a circulating medium and receivable in exchange for United States bonds bearing interest at the rate of 3.65 per cent. per annum of the denomination of ten, twenty, fifty, and one hundred dollars. These bonds have all the attributes of a medium and an investment. The amount, the facility with which the interest can be computed, and their negotiability by delivery will give them popularity with the people as money and as an investment.

If they should not circulate as a medium they are exchangeable for United States notes, so that they could be readily converted into money at the will or convenience of the holder. This exchangeable quality would make the currency adjust itself to the demands of trade and maintain steadiness in the value of property and products. During the business seasons, when crops are put upon the market, they could and would be exchanged for notes. And in the intervals of quiet the notes would be exchanged for bonds. The markets in this way would be relieved from the extortion and speculation of the banks. Thus the business necessities of the country would be supplied with a currency as occasion required and capitalists, large and small, with the means of a safe investment at a seasonably remunerative interest.

The fourth section of the bill provides that all moneys received into the treasury in pursuance of this act shall be applied exclusively to the redemption of such bonds of the United States as are redeemable at the pleasure of the government; and the Secretary of the Treasury shall call in of such bonds those that bear the highest rate of interest.

The object of this bill is to refund the public debt in securities bearing a lower rate of interest, payable in currency, change our foreign debt into a debt due to our people, and the postal savings-bank system is adopted as the means of raising the money to pay existing bonds. In discussing this bill and kindred measures two questions arise: Is the object desirable, and is the plan practicable? I maintain the affirmative of both propositions. Reference has already been made to the amount of the public debt and the unwise and unjust legislation with regard thereto as the principal cause of our present troubles. The total public debt, less cash in the treasury, February 1, 1878, is $2,044,287,366. Of this amount $1,726,933,750 bears interest in coin at the following rates:

Bonds at 6 per cent.............$	748,667,100
Bonds at 5 per cent............	703,266,650
Bonds at 4 1-2 per cent..........	200,000,000
Bonds at 4 per cent.............	75,000,000
Total principal ....$	1,726,933,750

The interest due on this debt on the 1st day of January, 1878, amounted to $21,827,524. Of the 6 per cent. bonds $660,000,000 are redeemable at the pleasure of the United States, and of the whole $1,452,000,-000 are redeemable on or before the 1st day of May, 1881. The amount of the public debt held by foreigners is variously estimated. The best English authorities, Seyd and Baxter, estimate the entire amount of the debts of this country held abroad, including public and private debts of all descriptions, at between twenty and twenty-two hundred millions of dollars. Mr. Edward Young, Chief of the Bureau of Statistics, estimates the national, State, municipal, and railroad debts held abroad at $1,050,000,000. This does not, of course, include private or individual indebtedness. There is no means of ascertaining precisely the amount of this debt. All, however, agree that it is immensely large. The Secretary of the Treasury estimates the debt of the United States government held abroad at six hundred millions.

There are many and cogent reasons why it is desirable that this debt should be changed from a foreign into a domestic debt, should be owned and held by our own people. Debt is but another name for slavery. The debtor is always to a greater or less extent in the power of the creditor. That a large amount of bonds was held in Germany I suppose was one of the reasons that induced the German Empire to demonetize silver. That its demonetization in the United States was procured here by the bondholders in conspiracy with the creditors there I do not doubt. The financial independence of the United States, therefore, requires the ownership of the public securities at home. The export of gold to meet the constantly accruing interest on this debt drains the life-blood from the heart of the nation.

If this debt were refunded in bonds held by our own people it would stop the exportation of gold to pay the interest. The balance of trade, which last year amounted to the sum of $47,202,682, would turn the tide in our favor and bring to us an annual influx of gold, varying only in amount with that balance. We would thus not only not send abroad large amounts of gold as now to pay interest, but it would be paid to our own people, and we would receive from abroad the excess of our exports over imports in coin. The people of no government on earth that owes a large foreign debt bearing a high rate of interest ever was or ever will be prosperous long. But it is true that great national prosperity may co-exist with a large public debt held at home and for the reason already given.

The British government is a signal illustration of this

truth. The public debt of England to-day amounts to $3,850,000,000. It is held by 126,331 of her own people. This debt bears only 3 per cent. interest. It consists of annuities sold by the government to the people without any time fixed for redemption and with but little prospect that they will ever be redeemed. Yet with this immense debt upon the Government the English are comparatively prosperous. This debt is kept at home and the interest is paid to the English people and constitutes that much of their general wealth. The vast commerce of the Kingdom brings into it constantly large quantities of coin and bullion, and the government maintains a financial policy that keeps all it gets. When we obtained the Geneva award of $15,500,000 in gold, England kept the gold and paid us in our bonds. With our national debt amounting to but little more than one-half of that of Great Britain, owned by our own people and bearing a low rate of interest, we would be independent of foreign creditors and foreign governments. And with our immense resources, mineral, manufacturing, agricultural, and commercial wisely developed, we would speedily become the richest as well as the most powerful nation of the world.

The Republic of France is a still more striking proof of the proposition that a government may owe its own people a large debt and yet be prosperous. The civilized world beheld with amazement as well as with admiration what seemed almost a financial miracle in the payment of the Prussian war indemnity. France paid in less than two years, in gold and silver, $1,000,000,000, at a time when her expenditures exceeded her revenues. It was paid at the close of a war in which two immense armies had trampled down the whole face of the country. Her capital was riddled with Prussian shells and reddened in communistic blood. The sceptre was passing from a perishing dynasty and her unsettled form of government in transition through anarchy to a republic. How was this grandest financial achievement of all time and history accomplished?

It was done in this way: the French government put upon the market 5 per cent. *rentes* or bonds and appealed to the French to buy them, and they promptly took $1,640,000,000, advancing to the government money therefor. A second loan was so eagerly sought by them that the subscription covered the amount called for thirteen times over, compelling the government to award the *rentes* among the subscribers *pro rata*. As long ago as 1867 the debt of France was held by 1,095,683 persons of her own people, and now by a much greater number. The public debt of France, with a population of only 36,905,788 and an area of only 201,900 square miles, amounts to the almost fabulous sum of $4,695,600,000—more than twice as much as our own. Her revenues are $514,605,716, while her expenditures reach the sum of $519,334,162, an excess of expenditures over revenue of $4,728,446. Yet France has never repudiated any portion of her debt, has never dishonored her own paper, which is now at par with coin, and has never passed a resumption act, and her people are prosperous and happy.

There must be some solution of this prosperity. It can not be found in the extent of value of her commerce.

I was astonished to find that for the year 1876 her imports were only $4,111,000, and her exports $9,280,-000, leaving a balance in her favor of only $5,179,000. It must be accounted for mainly by the fact that the national debt is due to the French people; that the interest is paid to them, and by them kept at home, constituting a part of the common wealth, and to the further fact that France floats a larger circulation *per capita* than any other civilized nation on earth. At all events, it is true that the national debt of France is held by the French people; that the circulation is more *per capita* than that of any other nation, and that her people are more prosperous and suffering less financial distress than those of any government in the world. This state of affairs does not result from the form nor the stability of the government. These are the facts of history, and the light they shed upon the question under consideration is worth infinitely more than the speculations of a thousand theorists. Who doubts that, with the public debt refunded at a lower rate of interest, owned by our own people, the country would soon be prosperous? The government would certainly be independent of foreign capitalists and domestic stock-jobbers and bullion-brokers. The object of this bill is the accomplishment of this result.

The refunding of the public debt at a lower rate of interest, and the change of its ownership from foreigners to our own people, in the judgment of a majority of the Committee on Banking and Currency, in which I concur, will be secured, by the passage of their bill. And if this object is attained the first important step will have been taken toward the ultimate extinction of the debt. But is this postal savings-bank system a practical one? Will it enable the government to raise the money? The light of experience is always a safe guide. The test of trial affords some evidence of what may be accomplished. I insist that this plan is feasible. The system proposed by the bill of the Committee on Banking and Currency is almost exactly the British system.

That system was inaugurated in Great Britain in 1863. It started with 301 postal savings-banks. It has since extended over Ireland and Scotland. In 1876 the number was 5,448 with 1,702,374 depositors, 1 in 19 of the whole population. The aggregate deposits amounted to the sum of $134,982,750. Only the poor deposit in this institution; it was intended only for them. The law establishing them limited the amount that could be deposited by one person and contained a prohibition against depositing in more than one bank. This system has been a success in Great Britain. Why should it not be a success here? It was a favorite with the people and continues to be. It greatly diminished the deposits in the independent savings-banks, showing its popularity over these independent savings-banks with the English people. It would no doubt do the same here. But what if it did? Who has a right to complain? Certainly the depositors have the right to place their money where, in their judgment, it will be safest.

The confidence of the American people in these institutions will be shown by the amount of money they place in them. What is that amount? The deposits now held by the savings-banks in twelve States of the

Union, as far as can be ascertained, as has already been shown, are $843,154,804. The report of the Comptroller of the Currency for 1875 shows that the deposits for that year in the savings-banks, State banks, and trust companies of the United States amounted to $1,346,014,813. This estimate is based upon imperfect reports. The amount is unquestionably larger. It may be safely assumed to be $1,500,000,000. I take it for granted that a very large portion of these deposits will be withdrawn, put into the institution created by this bill and invested in the bonds for the issue of which it provides, because of the superior security to the depositor and because of the facility with which the deposit can be changed into a currency or an investment.

There is very nearly enough money lying inactive or drawing a small interest in the savings-banks, State banks, and trust companies to pay the bonded debt of the United States. This bill makes it to the interest of the holders of this money to put it where the government can use it for that purpose. The system we propose establishes forty-one hundred and forty-five postal savings-banks located at convenient and accessible points in every State and Territory in the Union, affording facilities to almost every community in the entire country for the preservation and investment, without trouble and without expense, of the proceeds of the labor and industry of the people. And at the same time it enables the government, without additional taxation, to raise the money to pay off the public debt now existing and refund it at an interest but little over one-half as much as it now pays. Does any one doubt the popularity of these savings institutions in the light of experience in Great Britain and the United States? And in view of their popularity does any one doubt that with the increased facilities afforded and incentives inspired by this bill if it become the law, a sufficient sum would be raised to enable the government to refund the public debt in the bonds proposed, and thus relieve the country from the high rate of interest it now pays, and that too within a very few years? With this accomplished, payment of the national debt, now pressing like an incubus upon the prosperity, the property, the hopes, and the hearts of the people of this country, would speedily follow. Then syndicates, money-rings, and combinations would be unable to shape the policy of the government and control the destiny of the country. There is no conflict between capital and labor. Each is equally an important and indispensable factor in the solution of the problem of civilization. Each is the complement and the auxiliary of the other. Capital supplies labor with employment and rewards its endeavor. Labor furnishes to capital the means of profitable investment and opens new fields for adventurous enterprise. Each is equally entitled to legislative protection and encouragement, and to each is the world and the race equally indebted for their progress.

It is not against capital in the abstract nor when legitimately employed that complaint is made. But it is the corrupt and illegitimate use of money by bullion-brokers, stock-jobbers, and gambling combinations in the accomplishment of legislation in their own interest and against the public interest that the country condemns and denounces—that class of money-rings that produce corners in gold and panics in business to satiate an accursed thirst for gold that shames even that of Pizarro and his robber band. We have recently witnessed the humiliation of a great State by the bribery of the Legislature to enact a charter for the government of the greatest city in the Union that enabled one of these rings to rob the honest tax-payers of that city of millions of dollars. It is that greed for gain that acts from no motive but interest, that recognizes no law but selfishness, and worships no god but gold, that finds its fittest expression in the howlings of the maniacs around the counters of the exchange on Black Friday.

It is against these that the people of this country enter their solemn protest, and it is against these that every interest of this country demands protection. I honor the men who by energy and industry acquire fortunes, and who while they increase their means aid public enterprise and advance the public prosperity. And I honor men even more, like Peabody dead, and Corcocan living, who having acquired fortunes by the same honorable means dedicate them to great benevolent and humanitarian purposes. But capital is protected. We must not forget protection to the poor, says Sismundi in his political economy:

On whatever side we look the same lesson meets us everywhere—protect the poor—and ought to be the study of the legislator and the government. Protect the poor, for in consequence of their precarious condition they can not contend with the rich without losing every day some of their advantages. Protect the poor, that they may keep by law, by custom, by a perpetual contract, that share of the income of the community which their labors ought to secure to them. Protect the poor, for they want support that they may have some leisure for intellectual development in order to advance in virtue. Protect the poor, for the greatest danger to law, and to public peace and stability, is the belief of the poor that they are oppressed. Protect the poor, if you wish industry to flourish, for the poor are the most important of consumers. Protect the poor, if your revenues require to be increased, for after you have carefully guarded the enjoyments of the poor you will find them the most important of contributors.

This bill makes no distinction in classes. It is exactly equal in its operations on all, as all laws should be, and still its passage, in my judgment, would be a peculiar blessing to the poor for the encouragement to industry which it gives and the means of preserving the rewards of that industry which it affords. Again, if it should accomplish the results claimed for it, and I doubt not it will, it will supply the money to pay the foreign debt and refund the national debt at a lower rate of interest in securities that will be held by our people. It would enable us to accomplish another most desirable object, the reduction of taxation and the reform of a revenue system that is unjust in its discrimination, oppressive in its amount, unwise in its policy, and a disgrace to the civilization of the nineteenth century in the mode and instruments of its enforcement. Fruitless efforts are made at each session of Congress to mitigate the burdens which it imposes upon the people. We are informed by the Secretary of the Treasury that we must diminish appropriations or increase the revenues.

If the interest on the public debt can be reduced, as proposed, nearly one-half, the gold sent abroad to pay the interest kept at home and paid out to our own people, with the influx of gold from abroad which the balance of trade gives us, then taxation can and will be reduced. But so long as we are compelled to raise money to pay the interest on the public debt at its present rate I see but little hope of less taxation.

Another benefit resulting from this measure is the identification of all classes in every section of the Union and in almost every community of each section with the credit of the government. They will scrutinize more closely its financial policy and guard more vigilantly its expenditures and hold to a more strict accountability its officers and agents, and may prevent the precipitation upon the country of the question of repudiation.

Nearly one-half of the families of France have money in the public funds—are creditors of the government. To have their names in the *grand livre* of the public debt is esteemed an honor. It is an honor that is eagerly sought, as the promptness with which the *rentes* were taken shows. One of the effects of this wide diffusion of the public securities among the people of France is to unite them in maintaining the public credit. Of course they look upon the public debt as a most sacred obligation. The reason is obvious; it is due to themselves, and for it they paid a full consideration. They therefore maintain the public faith from motives of interest as well as sentiments of patriotism.

This sentiment does not change with a change in the form of their government. It is the same in the republic and in the monarchy. In our system of government, based upon the popular will and resting for support upon the popular affection, it is of the first importance that the people should be identified in interest as well as in sympathy with the Government in its policy as well as its principles. The public debt of the United States, held by nearly fifty millions of people scattered all over our vast territory, would take from the financial question its sectional element, with the animosities which will always attach to it so long as it remains sectional. It will take from it its class element. And if this debt is refunded it will avoid the question of the consideration of the debt which the American people may be driven to the necessity of raising unless we change our financial policy.

Another vital result of this measure will be the general diffusion of the money paid out for interest over the whole country. It will not only not go out of the country, as now, but it will not be concentrated in one or two great money centers. It will flow out from the treasury like the blood from the heart, to the extremities of the country in every direction and through all sections, vitalizing industry, rewarding labor, and stimulating enterprise.

My conviction is thorough that, with silver remonetized and that vast resource of national wealth utilized in currency, the resumption act repealed and any further contraction of the volume of the currency prevented, this bill passed into a law and faithfully administered, the whole public debt of the United States can be speedily refunded at a rate of interest but little more than half what we now pay, and the current of specie changed from foreign countries to us instead of from us to them, and that "gravitation shifting will turn the other way," from depression to activity, from bankruptcy and ruin to prosperity and wealth.

Then we can develop the grand and diversified resources of this magnificent country, whose vastness and variety defy and fatigue the computation of mathematics.

Then we can abolish a revenue system that violates the Constitution, that outrages popular sentiment, that wrings from honest toil the earnings of its sweat, and that exhausts the substance of the people by the enormity of its demands.

Then the sound of hammers, the blasts of furnaces, the whir of wheels, the hum of spindles, and the whistle of engines will fill the land with the music of industry. Then the Government can demand her awards against foreign powers in gold, and not be compelled to receive them in its own bonds. And then the people of this country, disenthralled from the financial slavery fastened upon them through the forms of law by bondholders and syndicates, can reap the fruits of their toil, rest in the protection of the law, and rejoice in the possession of their country.

Mr. HUMPHREY. I move that the House do now adjourn.

The motion was agreed to; and accordingly (at ten o'clock and five minutes p. m.) the House adjourned.

Speech of the Hon. Hiram P. Bell, of Georgia, Delivered in the House of Representatives, January 23, 1879, in Support of the Bill Reported by Mr. Goode from the Committee on Education and Labor, to Set Apart the Proceeds of the Public Land for the Education of the People.

The House being in Committee of the Whole, and having under consideration the bill (H. R. No. 3542) to apply the proceeds of sales of public lands to the education of the people, &c.—

Mr. Bell said:

Mr. Chairman: The bill under consideration forever consecrates and sets apart the net proceeds arising from the sale of the public lands for the education of the people. It does not change, nor affect in any way whatever, any law now in force authorzing the preemption of public lands, nor the entry of public lands for homesteads, nor does it interfere in any manner with the power of Congress over the public domain. It provides after paying the expenses of sale, that the whole of the net proceeds shall be distributed among the several States, Territories and the District of Columbia upon the basis of population between the ages of five and twenty-one years. For the first five years—the

27

whole of said proceeds and for the next five years one-half to be apportioned to the several States and Territories and the District of Columbia, according to the numbers of their respective population of ten years old and upward who can not read and write, as shown from time to time by the last preceding published census of the United States. It further provides that one-fourth of the money appropriated by this act shall be given to the colleges shown as agricultural colleges, established or hereafter to be established in accordance with the act approved July 2, 1862, unless in any case the Legislature of a State or Territory shall otherwise direct.

In a word, it gives three-fourths of the amount to the cause of popular education and one-fourth, subject to the control of the State and Territorial Legislatures, to the aid of agricultural education. It provides that after ten years the whole amount shall be invested in bonds of the United States bearing a rate of interest at 4 per cent. per annum, principal and interest payable in coin, the interest thereon to be applied to free education in conformity with the provisions of the bill.

This bill contains ample provisions to secure the application of the fund to the object intended and appropriate penalties for its misapplication.

I apprehend that no great difference of opinion exists and that no controversy will arise upon the details of this measure. Nor can any question of constitutional power arise.

The second clause of section 3, article 4, of the Constitution declares that "The Congress shall have power to dispose of and make all needful rules and regulations respecting the territory or other property belonging to the United States; and nothing in this Constitution shall be so construed as to prejudice any claims of the United States, or of any particular State."

This provision grants plenary powers to Congress to dispose of the public domain. No one will hazard his reputation for intelligence by denying that the power to dispose of the territory necessarily includes the power to dispose of the proceeds of the territory. The ownership of the territory necessarily involves the right and power, in the absence of any constitutional qualifications or limitations, to dispose of it and its proceeds.

But the question upon which a difference of opinion may exist is whether the disposition proposed by this measure is wise. And to the consideration of this great question the attention of the country is invited, and upon it the favorable action of Congress invoked. It has passed into a maxim that the preservation and perpetuity of our institutions depend upon the virtue and intelligence of the people. The question of man's capacity of self-government is still an unsolved problem. Every effort hitherto made has resulted in failure. We are now making the world's last experiment under conditions more favorable to success than any that history records. The recognition of power, of sovereign political power in the people, is the distinguishing attribute, the very genius of our system. The rights, duties, and powers of executive, legislative, judicial, and ministerial officers are all defined, prescribed, and limited by law. The untrammelled ballot—the sole peaceful instrument of original, inherent, political power—is the power behind the throne that is greater than the throne. Every ballot is a vital factor in determining the destiny of millions. It therefore follows that upon the intelligent and wise exercise of this power all the great moral, social, and civil interests of society in this country depend. This question is not ephemeral in its nature, sectional in its character, nor local in its influence. It is as wide in its range as the wants of humanity, enduring as the quenchless fires of intellect, and deals with the destiny of races. There is no question of public expenditure, except the expenses of administering the government and payment of the public debt, so purely national in its object as this.

All expenditures for railways and canals, the improvement of rivers and harbors, the erection of public buildings, &c., contain local as well as national elements, and not unfrequently engender local and sectional prejudices and animosities. But every State, every section, and every individual in the Republic is deeply interested in the qualifications of every citizen to discharge the obligations and meet the high responsibilities of American citizenship.

The public domain was acquired by the common blood and the common treasure of the people, and it seems to me that there is a peculiar fitness in devoting it to their education. Then the basis of distribution is one of perfect equality—illiteracy for ten years and population thereafter. It may be urged that the basis of illiteracy is unequal because it gives the larger portion of this fund to the South for ten years. It is true that the South would get the larger portion for that period, but it does not follow that the distribution is unequal for that reason. Equality and justice consist in meeting the necessities of the case. The education of the illiterate is the object, and this distribution recognizes the right of every illiterate child to an equal participation in this benefaction. But this issue of inequality or injustice is an unfortunate one for the opponents of this bill to raise. While Georgia and Virginia, receiving only an equal amount *per capita* for their illiterate with all the other States, would receive in the aggregate more than any of the others, it may be interesting to inquire what contributions to the national Treasury these two States have made by the cession of their territory, and how they compare with the contributions of the other States, and also what States have been the beneficiaries of the Federal Government in the way of internal improvements and public works.

From 1789 to 1873 the Federal Government expended in public works, railroads, canals, and wagon-roads, the sum of $207,999,664.77. Of this $18,594,-049.46 was expended in the sixteen Southern and border States, $174,885,371.21 in the Northern and Western States and Territories, and $15,520,224 in the District of Columbia. Of the aggregate sum of $207,999,664.77, $103,294,501.35 were appropriated in bonds and money to public works from 1865 to 1873; the remaining

$104,705,163.43 to railroads, wagon-roads, and canals from 1789 to 1873. Of this sum neither Georgia, Texas, nor West Virginia received one dollar. Virginia, North Carolina, Florida, Alabama, Mississippi, Louisiana, Arkansas, Tennessee, Kentucky and Missouri received $5,480,172.94, while the other States and Territories received $99,224,990.49.

Georgia ceded to the Federal Government the territory now constituting the States of Alabama and Mississippi with the express stipulation in the deed of session that "it should be considered as a common fund for the use and benefit of the United States, Georgia included." The Government realized from this magnificent domain $40,000,000 in cash, while in the distribution of $104,705,163.43 for works of internal improvement among the States, Georgia did not receive one cent. Besides, the United States this day owe her $36,000 for money she expended for the common defense in the Revolutionary war. The State of Virginia ceded to the Government the territory comprising the greater part of Ohio, Kentucky, Indiana and Illinois, containing an area of 137,860 square miles, property worth $10,329,669,974, while she has received of the $104,705,163.43 only $57,538.27. The Government had received up to 1850 from the sale of public lands ceded by Virginia $80,000,000.

This grand old Commonwealth, after having given away an empire, stands "like royalty in ruins," struggling with misfortune, poverty and debt, with elevated crest and unbroken spirit. She urns in her heart the ashes of her heroes and statesmen; the lofty device of *sic semper tyrannis* still emblazons her shield. Wrapped in the imperial robes of her ancient sovereignity, she stands not at your door a mendicant asking alms, but the mother of States and of statesmen, demanding for her illiterate children an equal participation in the treasure her bounty bestowed.

Georgia shelters her two hundred and seventy-five thousand illiterate under her arch supported by wisdom, justice, and moderation, and in the calmness of conscious dignity points to the magnificent domain of Alabama and Mississippi and the forty millions the Government received from the gift as the evidence of her right to an equal share of this treasure. In the presence of these facts avarice itself must stand abashed, and no whisper of inequality or injustice be heard or breathed.

The last census discloses the humiliating fact that there are nearly six millions of children in the United States over ten years of age who can neither read nor write. Every chapter of our legislative history recognizes the constitutional power of Congress to aid the education of the people. Many laws have been passed and a vast amount of the public lands donated for this purpose. Individual effort and parental affection and solicitude have contributed much toward the intellectual development and cultivation of the people of this country. The different religious sects throughout the country, stimulated by a legitimate denominational pride, animated by a generous emulation and inspired by the loftier sentiment of Christian philanthrophy, have employed all their energies and exhausted all their resources to promote the cause of education and advance the standard of a Christian civilization. Eight hundred and thirty-four thousand four hundred and eleven noble men and women, worthy to wear "the red wreath by martyrs won," instruct weekly in Sunday-schools over six millions of children. States have endowed and maintained colleges and universities.

Every section and every State bristles with spires of colleges, male and female. I believe every State in the Union now has established by organic law a system of free public schools supported by taxation; still the deplorable fact meets us everywhere, and at all times, that there are six millions unblessed by any and all of these agencies, with the light of learning, who are starving at a banquet and famishing at a fountain. And yet these children are soon in part to bear the ark that contains the oracles of popular liberty and the covenant of free institutions. The education of the masses in this country, at least in the rudimentary principles of learning, is demanded by every consideration that patriotism, philanthropy, and religion can urge. Neither denominational church enterprise nor private effort, much as they have done, can accomplish this most desirable object. Experience has shown that some system established by law, harmonious in its machinery, universal in its operation, and perpetual in its duration, is required. Experience has also demonstrated that the establishment and maintenance of such a system is an undertaking of the greatest difficulty, involving the utmost exercise of patience, the largest share of liberality, and the highest order of statesmanship; for the reason that its establishment and successful operation depend upon so many conditions rarely found to exist in combination.

The people of the Southern States are engaged in a heroic struggle with these difficulties, which are numerous and formidable. The system encountered at the threshold the opposition of enemies, the fears of the timid, the doubts of the faithless, the apprehension of friends, and the poverty of all. Every step taken discovered some new obstacle in the way of success. There are but comparatively few large cities and towns in the South; the greater part of that section of the Union is rural, the people are engaged in agricultural pursuits, the population in the country is sparse, and great difficulty was found in the location of school-houses so as to accommodate the largest number and equally distribute the benefits of instruction. But the greatest difficulty with which they had to contend, and which it is the object of this bill to obviate, to some extent at least, was the want of means. All will readily recognize money as an indispensable element of success; and that we do not possess. The losses resulting directly and indirectly from the war, the overwhelming burden of debt, public and private, with which the people are crushed, and the enormous taxation necessarily imposed upon them, make it doubtful whether the system of free public schools in the Southern States, so courageously inaugurated, will not have to be abandoned in despair or left to languish and ultimately perish for want of support unless timely aid comes from some quarter. Those who have not taken the trouble to examine into the extent of these losses have but little conception of their magnitude. Take, for illustration, the State of Georgia:

The taxable property in Georgia was valued under oath by the tax-payers in 1860 at	$672,322,777.
In 1868 it was valued at.............	191,235,520
A loss of......................	481,087,257

This includes 450,000 slaves, valued at $302,694,833. The losses, aside from the slaves, amounted to $188,-392,424, an amount nearly equal to the whole taxable property in 1868. It will be borne in mind that this property was valued at a time when cotton brought a high price, when the volume of the currency was large, before the contraction policy of Secretary McCulloch was inaugurated and before the war values had shrunk to a normal condition. If we add to these losses the duplication of the public debt, the consequent increase of taxation, the subversion of our labor system, and the revolution in our modes, habits, industries, and economies, not only of a life-time but of time immemorial, some just judgment can be formed of our poverty and condition to commence and prosecute an expensive system of popular education. And yet Georgia probably suffered less than most of the Southern States. I have purposely refrained from allusion to the crucifixion of reconstruction through which we passed. I have no fancy for rekindling the fires of hate and passion that deluged a continent in blood, nor have I any respect for the man who ignores the vital issues of the living present and coming future to indulge in crimination and recrimination for the low purposes of party or for any other purpose.

Under these circumstances of discouragement and difficulty we have inaugurated this system of public education, and are now struggling to maintain and make it a success. It has in every Southern State the sanction of organic law. The provision upon this subject in the constitution of Georgia is as follows:

There shall be a thorough system of common schools for the education of children in the elementary branches of an English education only, as nearly uniform as practicable, the expenses of which shall be provided for by taxation or otherwise. The school shall be free to all children of the State, but separate schools shall be provided for the white and colored races. Authority may be granted to counties upon the recommendation of two grand juries, and to municipal corporations upon the recommendation of the corporate authority, to establish and maintain public schools in their respective limits by local taxation; but no such local law shall take effect until the same shall have been submitted to a vote of the qualified voters in each county or municipal corporation and approved by a two-thirds vote of persons qualified to vote at such election, and the General Assembly may prescribe who shall vote on such questions.

Emancipation has immensely swelled the number to be educated, and therefore increased the demand for means. This increase in number occurred precisely at the time when the means were most diminished.

The additional number brings no material aid, except perhaps the single item of poll tax levied upon the colored people. Under the educational system of every Southern State the colored people are entitled to an equal participation with the whites in the school fund. There is no distinction, except that the white and colored schools are separate.

Whatever differences of opinion may have existed, or whatever theories may have been advanced or speculations indulged respecting the capabilities of the negro race for intellectual development and distinction, with proper facilities for culture, it is clear that the truth can be ascertained by the test of trial. This experiment the white people of the South have determined, if possible, shall be made. In making it they discharge an obligation while they dispense a benefaction. The history of the negro race is a sad one. It has been the sportive plaything of capricious fortune. Its destiny has been wrought by agencies over which it had no control. Hugging for countless ages the torrid zone, the influences of habit and climate developed the animal nature and emasculated the intellectual and moral powers, leaving barbarism as the result. The contact of the negro with the white race has hitherto been, in the main, under conditions that confined the means of their advancement to imitation and observation. Neither history nor tradition brings from them any contribution to civilization in the achievment of arms, the discoveries of science, or the inventions of art. I have said that the white people of the South are but discharging an obligation to the negroes in an effort to educate their children. They served us before emancipation, they were faithful to us in the dark days of the war, and they have, under the circumstances and temptations surrounding them, demeaned themselves well since the surrender.

What were the circumstances surrounding them? They were suddenly transformed from slaves to freedmen; they did not and perhaps never will know who was responsible for their enslavement. They would naturally hold their former masters responsible and regard the agents of the Federal Government as their deliverers; and thus the avenues to their confidence and credulity were opened. The Freedman's Bank was established to be plundered by knaves, and the Freedman's Bureau organized to control their political affiliations under the pretext of managing their affairs. Artful villians appealed to their communistic instincts by false promises of an agrarian division of property. Infamous adventurers swore them to deadly hostility to the whites in secret conclaves in the darkness of midnight, and aroused their superstition by administering the oath over skeletons and coffins. Newly clothed with the rights, privileges, and immunities of citizenship, they were marched and countermarched on election days to the stirring music of drum and fife around the polls in the presence of disfranchised patriotism and ostracised virtue and intelligence. They were elevated from prison cells to legislative halls, and converted from sweating convicts into pompous legislators, exchanging the humbler occupation of bearing burdens for the loftier business of making constitutions. And at last Federal legislation undertook to bridge the social gulf separating the races, established by nature and extending "down to earth profound and up to heaven," and invite them over to perfect social equality with the superior race.

Yet with all these powerful influences pressed upon them, let it be said to the infinite credit of the great mass of the colored people that they have conducted themselves with a propriety and exhibited a capacity for usefulness in society that has more than met the expectations of their most judicious friends. If occasional riots have attended or preceded elections, they have been instigated and manipulated outside of the South, or by the agents of parties outside, to inflame and control public opinion pending closely contested elections in other states, with the view of controlling important elections. And thus the colored people have been made the unwitting instruments of occasional disorders which have their conception in foul conspiracies outside of the South, and for which the white people of the South are falsely held responsible. The relations of friendship existing between the races in the South are not at all surprising; it is but the ligitimate effect of obvious causes and results from traditional family attachments not in any wise incompatible with superior and subordinate relations. The races are identified in interest and in neighborhood. The dealings of the white race with the black have been characterized by the strictest justice, fairness, and honesty; the colored people have received from them sympathy in their sorrow, assistance in their misfortunes, and encouragement in their struggles; all of their political rights have been conceded with cheerfulness and enforced with fidelity; an upright and learned bench always assigns for the defense of the accused who are unable to employ counsel the ablest lawyers the bar supplies; and now, in almost hopeless poverty, the white people are paying heavy self-imposed taxes to test the experiment of their education.

If the colored people are the "wards of the nation," if the Federal Government is the guardian of these people, this bill and this occasion furnish the finest opportunity it will ever have to discharge the most important duty of the guardianship—the education of the wards. They stand here by the millions through their representatives and insist that the Government will at least aid their late owners in this humane effort to improve their condition; and this appeal they emphasize with the pathos of helplessness, of poverty. How far their general education, if it can be accomplished, would affect their inclination to manual labor and impair their capacity for its performance, is a question that may well excite serious apprehension. Living as they do in a purely agricultural section, and adapted as their labor is to the climate and productions of that section, their manual labor is not only indispensable to their own support, but of the first importance to the prosperity of the whole country. But the consideration of this question is foreclosed by the general judgment of the country that the experiment shall be made. The practical question now is, how to secure the means to make it. Since the organization of the Government, Congress has donated to the cause of education, under different acts, land amounting in the aggregate to 95,737,714 acres, and the sum of $47,785,197.93 in money. The greater portion of the land was given to the Northwestern States by setting apart for educational purposes, in that section, sections 16 and 36. Upon her annexation to the Union the State of Texas reserved her public lands, and has therefore ample resources for the support of her educational system. But she stands the solitary exception among the Southern States, who have received only a trifling sum compared with the amount received by other States, Virginia and Georgia less than almost any of them, although each ceded to the General Government an empire in extent and wealth, and now in the extremity of their poverty, when the number of their illiterate population has been doubled, they invoke the aid which the bill proposes to extend. They do so in common with the other Southern States, not only to educate the white children within their borders, but to educate the ignorant colored race in which one-eighth of the sovereign political power of the Republic is vested by the Constitution and laws of the United States. Thirty-five Representatives of the American people on this floor symbolize the power of the negro race, two-fifths of which—fourteen in number—accrued from emancipation; to say nothing of the improvement of their intelligence, their morals, and their elevation in the scale of civilization. Does not the qualification for citizenship, which education alone supplies, demand imperatively that speedy and ample provision be made for that education?

Are not the institutions of this country imperiled by the ignorance of so large a number with whom political power is deposited, whose votes from ignorance, are liable to be controlled by prejudice or purchase? Is not the Government under some obligation to furnish the means to qualify these people for the enjoyment of the right and the exercise of the power which is so unceremoniously and bountifully thrust upon them? This bill provides that one-fourth of the money appropriated by it shall be given to the agricultural colleges unless the Legislatures of the States and Territories shall otherwise direct; thus devoting one-fourth of the sum to agricultural education. The judgment of Congress and the country has been made up upon the wisdom and propriety of fostering intelligence in the cultivation of the soil of this country. That judgment is recorded in the act establishing these colleges and appropriating a part of the public land to support them, and in the acts of the various Legislatures accepting the donation. The success of these institutions vindicates their claim to liberal support.

I but state what all know to be true when I assert that the agricultural is the paramount interest of this country, the basis of all prosperity, and the only original source from which subsistence and clothing come. There can be no reason why its votaries should not be as well educated as those of any other art or science, and there can exist no reason why cultivated intellect should not be employed in the discovery and the development of the resources of the soil. The North Georgia Agricultural College, established by the act of 1862, has accomplished more good in the few years of its existence than any two schools in the State within the same period; unfortunately its buildings were recently destroyed by fire.

To the products of the soil are we mainly indebted for the balance of trade in our favor, amounting for the last year to $309,309,741. It is the labor employed in agriculture and the products of that labor that enable us to dispute commercial supremacy with Great Britain. This labor is productive in the proportion that it is guided by intelligence.

If experience should show that one-fourth of this money could be more usefully employed in other departments of education, then it is perfectly competent for the Legislatures of the States and Territories so to employ it. It is within the control and subject to the direction of the State and territorial authorities. There can therefore, as it seems to me, be no well-founded objection to the bill because it gives a part of the money to this particular class of institutions. While this istruly a national question, still, regarding it from a local and sectional standpoint; in view of the necessities for aid to public education in the South, it is important to inquire what amount this measure will supply. Assuming, as estimated by the Commissioner of Education, that the sales will amount annually to $1,500,000, the amount that each of the Southern States would receive is exhibited in the following table:

Alabama	$101,534.56
Arkansas	35,347.50

Florida	19,034.61
Georgia	124,221.66
Kentucky	88,058.19
Louisiana	73,208.10
Mississippi	83,056.90
Missouri	58,960.03
North Carolina	105,425.63
South Carolina	76,978.02
Tennessee	96,679.35
Texas	58,772.35
Virginia	118,203.99
West Virginia	21,602.58
	$1,061,083.47

It will be seen that the State of Georgia would annually receive upon this basis $124,221.66, one-fourth of which, or $31,055.41, for five years would amount to $155,277. This would endow the agricultural college, leaving to the cause of popular education in this State each year $93,166.25, which amount would vary of course with the amount of the sales of the public land. We can form some estimate of the aid which this bill will render to the education of the people of the United States when it is remembered that the public domain, surveyed and unsurveyed, amounts to 1,154,-471,762 acres. Whether this domain shall be wisely and humanely devoted to the education and elevation of the masses of the people of this country, distributed upon the basis of necessity and equality, or given to rich and powerful corporations, and thus increase their means of fixing the price of labor and controlling legislation, is not a debatable question.

Mr. Chairman, the first century of our national existence vindicates the wisdom that founded our institutions and the beneficence that distinguishes their operation. Our career is the wonder and admiration of the world. We have extended our domain from a narrow strip along the Atlantic coast across a hundred degrees of longitude to the Pacific Ocean, increased the number of States from thirteen to thirty-eight and our population from three millions to fifty millions. We have a country that possesses every variety of climate and production, soil and scenery. It combines in prodigal profusion every element of individual and national wealth. It opens an inviting field to every industrial enterprise and bestows the richest rewards upon the efforts of labor. It has given to immortality the names of Franklin, Fulton, and Morse, and bequeathed to mankind the triumphs of their genius. Its discoveries in science and inventions in art have revolutionized the industries and commerce of the world. Her iron ships float upon every sea and bear to every port the treasures of her mines, her fields, and her forests.

Our skill has unlocked the arcana of nature and utilized her physical forces in constructing the temple of freedom, and American genius has brought its trophies of sculpture, painting, and poetry to adorn its columns and festoon its arches. American orators have eclipsed the famous masters of antiquity. American literature has attained a range of thought, a felicity of expression, and a purity of sentiment unknown to other ages and countries. We have sent back to the birthplace of civilization the inspiration of a new national life and aroused the East from the slumber of ages. Hoary systems are dissolving in the blaze of the star of empire that "westward takes its way." Vitalized by contact with us, China and Japan have adopted systems of popular education abreast with the demands of the age that rival the best models of modern times. But while we are dazzled with the splendor of these achievements that cultivated intellect has done so much to secure, we are confronted with the melancholy fact that six millions of American children are unable to read and write the language in which the historian records and perpetuates them.

If so much has been accomplished in the brief period of a century under existing disadvantages, what hopes are the least sanguine not authorized to indulge of the future grandeur and glory of our common country? Each conquest in this aggressive march to national destiny enlarges the desire and augments the power for new and grander results, and each new acquisition imposes additional obligations.

Next in importance to the obligation to preserve public liberty is the duty of providing the means for popular education. These will be the two great agents of advancement in the future, as they have been of success in the past. The possibilities of our future promise more than the realization of Utopian dreams. They spread out over the vast West a population numbered by hundreds of millions, combining the strength of the Roman with the culture of the Greek, uniting the chivalry of Bayard with the benevolence of Howard, and exhibiting in blended harmony the best elements of the Puritan and the Cavalier; a wilderness reclaimed from primeval solitude, yielding to industry harvests that fill the marts of the world with commerce and appease the hunger of nations with bread; great national highways substituting the dim trail of the receding Indian, magnificent cities occupying the place of abandoned wigwams, and the light of council-fires paling before the superior light reflected from galleries of art, halls of learning, and temples of worship, realizing the fulfillment of prophetic prediction:

"The wilderness shall be glad for them, and the desert shall rejoice and blossom as the rose."

This population under the protection of and this progress fostered by a Government under a written constitution, that explicitly defines the powers of the Government and expressly secures the rights of the people, we may here expect to witness the highest physical, social, moral, and political development of which the race is capable.

It was during the thousand years of darkness and blood, when cloistered monks monopolized the learning of Europe and Asia, leaving the masses in ignorance, that barbarous conquerors and ambitious prelates fastened upon the world the despotism of the Feudal system and the horrors of the Inquisition. Against this stupendous crime upon humanity its mind, heart, and conscience have never ceased to utter their protest. The revival of letters and the general diffusion of knowledge relaxed the grasp of the tyrant and broke the spell of tyranny; and cultivated intellect, inspired by patriotism at the expense of blood has erected and consecrated upon American soil the sacred temple of liberty, rebuilt her ruined altars, installed her banished priestess, and restored the worship of her divinity. And here, under the patronage of Republican institutions and universal education, liberty finds its freest expression, religion its purest model, and humanity its highest type.

Speech of Hon. Hiram P. Bell, Delivered Before the General Assembly of the State of Georgia in Special Joint Session, Dec. 3, 1901. Reported by Mr. McAllister. Subject:The Georgia Secession Convention of 1861.

Mr. President; Mr. Speaker;Gentlemen of the General Assembly of the State of Georgia; Ladies and Gentlemen:—

I can only wish that I deserved a tithe of the eulogiums which my friend has seen proper to pronounce upon me. I am really at a loss to know whether to accept it as a tribute of friendship, or as an example of the splendid ability of the president to round magnificient periods of oratory.

We live and have lived in a history-making epoch; and we are here to-night to consider the most important, certainly the most thrilling event in the history of this great commonwealth,—the secession convention of 1861. The decade that preceded that convention is crowded with the startling developments of the conflict of opinion in this country, upon the question of African Slavery. We thought—or the country thought—upon the admission of Missouri into the Union in 1821, that there would be a respite from the slavery agitation. There was comparative rest for a period of nearly thirty years. But Southern valor in the field, under the administration of a Democratic president, on the battlefields of Mexico, aided by Southern diplomacy at Guadaloupe, Hidalgo, had won for our common country an empire upon the Pacific slope. In 1847, Commodore Stockton captured California, in area nearly as large as New England, New York and Pennsylvania. A military government was organized, a constitutional convention was called. That convention framed a constitution excluding African slavery, which was submitted, under military authority, to a conglomeration of mongrels, Mexicans and Indians; *id et omni genus,* and with that constitution, thus irregularly and illegally framed, California applied for admission into the sisterhood of States.

That application was met with an indignant protest from the men of the section whose blood and valor had wrung the soil from the grasp of a foreign power. It kindled their chivalry like flame, and reopened the fearful conflict of opinion between the sections of our common country. Its solution was found in the compromise measure of 1850. The admission of California into the Union, the passage of the Fugitive Slave law, the abolition of the slave trade in the District of Columbia and the dockyards of the United States, all had their effect, and the fires thus kindled were never extinguished. The Southern people met in convention in Nashville under the presidency of a Southern Statesman, and protested. The people of Georgia assembled in convention in 1850, and while they acquiesced *ex necessitate rei* in existing conditions, they entered a vigorous protest, and announced that unless the aggressions of the Northern States upon the South ceased, they would be resisted to the disruption of every tie which bound Georgia to the Union.

This controversy resulted in a division of the Southern people and the Democratic party into two factions, marshalled respectively under the banners of Southern Rights and Union, and so complete was that division, and so well defined, that in 1852, when the party harmonized upon Pierce and King for the presidency and vice-presidency, the Democratic party of Georgia ran two electoral tickets. And so intense was this factional feeling in the sister State of Alabama, that the Democratic party of Alabama, although her ablest statesman was upon the ticket, nominated the lion-hearted Troup, of Georgia, and the chivalric Quitman, of Mississippi, for the presidency and vice-presidency.

Mr. Pierce gave to the country a comparatively conservative administration. In 1854, Stephen A. Douglas, chairman of the committee on Territories in the United States Senate, and Alexander H. Stephens, chairman of a similar committee in the House, reported the now famous and historic "Kansas-Nebraska" bill, the leading feature of which was the recognition of what was known as the doctrine of popular sovereignty. That rekindled the fires of slavery agitation. New England piety gathered from the slums of her cities her thugs, riff-raff and pluguglies, armed them with Sharp's rifles and sent them to the borders of Kansas to butcher men who had settled and were occupying the country. The result of that contest was the bringing forward of John C. Fremont for the presidency in 1856, and he failed of an election by a very small majority of the popular vote of the country.

In 1858, the celebrated debates between Stephen A. Douglas and Abraham Lincoln, took place in the State of Illinois, when they contested the United States senatorship before the people, the issue being the Congressional exclusion of slavery, maintained by Lincoln, or the right of the people to ordain their own government and institutions, maintained by Douglas. The result was the popular verdict for Lincoln, but the legislative triumph of Douglas. That campaign, and his Cooper Union speech made Abraham Lincoln president of the United States. He was the representative of a purely sectional party.

In the meantime, the Democratic convention for the nomination of presidential candidates assembled at Charleston. During this agitation there flourished a large secret organization of Southern patriots known as the Knights of the Golden Circle. A leading and distinguished Alabamian advocated the policy of a division of the party at Charleston and the defeat of the nomination of Douglas, who was the recognized leader of the party as to strength if not as to ability, and there is now in print extant a letter in which he announced that the policy of the fire-eating element of the South was to defeat the nomination of Douglas for the presidency, divide the party, secure the election for Lincoln, and precipitate the Cotton States into revolution.

The convention was divided. Douglas was within a fraction of a vote of receiving the requisite two-thirds. One wing of the party nominated Breckenridge and Lane; another nominated Douglas and Johnson. The Republicans nominated Lincoln and Hamlin. The National party nominated Bell and Everett.. These parties represented these distinctive political positions upon the everlasting slavery question: Breckenridge represented the proposition of Congressional protection to slavery in the Territories; Lincoln, the Congressional exclusion of slavery from the territories; Douglas proclaimed the inherent popular inalienable right of the people of the Territories, as well as elsewhere, to determine their own institutions as they might wish. Bell represented a platform with ten words: "The Constitution, the Union, and the enforcement of the law." That contest was upon those issues. Lincoln won in the electoral college by a large majority, but was defeated in the popular vote by over a half million. There was no election in Georgia,—I mean no election by the people.

In the autumn of 1860, the Legislature of Georgia assembled, the State all ablaze with interest, with excitement and with apprehension. There were those in Georgia who insisted upon the secession of the State from the Union by the Legislature. Wiser counsels prevailed, however, and on the 20th of November, 1860, a bill passed the Legislature calling a convention of the people of the State of Georgia to consider the gravity of the situation and adopt the line of policy that Georgia desired to pursue.

That convention met on the 16th day of January, 1861. In some counties the distinct issue was made—in a few, not a great many. In a great many other counties the Southern Rights party had no opposition. In many other counties what was known as the Union or Co-operation Party had no opposition. In still other counties, there was a union of the two parties in the selection of candidates.

That convention met to wrestle with the weightiest question that ever oppressed patriot hearts. I shall never forget my approach to the capitol on that occasion. I had never been in Milledgeville. The first view I had of the capitol of my own State, after a Presidential campaign in which I had made in every county in my Congressional district the best Glorious—Union—and—Star—Spangled—Banner speeches of which I was capable, presented to my gaze a tremendous flag floating from the capitol building, with a rattlesnake in coil, its mouth open—the symbol of the creature that withered Eden's bloom with the slime of sin. The cold repulsion upon my heart and my feelings is simply beyond the power of language to express. I had loved the glorious old Stars and Stripes. It had sheltered Washington and his shivering soldiers in the snows of Valley Forge. It was borne by Scott and Harrison at Lundy's Lane and the Thames, when British grenadiers that fought with Wellington in Spain and won with Wellington at Waterloo, fled. It shadowed the brave De-Kalb as he lay bleeding on the smoking plains at Camden. It was christened in a baptism of the richest blood from the heart of Jasper, and had floated in triumph from the dome of the capitol of the Aztecs.

> "Flag of the free heart's hope and home,
> By angel hands to valor given,
> Its stars have lit the azure dome,
> And all its hues were born in Heaven."

I call your attention now to the personnel of the convention of 1861. It was composed of 296 men representing every interest of the State, representing every department of industrial endeavor, representing every type and class of ability in Georgia. There was a constellation of Georgia's most brilliant stars at the head of that memorable and historic body. Ex-Secretary of War George W. Crawford, ex-Governors of Georgia Crawford and Johnson, ex-United States Senators Toombs and Johnson, ex-Justices of the Supreme Court Benning, Nisbet, Stephens and Warner, ex-Congressman Stephens, Toombs, Colquitt, Poe, Bailey, Nisbet, Chastain and Murphy, (Murphy died the day the convention assembled), and ex-judges of the superior court almost innumerable,—Hansell, Tripp, Rice, Reese, Harris and Fleming; all men of the highest ability and the purest patriotism, who had held the highest offices of the Government, save that of President of the United States. In addition to these able statesmen, three lawyers were in that convention who stood in the very forefront of the bar in all the South: Benjamin H. Hill, Thomas

R. R. Cobb and Francis S. Bartow. Divinity and scholarship were represented by Nathan M. Crawford, president of Mercer University, and Alexander Means, ex-president of Emory College. The bar, the pulpit, the farm, the counter, the doctor-shop, the office—everywhere, everybody had the very best specimens of the race for representatives in that convention.

When we met everything was in uncertainty, everything was in doubt. There has never been a question in my mind but that at the time of the election of those who were opposed to secession *per se,* were immensely in the majority. Nobody knew what would be done, or what could be done, to chain the cyclone. The feeling was so intense as to make men stand aghast as they looked into the face of their fellows. The very air quivered with the intensity of feeling, solicitude and apprehension. The co-operationists called a caucus on the evening of the 15th, at which Alexander H. Stephens, Linton Stephens, Hiram Warner, and, as I remember, Benjamin H. Hill, and my distinguished friend, ex-Governor McDaniel, and many others of us, met with a view to arranging some sort of a platform upon which we could stand, and it was finally arranged that Governor Johnson should prepare a substitute to the proposition to secede immediately, which he did.

Next morning the convention met. Of course, we knew not what the other side was doing, except as it developed in the infinite shrewdness of their policy. When we met, Asbury Hull moved that George W. Crawford should be elected president by acclamation. The significance of that selection lay in the fact that

Hull was the embodiment of conservatism, purity of character and the absence of madcap passion. He was a type of magnificent, moral, conservative and intellectual manhood. Of course, the motion was adopted. The next proposition was to elect a secretary, and Muscogee, always in evidence when a good officer is needed, came to the front with Albert Lamar, with a blue cockade in his hat, and he was elected. Then they manœuvered. These parties skirmished, neither knowing exactly where the majority would lie. Everybody anxious, everybody scared—I pledge you my word I was completely dazed. I didn't know what would happen. I felt like I was standing in the shadow of some great event that had been cast before, and nearly everybody felt the same way. There was no jubilation, no fun, no frolicking, no absence from that convention on free passes. Every delegate was in his seat.

Well, they manœuvered about in the adoption of rules until the 17th. The Commissioner of South Carolina was on hand, and ex-Governor Shorter, of Alabama, was there also, and at the proper time they were invited to address the convention, on the 18th. All was going along nicely, and all running in one current. When the convention met on the 19th, Mr. Hull moved to go into secret session, and so soon as the doors were closed, one of the finest historical characters that I ever knew arose,—small, elegant, he looked as if he had just been withdrawn from a bandbox in his wife's boudoir. Cold as a Siberian icicle, clear as a tropical sunbeam, pure as the down on a seraph's wing,—such was Eugenius A. Nisbet. I would not trust my memory to quote his language, but this is the resolution which he presented to the convention:

"The doors were then closed, and Mr. Nisbet offered the following resolutions, which were taken up and read: 'Resolved, that in the opinion of this convention, it is the right and duty of Georgia to secede from the present Union, and to co-operate with such of the other States as have or shall do the same, for the purpose of forming a Southern Confederacy upon the basis of the Constitution of the United States.' Resolved that a committee of —— be appointed by the chair to report an ordinance to assert the right and fulfill the obligation of the State of Georgia to secede from the Union."

History has recorded the consequences that followed from that resolution; and you will be surprised to hear that that pure, clear and able man, in about a twenty minutes speech, argued in favor of the adoption of that resolution, and based his argument solely upon the ground that it was the only way to prevent war! The argument was that if we did not secede we would fight among ourselves. There was no sort of idea of any war with the United States if we did secede. When he took his seat, Governor Johnson arose and presented a very remarkable paper, which you will find by reference to the Journal of the convention. In the magnificent, Macaulay-like style peculiar to him, as faulty in logic and as untrue in practicability as a composition of that length could well be, it was the best we could do to catch in falling. Well, I expected debate like that war of the fabled gods, which shook nations and realms in its jar. Governor Johnson made perhaps a fifteen or twenty minutes speech, which was an attempt to defend his substitute. The truth is, that we were like Atlas, crushed by the superincumbent burden of the world. The question was too deep, and the consequences too great, and those great and glorious orators trembled, as I thought then and as I think now. They certainly failed to come up to my expectations.

When he sat down, Thomas R. R. Cobb arose, free from passion, earnest, calm, pure, patriotic, and made a short speech, taking it for granted that of course we were going to secede, and down he sat. When he took his seat Alexander H. Stephens arose, under a high tide of excitement. I was associated with him pretty closely for four years, but I had never seen him so excited. He went on to picture the cost and suffering and sacrifice that the Union involved. He spoke of the benediction it had been to the people. He spoke of the glory and grandeur that it was destined, undissolved, to accomplish. "But," said he, "if you ever intend to secede, the sooner you do so, the better," which was a confession of judgment in open court. Mr. Toombs then arose, that combination of Cato, Agamemnon and Mirabeau, and for about ten minutes, with the skill of a master he told of the persecutions in legislation and of the aggressions of the North upon the rights of the South. He spoke of the benefactions that they had received from the Government in the way of high protective tariffs, in fishing bounties and in the coast trade, and he charged upon them the intended destruction of the institution of slavery by the election of a sectional president pledged to its exclusion by law from the Territories and its confinement within the then existing limits. He closed with this remark: "Mr. President and gentlemen, these are facts. South Carolina has withdrawn. It remains for you to grasp in fraternity the bloody hand of Massachusetts, or align yourselves with gallant South Carolina!" That is the only sentence that ever shook my views upon the question. When he concluded Dr. Means arose and made a Star-Spangled-Banner speech, such as only he could make. Judge Reese, of Madison, made a strong, sturdy little talk. Just as the dinner hour approached, and the convention was about to adjourn, Benjamin H. Hill took the floor and by common consent, or as we call it now, unanimous consent, he was recognized. He opened his speech with, I think, the most thrilling eloquence I have ever heard. Said he, "Mr. President and Gentlemen of the Convention, we now witness the dying throes of the grandest government God Almighty ever vouchsafed to man. Let us not be in haste to wrap around its corpse the winding-sheet." And for thirty or forty minutes, with a power of speech, with a thrilling eloquence and with a logic characteristic of Benjamin H. Hill alone, he addressed that convention; and yet that speech, which ordinarily would have stirred multi tudes to madness, fell upon that convention like the arrows aimed at the heart of Priam,—bloodless to the ground. Francis S. Bartow, far back in the Representative hall, arose, all on fire, and with decided power and energy and vim (I like to have said vindictiveness) he made a telling speech. So soon as he sat down, Marcellus Douglas arose, pointed at him and said: "That man is Charles Carrol of Carrollton."

The vote was taken; ayes 166, noes 130. The ordinance carrying the resolution into effect was adopted. George W. Crawford, the president, announced: "Gentlemen of the Convention, I have the pleasure to announce that the State of Georgia is free, sovereign and independent!" A question arose with some of the Union delegates about signing the ordinance, and there were some that were disinclined to sign. When, however, the convention at length adopted a resolution requesting them to sign, all of them except seven did so. Latimer and McRae, of Montgomery, Simmons, of Gwinett, Welchel and Byrd, of Hall, and Simmons, of Pickens, were those who refused to sign the ordinance, but it is due to their memory to state, that whilst they signed a protest against its passage, they pledged, like our forefathers, their lives, their fortunes and their sacred honor for its vindication. William C. Fain, of the county of Fannin, refused to sign either the ordinance, or the protest. He was killed early in the War by scouts near his own home.

I have remarked that a good many hesitated about signing the ordinance. W. T. Day, of Jasper, and Anderson and Farnsworth, of Murray County, had quite a discussion over the question. They thought about it all of one night, and the next morning when they arose, Farnsworth said to Day: "Day I have been pondering this thing over all night, and I have concluded that I will sign the ordinance as a witness that the damned thing has passed."

What followed, my fellow-citizens, is a matter of history. The theory of secession was Paradise promised; its realization was Hell endured. When that Ordinance of Secession was passed, Georgia was worth seven hundred millions of taxable property, according to the official message of the Governor; four years from that day our heritage was ashes and ruins, ground and glory and graves. I am not repining at the result; but it was, and it always will seem strange to me, that men of experience, men of statesmanship, men of patriotism, men of wisdom, could be so immensely mistaken, as to suppose that the spirit which had organized a sectional party, elected a sectional president and overthrown and subverted the Constitution which they had sworn to support, would let us depart in peace. Seven years after this event, free negroes, carpet-baggers, bounty-jumpers and Federal army officers were assembled in this capitol, making a constitution for Georgia; not free, but for disfranchised virtue and patriotism. I do not blame anybody. I am dealing with historic facts. But I can not relieve my mind and my heart of the conviction that sometime, somewhere, somebody will have to answer for the blood and slaughter of 1861. And the years following, we had no government; we had no constitution; we had no army; we had no navy; we had no commerce; we had no commercial relations with the world; and the united judgment of the civilized world was against us upon the controlling issue of that controversy,—African slavery. And yet, in the absence of all this, more statesmanship and more patriotism were never exhibited, in my judgment, than was by the statesmen of the Confederacy after we got into the struggle. The grandest Congressional delegation, in my opinon, in history, was the delegation of Georgia to the Provisional Congress. Think of it! Bartow, Crawford, Kennan, Stephens, Toombs, Howell Cobb, Thomas R. R. Cobb, Benjamin Harvey Hill and Augustus R. Wright! The trouble was that the world was against us! The grandest army that ever trod the planet was the Confederate Army. It grasped the sparkling gem of victory from the cannon's smoking mouth, on a hundred bloody fields, and spangled the milky way of glory with its gorgeous jewelry of stars!

On the 28th day of January the convention appointed to the several Southern States the following commissioners, charged with the duty of presenting to the officers of said States, the Ordinance of Secession with the reasons which induced its adoption. The commissioners were for Virginia, Henry L. Benning; Maryland, Ambrose R. Wright; Kentucky, Henry R. Jackson; Tennessee, Hiram P. Bell; Missouri, Luther J. Glenn; Arkansas, D. P. Hill; Delaware, D. C. Campbell; North Carolina, Samuel Hall; Texas, J. W. A. Sanford. After the passage of various ordinances to adjust the relation of the State to the new condition, the convention took a recess, to meet at Savannah upon the call of the president, in obedience to which it reassembled in the city of Savannah, March 7, 1861. On the 15th of March the permanent Constitution of the Confederate States of America adopted by the Provisional Congress at Montgomery was presented by the president of the convention. On the day following, on motion of Alexander H. Stephens, the Constitution was unanimously ratified.

On the 23rd of March the convention adopted and submitted to the qualified voters of the State for ratification, the State Constitution, which was duly ratified on the first Tuesday in March, 1861.

The convention adjourned *sine die* March 23, 1861. Thus the issue made up between the Northern and Southern sections of a once common Union was submitted to the determination of the sword, the *ultima ratio regum*.

I have spoken of a past event. I know now of but eight solitary survivors of all those who participated in that event. I am delighted to see my distinguished friend, ex-Governor McDaniel present. He is one. Augustus H. Hansell, of Thomasville, Jefferson Jennings, of Jackson, Henry R. Harris, of Meriwether, William T. Day, of Pickens, William A. Teasley, of Cherokee, L. H. O. Martin, of Elbert, and your speaker of this evening is the eighth.

Oh, how time flies; and how these reminiscences of past mistakes and troubles and sorrows should incite us to the faithful discharge of patriotic duty while our short probation exists.

I thank you, gentlemen of the General Assembly and Ladies and Gentlemen, for the kind attention that you have given me.

Memorial Address of Mr. Bell, of Georgia, on the Life and Character of Julian Hartridge.

Mr. Speaker: The whole country received the announcement that Julian Hartridge was dead, with consternation and sorrow. The people of Georgia have enshrined his memory in their hearts and placed upon his bier their immortelles, dripping with the tears of their anguish. The summons came to him in the vigor of his manhood and the full maturity of his powers, and closed a useful and brilliant career with scarcely a note of warning. We are prepared for the demise of the aged and infirm, and we watch the flickering of life's lamp in them with emotions similar to those with which we look upon the mellow glow of sunset. The grave then loses something of its terrors as we contemplate it as the resting-place of a weary pilgrimage. Ignoring the sad truth that humanity is subjected to the universal law of suffering and death, we assign to life's duration the limit which age alone prescribes. We seem to forget that—

> Leaves have their time to fall,
> And flowers to wither at the north wind's breath,
> And stars to set;—but all,
> Thou hast all seasons for thine own, O death!

Death palsies the arm of the warrior, and he drops from his nerveless grasp the shattered spear. It stills the tongue of the orator, and the senate and the forum are silent. It severs the chord in the tide of song, and the harp of the minstrel hangs upon the willow. It drinks from the blushes of beauty the mingled hues of the rose and lily, and the reptiles of the grave banquet upon the lips our love has pressed. Every age and every clime is monumental with its symbols and strewn with the trophies of its conquests.

And still we are startled when its victim is selected from the strong, suddenly stricken down in the full-orbed splendor of manhood's high meridian, leaving exalted position vacant, and forever blighting the promise of future honor and usefulness to country and kind. The estimation in which the lamented Hartridge was held by the people of his native State is shown by the honors conferred upon him living, and the grief with which they mourn him dead. He was born in the city of Savannah, and spent the gambols of his childhood and won the triumphs of his manhood in that beautiful city that keeps vigil like a weeping vestal over the repose of his ashes.

Julian Hartridge commenced his education in the schools of his native State and completed it at Brown University in Rhode Island, graduating with high distinction. He selected the law as his profession and for a period attended the law school at Cambridge, Massachusetts. Soon after his admission to the bar the people of his country, always distinguished for their wisdom in selecting their ablest men for official trusts, returned him to the Legislature, in which, at a bound, he placed himself in the front rank of the wise men of the State as an eloquent speaker, ready debater, and practical legislator. He was a delegate to the historic national Democratic convention that met in Charleston in 1860. Returned to the Confederate Congress in 1861, he was re-elected in 1863 and served as a member of that body during the existence of the Confederacy.

He was chosen chairman of the executive committee of the Democratic party of the State of Georgia in 1871, delegate for the State at large to the national Democratic convention in 1872, an elector for the State at large on the Greeley and Brown ticket in the presidential campaign. He was elected a representative from the first district of Georgia to the Forty-fourth Congress and re-elected to the Forty-fifth, of which he was an honored and useful member at the time of his death. He was always fully equal to the emergency surrounding him, discharging the duties of every official position to which he was called to the gratification of his friends and the admiration of his enemies. He recognized in the law a jealous mistress, and paid chivalric court to her shrine. He entered the lists for professional trial and professional triumph with a bar illustrated with the learning and adorned with the virtues of Berrien, Charlton, and Law, and soon the lance of the youthful knight was gleaming at its head. He was elected by the Legislature solicitor-general of the eastern judicial circuit, and the certainty with which criminals were convicted and crime punished attested the ability and fidelity with which he met the obligations and discharged the duties of that responsible office.

His thorough culture, his sense of justice, his love of right, and his powers of analysis eminently fitted him for success at the bar. His statements of the questions of law in his case had the clearness and force of argument, and his representation of the facts the merit of fairness and candor. Repudiating mere *dicta* as authority, he venerated the precedents established by the great lights of the law based upon authority and sustained by reason. He seized with promptness the controlling points of his case and fortified them with authority until his position was impregnable, and then assailed his adversary in his weak points by harrassing sorties from his chosen stronghold. His position thus taken and his authorities arranged, he brought to his argument the aid of a style of singular vigor and perspicuity. He aroused the indignation of juries against wrong with blistering invective and won them to his cause and his client with the appeals of melting pathos.

He added to a handsome person the accomplishment of graceful action and the power of a charming voice. His elocution was faultless; you could neither add nor reject a word without marring its beauty or impairing its harmony. The sentences were so constructed as to evolve the exact thought with the greatest possible force, and to flow in "Pierian streams, transparent, cool, and sweet." The multitude hung like the bees of Hybla upon his lips to catch the sweetness his eloquence distilled. His mind, trained in the disputations of the forum, in intellectual gladiatorship with lawyers of the highest order of ability, who came together like electric clouds, flashing as they met, acquired wonderful powers of activity and concentration; and these powers, marshaled by him for the ascertainment and defense of truth, were wielded with the skill of a master.

The truth was his guiding star in all his investigations. He sought it by the nearest ways and plainest methods that earnest inquiry and thorough research could discover. His resources of learning supplied him with rich stores of classical illustration which were used not to embellish, but to intensify his logic. Criminal prosecutions involving the death penalty fully developed his transcendent powers of advocacy. The announcement that Hartridge would address the jury in a murder case was the signal for an admiring multitude to crowd the court-room. The reports of the Supreme Court of Georgia contain the evidence of his research, and learning as a jurist. He was averse to the irksome drudgery of routine labor, but delighted in the investigation and solution of new and difficult problems of law and political economy. Brave as Cæsar, he was modest as a maiden. He had an exalted conception of the amenities and proprieties of life in its private, professional, and public relations.

He seldom spoke in the House of Representatives, his sensitive nature revolting at the struggle for the floor which frequently characterizes its proceedings, and his modesty recoiling at the thought of thrusting a speech on unwilling auditors; but when he did speak he always confined himself to the question, enlightened the House, and commanded its attention. His speech on the electoral commission, and the one delivered at the last session on the bill to prevent the introduction into the United States of contagious and infectious diseases, are fine models of parliamentary eloquence. The world is unwilling to concede excellence in more than one department of intellectual superiority, but his professional brethren who knew him best have accorded to him rare powers of advocacy and great learning as a jurist, and by common consent have assigned him his position at their head.

Of his statesmanship it is scarcely necessary to speak in this presence; decided in his convictions, ardent in his patriotism, comprehensive in his views, and intensely devoted to the Constitution of his country, he was a model representative of an intelligent and patriotic constituency. To appreciate the social qualities of Julian Hartridge it was necessary to know him intimately. Beneath an apparently cold exterior was concealed an affluence of genial nature, warm frienship, and tender sensibility. At his desk during the last session of Congress, he grasped my hand warmly, and in the absence of any suggestion leading or referring to the subject, with evident emotion said:

"I am regarded as cold, distant, and proud, but no man has ever been so misunderstood; there never was a greater mistake. There never was a warmer heart than mine. The truth is, it arises from a defect in my vision. I am near-sighted, and can not recognize my dearest friends at any distance from me. I would give the world if it were otherwise."

Although I had been acquainted with him for twenty years, I never knew nor appreciated him until that moment. It developed in him the possession of a large endowment of these rare and high qualities which constitute the charm of social life, beautifully and comprehensively called—

The softer green of the soul.

His countrymen have twined for his memory the wreath of laurel and cypress—the insignia of their pride and the symbol of their sorrow; and his friends have dropped upon his new-made grave friendship's last offering, the tribute of their tears.

But strew his ashes to the wind
Whose sword or voice has served mankind—
And is he dead, whose glorious mind
Lifts thine on high?
To live in hearts we leave behind,
Is not to die.

In the death of my late colleague the Republic has lost a patriotic citizen and a wise statesman, the profession an eloquent advocate and a learned jurist, society a courtly gentleman and a brilliant ornament, and his family a devoted husband and affectionate father. All that is left to them of Julian Hartridge is the heritage of his wisdom, the light of his example, and the memory of his virtues. Time will mitigate our grief, and in the rush and whirl of busy life other thoughts will engage our attention, but there is a sad home in the sunny South within whose broken circle there are bleeding hearts for the healing of which earth has no balm.

For time makes all but true love old;
The burning thoughts that then were told
Run molten still in memory's mold,

And will not cool
Until the heart itself be cold
In Lethe's pool.

The influence of wealth, the resources of learning, and the authority of power, all stand dumb and helpless in the presence of death. It is the solution of all the rivalries, struggles, and achievements of time. Surrounded with blighted hopes and funeral trains, the broken heart of humanity through all time has pressed the question of the suffering patriarch of Uz, "If a man die shall he live again?" The quivering spirit whose insatiable thirst for immortality attests the divinity of its origin and the duration of its destiny, kindles with joy as it catches the response from the rejected Nazarene at Bethany, "I am the resurrection and the life; he that believeth in Me, though he were dead, yet shall he live."

Poor wanderers of a stormy day,
From place to place we're driven,
And fancy's flash and reason's ray
Serve but to light the troubled way,—
There's nothing true but Heaven.

And false the light on glory's plume,
As fading hues of even,
And love and joy and beauty's bloom
Are blossoms gathered for the tomb,—
There's nothing *lives but* heaven.

Stonewall Jackson.

(The following was written for a school boy's declamation.)

It has been said that a great man is the gift of a century. Stonewall Jackson stands alone in the nineteenth century in the isolated grandeur of his greatness. Indeed, the student of the annals of his race will look in vain, along the lists of illustrious names that genius has apotheosized among the demi-gods of history, for his peer. It was the exultation of Pompey the Great, that an army would rise at the stamp of his foot, yet he fled from the disaster of Pharsalia and fell at the hands of an assassin. The eagles of Cæsar flashed the triumph of Rome over a hemisphere, yet he fell the victim of treason leaving a name the synonym of conquest and ambition. Hannibal disputed for years the power of Rome, but the stars of Carthagenian glory went down in blood and her great chieftain died in exile. Europe trembled, thrones crumbled and kings fled at the advancing footsteps of the Man of Destiny; but the fate of Waterloo bound Napoleon, like Prometheus to the rock, the prey of Bourbon vultures. But the living light of victory blazed upon Jackson's peerless banner, on every field. The invincible legions under his leadership charged the enemy's batteries with the tread of fate and the sanction of a God. He grasped at the "cannons smoking mouth," the burning palm of victory and mingled its light with the stars that sparkled upon his country's banner. "His was the hero's soul of fire—and

> His the martyr's deathless name,
> And his love was exalted higher
> By all the glow of chivalry."

The Goddess of Liberty touched his heart with a vestal spark from her altar, and he sprang, like Minerva from the brain of Jupiter upon the plains of Manassas, and valor sealed to him in a baptism of blood on his first field the enduring name of Stonewall. She festooned his brow with the laurels of triumph and he hung them in garlands of faith, upon the cross of Calvary. Some conquerors have been stimulated to great achievements by the love of glory; others by the thirst for power, but the sentiment that nerved the arm, absorbed the thought and thrilled the heart of Jackson, was love of country.

"Breathes there a man with soul so dead, Who never to himself hath said, This is my own, my native land." The heraldic insignia that emblazoned the shield of Jackson is not alone stamped with the blood of revolutionary conflict. Virtue intertwined with the laurel with which she wreathed his brow, the evergreen of immortality, the sublime symbol of the Christian's hope and faith, and the hero that wrested victory from the enemy's standard, cast it, as the trophy, at the feet of the Divinity his soul adored. There was no niche for the God of Ambition in the temple in which he worshipped. He poured upon his country's shrine from a spotless heart, liberty's last libation, with the profusion of a Prince and the adoration of a Priest.

This luminary was extinguished in the blaze of victory his valor had won, and by a mysterious Providence, he fell at the hands of his own comrades, and with him expired the cause, vindicated by his sword, illustrated by his patriotism and consecrated in his blood. The grief of ten millions of stricken hearts wailed his funeral dirge.

"Bury me," said the dying hero, "at Lexington in the valley of Virginia," and his redeemed spirit crossed "over the river to rest under the shade of the trees." His ashes repose in the bosom of the Old Dominion with those of Washington and Jefferson and Madison and Henry and their compatriots of revolutionary fame. And Virginia pours the tribute of her tears upon her hero's grave.

"Such graves as his are pilgrim's shrines,
Shrines to no creed or code confined,
The Delphian vales, the Palestines,
The Meccas of the mind."

Hon. Hiram Parks Bell
"The Demosthenes of the Mountains"
Last Surviving Member of Confederate Congress
Colonel, 43rd Georgia Volunteer Infantry
Confederate Representative 1863-1865
United States Representative 1873-1875, 1877-1879
Georgia Representative 1898-1899
Georgia Senator 1861-1862, 1900-1901

Epilogue

Hiram Parks Bell passed from this life to the next on August 16, 1907 at the home of his son, George L. Bell, at 20 Spruce Street in Inman Park in Atlanta. *Men and Things* had been completed by the printer that very week, soon before Hiram was laid to rest in the red soil of his native state in the Cumming City Cemetery.

> "His four score years were spent in contact with the most distinguished and therefore the most congenial men the South has ever produced. His reminiscences of "Men and Things" as he saw them – *magna pars fui* – have recently come from the press, and give us an insight of the stirring period through which he passed.
>
> In peace and war he was a Georgian of whom the whole state may well be proud. Born on her old red hills, his entire life was spent here, except during the periods when he was serving her in deliberative halls elsewhere. He goes to his grave full of years and honors, leaving behind him a record which the youth of the state could not do better than emulate."

The Atlanta Journal

Saturday, August 17, 1907

"The highest evidence of right
to public gratitude
which the citizen of this or
any country can give
is the offering of his blood and his life
to the government in
the defense of its liberty,
the vindication of its rights,
and the honor of its flag."

-Hiram P. Bell
February 9, 1878